# SPOTLESS
2

Other titles by
Shannon Lush and Jennifer Fleming

*Spotless*
*Speedcleaning*
*How to be Comfy*
*Save*

Shannon Lush & Jennifer Fleming

# SPOTLESS 2

**MORE STAINS AND SOLUTIONS TO DOMESTIC DISASTERS**

ABC Books

DISCLAIMER: Every effort has been made to ensure that the information in this book is as accurate as possible. It is made available on the understanding that neither the auhors nor the publisher are engaged in rendering professional advice.

The ABC 'Wave' device is a trademark of the Australian Broadcasting Corporation and is used under licence by HarperCollins*Publishers* Australia.

This edition first published in 2009 by ABC Books for
the Australian Broadcasting Corporation.
Reprinted by HarperCollins*Publishers* Australia Pty Limited
ABN 36 009 913 517
harpercollins.com.au

Copyright © Shannon Lush and Jennifer Fleming 2009

The right of Shannon Lush and Jennifer Fleming to be identified as the authors of this work has been asserted by them under the *Copyright Amendment (Moral Rights) Act 2000*.

This work is copyright. Apart from any use as permitted under the *Copyright Act 1968*, no part may be reproduced, copied, scanned, stored in a retrieval system, recorded, or transmitted, in any form or by any means, without the prior written permission of the publisher.

**HarperCollins***Publishers*
25 Ryde Road, Pymble, Sydney, NSW 2073, Australia
31 View Road, Glenfield, Auckland 0627, New Zealand

National Library of Australia Cataloguing-in-publication data:

Lush, Shannon.
 Spotless 2 ... more stains and solutions to domestic disasters / Shannon Lush.
 1st ed.
 ISBN: 978 0 7333 2532 8 (pbk.)
 Includes index.
 1. House cleaning, Spotting (Cleaning)
 Other authors/Contributorrs: Fleming, Jennifer.
 Australian Broadcasting Corporation.
648.5

Cover by Luke Causby, Blue Cork Design
Cover image courtesy Getty Images
Internal design and layout by Judi Rowe, Agave Creative Group
Printed and bound in Australia by Griffin Press
70gsm Classic used by HarperCollins*Publishers* is a natural, recyclable product made from wood grown in sustainable forests. The manufacturing processes conform to the environmental regulations in the country of origin, Finland.

8 7 6 5 4         10 11 12 13

# CONTENTS

Acknowledgements  vi

Who we are  vii

Introduction  1

How to use this book  3

Useful Ingredients  5

The Kitchen  23

The Bathroom  63

Lounge, Dining and Family Rooms  83

Floors, Walls and Windows  123

The Bedroom  205

Clothing and Shoes  225

Kids' Stuff  275

The Laundry  293

Quick stain removal guide for fabrics  298

Outside  321

Formulas  357

Index  368

# Acknowledgements

Once again, the list of people to thank is a long one. Thank you to all of the wonderful radio producers and presenters I've worked with, including James Valentine, Richard Fidler, Annie Gaston, Kathie Bedford, Ingrid Just, Louise Saunders, Carol Whitelock, Genevieve Jacobs, Kirsten March and Glenn Barndon from the ABC; George and Paul from 2UE; and Graham Hill from Radio Live New Zealand. Thanks to the team at ABC Books including Jane Finemore, Karen Penning, Brigitta Doyle and too many others to list. A special thank you to all the people who send their questions to the magazines and newspapers I write for, or who call the radio stations for advice. Thanks to my partner in grime Jennifer Fleming, and my agent and friend Elizabeth Troyeur. Thank you to my friends Sanna Mrad and Ronnie Petersson, who always encourage my dreams. But most of all, thank you to my wonderful, crazy, talented and supportive family. A special thanks to my husband, Rick, and daughter, Erin.

### Shannon

I wrote this book under a layer of renovation dust – during breaks in writing, I sanded, painted and rued my decision to take on so much. Thanks to Shannon Lush for her continuing collaboration. Thanks to our agent, Elizabeth Troyeur, for her unfailing calm. Editor Megan Johnston performed another great job of mending, tidying and shaping the text. Karen Penning, Brigitta Doyle, Jane Finemore and Judi Rowe at ABC Books worked their special magic. And heartfelt and unending thanks go to my parents, John and Pat Fleming, who not only gave suggestions for the book but helped me renovate my home as well.

### Jennifer

# Who we are

## Shannon's story

I'm a wife to my wonderful husband, Rick, and a mother to my beautiful daughters, Tamara and Erin (and anybody else who will let me mother them, too). I am also an artist and fine arts restorer who works in 27 different mediums. I love to collect handy hints and to understand the chemistry behind them. Every week I take talkback questions on numerous radio programs around the country, and so far I have never been stumped by a 'how to' question relating to the home. I enjoy coming up with creative solutions to everyday problems, from removing stains to finding alternative uses for old banana peels, tea bags and even dental floss, and I love it when other people get a kick out of the wonder and beauty I find in the simplest things. Some of my solutions are quirky, some are hilarious, but all of them have a practical bent. I would love to be available to answer all of your stain questions 24/7 but as that's just not possible, I hope this book fills in the gaps and gives you the answers you need.

## Jennifer's story

When it comes to cleaning, I admit that I'm a late bloomer. As a child, I didn't spend hours at my mother's side learning the domestic arts. But that also meant I was at a bit of a loss when dealing with a spill or stain. I've now embraced the cleaning and stain removal techniques outlined in this and our other books. And while I wouldn't describe my house as 'spotless' (I'm not a neat freak), it's clean, comfortable and hygienic. If you look inside my cleaning cupboard, you'll find bicarb and white vinegar – no smelly packaged cleaners for me! Also sitting on the cleaning shelf are lemon oil, lavender oil and, of course, oil of cloves. And the best thing: the transition to this way of cleaning and stain removal has been easy and saved me money. Good luck in removing your stains – I hope you find this book helpful.

# Introduction

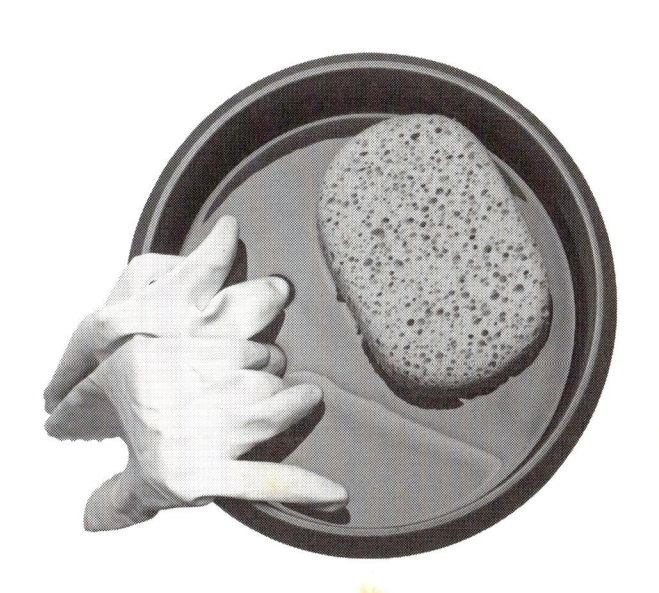

It doesn't matter how careful you are, at some stage you'll have to deal with a stain. It could be soy sauce on your shirt, red wine on your carpet, pen marks on your couch, a scratch on your timber table, curry on your benchtop, a water stain in your toilet, bird droppings on your deck or grease on your driveway—the list of possible stains is almost endless. When we wrote *Spotless*, we didn't include every stain imaginable because the book would have been too heavy to hold in one hand (while you cleaned with the other). Our aim was to give a general overview of common household stains with easy-to-follow instructions on how to fix them—all with a fun approach.

*Spotless 2* contains hundreds of brand new stains, updates and revisions, as well as some *Spotless* classics. It includes real-life questions from people who've called ABC radio from all over Australia. Other questions have come through our 'Stain Clinics', our website **www.homepalette.com.au** and Shannon's magazine and newspaper columns. There's a whole chapter devoted to common clothing stains and an extended chapter on carpet stains. There's even a chapter of cleaning formulas with a stain diagnosis guide to help you work out what is in the stain.

We hope *Spotless 2* helps you solve more of your domestic disasters. Whatever you do, don't stress about it. Stains happen! And so does stain removal.

# How to use this book

*Spotless 2* is set out a bit like a cookbook. It has lists of 'ingredients' or cleaning items followed by stain removal 'recipes', and these methods need to be followed exactly. You can't substitute one cleaning ingredient for another, just as you can't replace sugar with salt, or add extra eggs to a cake batter and expect the texture to be the same. **Stain removal solutions are not interchangeable.** Each chapter has an overview of various surfaces and materials and we strongly recommend that you read these before attempting any stain removal.

There are other guidelines to keep in mind. More is not better. You don't want to create a ski-field with bicarb; use it sparingly, the way you would dust icing sugar on a cake. Don't tip a whole container of white vinegar over your carpet or it will create another stain. If in doubt about a stain removal technique, first do a test on an area that no one can see. And don't throw just anything on a stain and wonder why it's worse than ever. Each thing you add changes the chemical signature of the stain and has to be removed before the right solvent can be applied. Work out what the stain is, what the surface is made of, determine the correct solvent and then apply just enough to remove the stain. Even though you're using less toxic cleaning items, because they're undiluted they can be very strong, so never overdo it!

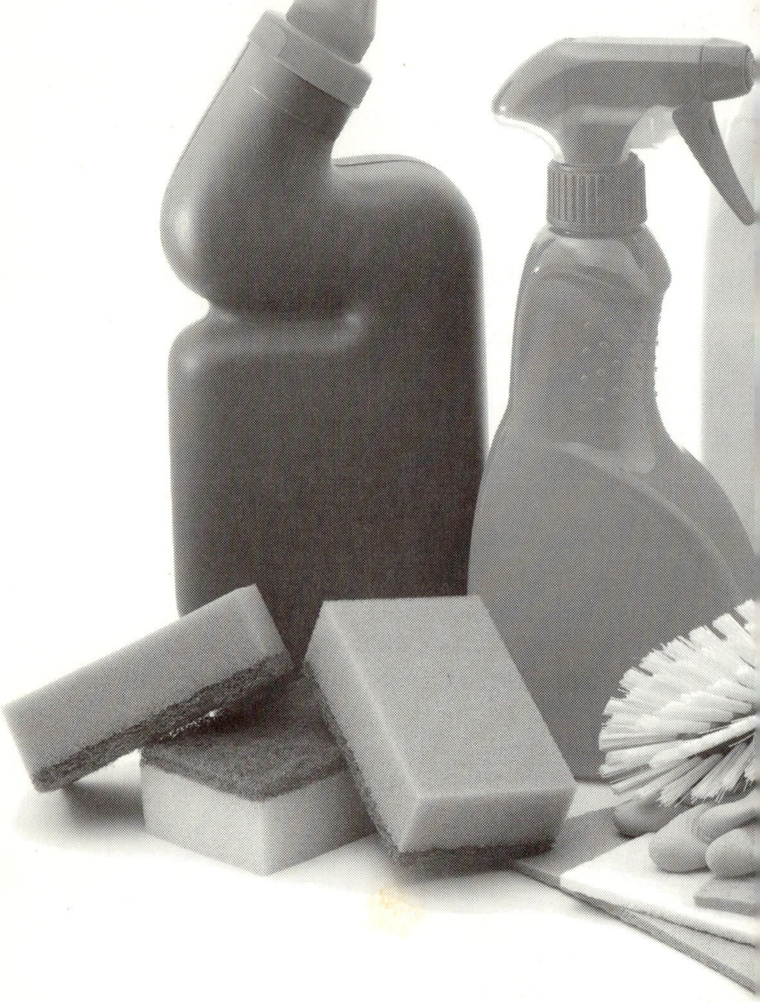

# Useful Ingredients

**Acetone** is a volatile, flammable ketone. It's a liquid solvent for resins, primers, nail polish, superglue, acrylics and heavy plastics. It's available at the supermarket and hardware stores.

**Baby Oil** also known as mineral oil. It's a lubricant, skin ointment and dilutes dark oils. It's available at the supermarket or chemist.

**Bay Leaves** are a moth and weevil deterrent. They're available at the supermarket.

**Beeswax** is the wax produced by bees when making honeycomb and is used as a polishing, lubricating and sealing agent. It's available at hardware stores, chemists and some supermarkets.

**Bicarb (bicarbonate of soda)** is a salt and alkaline that neutralises acid. When added to an acid (such as white vinegar) it releases carbon dioxide and water. It penetrates stains and dissolves grease. It's available at the supermarket in the cake baking section.

Useful Ingredients

**Bleach** is a whitening agent. It doesn't kill mould, just whitens it. Use with care and don't breathe the fumes. It's available at the supermarket.

**Blood-heat water** water at body temperature.

**Borax** is crystalline sodium borate and is used as a fungicide, insecticide and detergent booster. It's mildly toxic and should be used with care. Avoid contact with skin and avoid ingestion. It's available at the supermarket.

**Brasso** is a proprietary abrasive product that partially melts polyurethane. It's available at the supermarket.

**Broom** there are many sizes and varieties available. It's used to sweep over floors and access out-of-reach areas. It's available at the supermarket and hardware store.

**Bucket** these are available in various sizes – 9 litres is most common. It's available at the supermarket and hardware stores.

**Cake of Bathroom Soap** — a regular white cake of soap (not laundry soap)—the less fragrance it has, the better it is to clean with. Use it to remove protein stains. It's available at the supermarket.

**Camphor** is a ketone from the camphor laurel tree. It has a strong vapour which most insects, particularly moths, don't like. Cats and possums are also deterred by camphor. It's flammable so don't heat it. It's found in mothballs, naphthalene flakes and Vicks VapoRub. It's available at the supermarket.

**Carnauba Wax** is a hard, fine wax used in furniture and timber polish. It's available at the hardware store.

**Carpet Steam Cleaner** is used for DIY carpet cleaning. It comes with a bottle of chemicals and Shannon adds her own concoction (see page 135). It's available for hire at the supermarket.

**Cedar Chips** moth deterrent. They're available at the supermarket.

**Cera Wax** proprietary product used to wax marble surfaces. It's available through the internet.

Useful Ingredients

**Chalk Sticks**  normally used to write on blackboards but they're also very absorbent. You can tie white chalk sticks together and place them in areas that have a lot of moisture. They can be dried in sunshine and used again. Chalk is also handy to mark around urine stains. It's available at the supermarket, craft stores, newsagents and toy stores.

**Cigarette Ash**  from cigarettes, used to clean smoke stains. Get some from your local club or hotel.

**CLR**  stands for Calcium, Lime and Rust. It removes calcium deposits from glass and kettles, lime scale from coffee machines, toilets and sinks and rust from cement, porcelain, chrome and fabric. It can burn so wear protective gloves when using it and don't get it on your skin. It's available at the supermarket and hardware stores.

**Cloth**  old cotton T-shirts make great lint-free cloths.

| | |
|---|---|
| **Cloves** | are a spice from the dried flower bud of the clove tree. They can be used to deter silverfish. Clove oil is extracted from the clove flower bud and used to inhibit mould. It's available from chemists (see also Oil of Cloves). |
| **Cold Water** | the coldest tap water. Use when removing protein stains. |
| **Colour Run Remover** | (formerly called Runaway)—there are two varieties Colour Run Remover: Whites and Colour Run Remover: Coloursafe used to remove dye and colour run in fabrics and carpet. Place in a bucket with water and soak item overnight (unless wool). It's available at the supermarket in the laundry aisle. |
| **Cornflour** | is a starch of maize, rice and other grains. It's absorbent and a very fine abrasive. It's available at the supermarket. |
| **Cotton Ball** | use over specific areas. They're available at the supermarket. |

Useful Ingredients

**Cotton Bud**  use to wipe over and absorb stains. They're available at the supermarket.

**Damp Cloth**  means a cloth that's been run under water and then very well-wrung or a cloth just dabbed with water.

**Deck Scrubber**  a stiff bristled brush.

**Denture Tablets**  used to clean dentures but also useful to whiten porcelain and ceramic surfaces. They're available at the chemist.

**Dishwashing Liquid**  removes grease. Add a couple of drops to your fingers and massage into oil and grease stains. They're available at the supermarket.

**Disposable Rubber Gloves**  use to protect your skin from harsh chemicals. They're available from the supermarket.

**Eraser**  (pencil and biro)—made of rubber and removes lead pencil and biro marks on some surfaces. They're available at the supermarket or newsagency.

**Eucalyptus Oil** an essential oil distilled from the leaves of certain eucalyptus trees. It's a paint and dye stripper, solvent for adhesives and some resins, and releases vapours that inhibit some insects. It's available at the supermarket and chemist.

**Fuller's Earth** is a calcium clay with bleaching agent and is very absorbent. It's a wool relaxant and used to shrink and unshrink woollens. It's available at the chemist.

**Glycerine** is a clear liquid used as an agent in cosmetics, toothpaste and shampoos. It's water and alcohol soluble. Glycerine helps loosen stains, particularly tannin stains. It's available at the supermarket or chemist.

**Grout Rake** a hand-held device with a flat tungsten tip which is run against grout to remove it, making it powdery. It's available at the hardware store.

**Gumption** is a greyish cleaning paste with many uses. It contains a mild bleaching agent and is an abrasive. It's available at the supermarket.

## Useful Ingredients

| | |
|---:|:---|
| **Hairbrush** | use to fluff sheepskin as it's drying. It's available at the supermarket. |
| **Hair Conditioner (cheap)** | cheap hair conditioners have fewer perfumes and additives. Use to soften woollens. It's available at the supermarket. |
| **Hair Dryer** | speeds drying time and helps melt wax and crayon. It's available from department stores. |
| **Hydrogen Peroxide (3%)** | an oxidising liquid used as an antiseptic and bleaching agent. It's available at the supermarket. |
| **Iron** | is a regular, household iron. It's available from department stores. |
| **Kerosene** | is a combustible liquid hydrocarbon used as a solvent. It's available at the hardware store and some supermarkets. |
| **Kitty Litter** | absorbs moisture. It's available at the supermarket and pet stores. |
| **Laundry Detergent** | used in the washing machine to lift dirt and stains from fabric. It's available at the supermarket. |

**Lavender Oil** is from lavender flowers and has many uses including insect repellent, dog inhibitor and air freshener. It's available at the supermarket, chemist and health food stores.

**Leather Conditioner** used to treat leather. It's available at shoe repairers and hardware stores.

**Lemon Oil** is the oil in lemon peel and is used to deter spiders, polish pale timbers and provide a fresh fragrance. It's available at health stores.

**Lemon Juice** is the juice from lemons. It's used to remove rust stains and to lighten or bleach colour. It's available at supermarkets.

**Marble Floor Wax** (such as Cera Wax) used to wax and seal marble. It's available from hardware stores and through the internet.

**Metal Lice Comb** used to remove nail polish from carpet. It's available at chemists.

Useful Ingredients

| | |
|---|---|
| **Methylated Spirits** | is a raw alcohol with menthol. It's a solvent for some paint and marker inks, and helps release stains and smells in synthetic materials. It's available at the supermarket and hardware stores. |
| **NapiSan Plus** | chlorine-based soaker and bleach. Not advised to use on leather, silk, wool, chiffon, satin or embroidered garments. It's available at the supermarket. |
| **NapiSan OxyAction MAX** | its active ingredient is sodium percarbonate, a detergent and bleaching agent which removes some stains. It's available at the supermarket. |
| **Non-iodised Salt** | salt that doesn't contain iodine. The iodine in salt can stain some fabrics. It's available at the supermarket. |
| **Nylon Brush** | regular dishwashing scrubbing brush. It's available at the supermarket. |

SPOTLESS 2

**Oil of Cloves** cold pressed oil from the dried flower bud of the clove tree. It's a mould inhibitor, insecticide, toothache soother and an ingredient in cooking. It's available at the chemist.

**Oil of Pennyroyal** is oil from a small-leafed mint. It deters moths, bed bugs and fleas but is **harmful to pregnant women and pregnant pets**.

**Pantyhose/ Stockings** normally worn over your legs. The weave and fibre make a great scrubber and polisher. They're available at the supermarket.

**Paper Towel** used to polish glass, and absorb stains and excess moisture. It's available at the supermarket.

**Petroleum Jelly (Vaseline)** is a mixture of mineral oils, paraffin and microcrystalline waxes. It acts as a water barrier and inhibits snails. It's available at the supermarket and chemist.

**Pillowcase** used to cover pillows. Use them to hold items and protect delicates in the washing machine. They're available at department stores.

Useful Ingredients

Plastic Bag
: protects items being placed in the freezer. Reuse shopping bags. Don't store clothes in them for an extended time because plastic sweats and fumes.

Plastic Wrap
: cling film. It's available from supermarkets.

Plaster of Paris
: white powder made of calcium sulphate which forms a paste when mixed with water and has absorbent properties. It's available from art supplies and hardware stores.

Ranex
: removes calcium, lime and rust. It's available at hardware stores.

Rotten Milk
: milk left in the sun to rot until it forms solids. Absorbs ink stains. Buy milk from the supermarket.

Saddle Soap
: used to clean leather. It's available through the internet.

Saline Solution
: for contact lenses—used to clean contact lenses. It's available at the chemist.

Salt
: table or pool salt. It's available at the supermarket.

| | |
|---|---|
| **Scraper** | triangle-shaped metal device with a handle. It's available from the hardware store. |
| **Shampoo (cheap)** | cheaper shampoos have fewer fragrances and are better for cleaning. Use to wash woollens. It's available at the supermarket. |
| **Silicone** | liquid gel that hardens once applied. It's used as a join sealant and is water impermeable. It's available at hardware stores. |
| **Spray Pack** | plastic bottle with removable nozzle head. Can have many concoctions added to it. It's available at the supermarket or hardware stores. |
| **Slurpex** | super-absorbent chamois block. Only available through the internet at **www.slurpex.com.au.** |
| **Stiff Brush** | brush with strong bristles. It's available from the supermarket. |
| **Squeegee** | implement with a rubber blade on one side used to wipe moisture from surfaces. It's available at the supermarket or hardware store. |

Useful Ingredients

**Sugar Soap** is a highly caustic soap. It comes in powder or liquid form. The powder has a mild abrasive. It's available at the supermarket and hardware stores.

**Sweet Almond Oil** is the oil from almond nuts. Use it to clean bone, ivory, bakelite and plastics. It's available from the supermarket or chemist.

**Talcum Powder** is a mineral powder. It's a super fine abrasive, lubricant and also absorbent. It's available at the supermarket and chemist.

**Tea Bag** used to make a cup of tea. Hang on to old ones to use when cleaning timber and aluminium and restoring tannins. It's available at the supermarket.

**Tea Tree Oil** is an oil extracted from the tea-tree bush. It's an antibacterial and removes glues and resins including chewing gum. It's available at the supermarket and chemist.

**Tissues** fine, soft paper. Use to absorb stains and moisture and protect surfaces. It's available at the supermarket and chemist.

SPOTLESS 2

| | |
|---|---|
| **Toothbrush** | used to clean teeth but also makes a great mini scrubbing brush. Keep old ones to clean in difficult-to-access areas and over grout. It's available at the supermarket and chemist. |
| **Turpentine** | is a volatile oil and resin distilled from trees and is a solvent for oil-based paints. It's available at hardware stores. |
| **Ultraviolet Light** | is used to fade stains. It's available from electronics stores, lighting stores or from ABC Shops in the form of the 'Dr Who' sonic screwdriver. |
| **Unprocessed Wheat Bran (not just any bran)** | is the ground husk of wheat. It can be used as a scourer and absorbent to clean fabrics and furs. It's available at the supermarket. |
| **Vacuum Cleaner** | sucks up dirt. It's available at department stores and specialist vacuum cleaning stores. |
| **Washing Soda** | is sodium carbonate and an alkaline. Use to clean dirt and grease. It's available at the supermarket. |

Useful Ingredients

**White Spirits** is a mixture of petroleum hydrocarbons and a solvent. It's also known as dry cleaning fluid or Murlex. It's available at hardware stores.

**White Vinegar** is an acid and used to clean and sanitise. It's available at the supermarket.

**Whiting** is a powder used in cleaning and polishing glass. It's available from leadlight stores.

**Zip-lock Bag** is a plastic bag with a top that clicks open and shut. It's handy to store items. It's available at the supermarket.

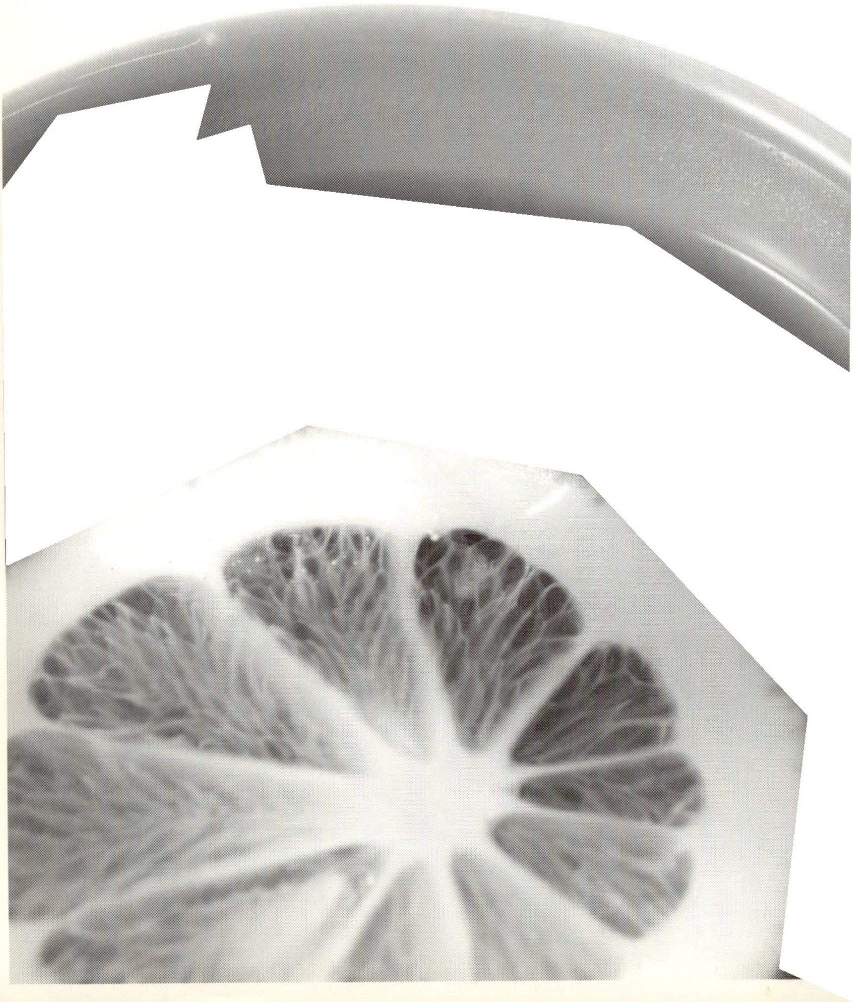

# The Kitchen

We're all taught about the dangers of germs but for some this can become an obsession. For years, advertising has told us we must get rid of these disease-carrying microbes with antibacterial cleaners. Now we discover their overuse has led to the development of antibiotic-resistant bacteria. Rather than overdoing it with harsh and harmful sprays, maintain a clean kitchen by wiping surfaces with a damp soapy cloth or sprinkle on bicarb, spray a little white vinegar and wipe with a clean cloth. Simple! These days the modern kitchen is often part of the living area so there's an extra incentive to keep it clean as it's on display when visitors pop over.

## NOT-SO-FANTASTIC PLASTIC: Sonia's story

**INCIDENT:** 'I have an electric stove but the hotplates no longer light up, so you can't tell when they're on. I keep my plastic water filter jug near the stove and you can guess what happened. I ended up resting the jug on top of the hot plate and it melted. My husband turned the element back on to re-melt the plastic but that didn't work and it smelt awful. Now I'm left with a plastic ring on the hotplate which I can't remove. What can I do?'

**SOLUTION:** When you heat plastic it spreads and is more difficult to remove. Make sure the electric stove is turned off and is cold. Put ice-cubes in a zip-lock bag and place over the stain. When the ice has almost melted, remove and sprinkle the stain with a little bicarb. Spray with a little white vinegar and, while it's fizzing, rub with a rolled up pair of pantyhose. If any stain remains, mix equal parts glycerine and talcum powder and rub with pantyhose. To make sure you've removed all the burnt plastic, wipe with a little vegetable oil and shine a torch over the area. If the light beam shows an irregularity in the surface, it means some plastic is still there. If so, repeat until all the plastic is removed.

## OVEN

Shannon's niece saw her clean the stove using bicarb, white vinegar and a rolled up pair of pantyhose and couldn't believe the result. She said it looked really easy. You don't need expensive cleaners to make your oven sparkle. Yes, you'll need to rub while the mixture is fizzing but this is far preferable to breathing nasty fumes (see *Speedcleaning* for oven cleaning instructions).

**TIP** To avoid warping and discolouration in your cupboards, install a heat-resistant metal panel between the oven and the surrounding cupboards.

## Q: 'My white oven door handle and surrounds are yellowing', says Sue. 'What can I do?'

**Problem:** **Yellowing oven door.**

**What to use:** **Glycerine, talcum powder, cloth, pantyhose, bicarb, white vinegar.**

**How to apply:** Plastic heat-resistant door handles can become yellow from heat, sunlight or the bleach in cleaning products. Mix a paste of glycerine and talcum powder to the consistency of thickened cream and polish on with a cloth. Leave for 10 minutes and polish off with a pair of pantyhose. If the burn is deep, this will only lighten the yellow. The oven surround is usually made of baked enamel and can be cleaned with bicarb and white vinegar. If you can't fix it, you can replace the handle or have the doors re-enamelled.

## The Kitchen

**TIP** Your oven will work more efficiently and food will cook more evenly if the hinges and seals are in good working order. If damaged, have them professionally refitted.
If your sponge cakes are flat or uneven, it could be from poorly fitted oven seals.

**Q:** 'I left the stove on and returned an hour later to find my house full of smoke', admits Jim. 'Fortunately, the house didn't burn to the ground. Is there a way to remove the smell of smoke throughout the house?'

**Problem:** **Smoky smell in house.**

**What to use:** **Bicarb, tennis racquet (or similar item to whack cushions), vacuum cleaner (upholstery); bicarb, white vinegar (hard surfaces); cigarette ash, bicarb, white vinegar, disposable rubber gloves, stiff brush (brickwork), warm water, soft broom.**

**How to apply:** Smoke travels throughout the house and gets trapped in the soft furnishings so everything in the house needs to be cleaned. For upholstered items and soft furnishings, scatter with bicarb and give them a good whack with a tennis racquet. Leave for half an hour, then vacuum thoroughly. If you have air conditioning, clean the filters. Wash curtains and other removable fabric.

SPOTLESS 2

For hard surfaces including painted walls (except marble), clean with bicarb and white vinegar. To clean brickwork, mix 1 part cigarette ash (you can get cigarette ash from your local pub or club), 1 part bicarb and 1 part white vinegar. Wear disposable rubber gloves (because this mixture can burn skin) and scrub the mixture over the bricks with a stiff brush. Leave for 5 minutes and scrub off with warm water on a soft broom. To clean wallpaper, rub over with slices of stale bread.

**(TIP)** Clean the grill after each use as you would the oven.

# COOKTOP

## Ceramic/Induction

If you have this type of cooktop, our advice is to clean it thoroughly after each use because it can become permanently etched and marked. Wipe with a damp soft cloth or pantyhose when it's cold (don't use detergent because it discolours the surface). If there's any food or gunk on the surface, carefully use a scraper (they are often supplied when you buy the cooktop) or a single-sided razor blade at a low angle to remove it.

The Kitchen

**Q:** 'My electric cooktop has rings around the hotplates', says Sue. 'How can I remove them?'

**Problem:** **Rings on electric cooktop.**
**What to use:** **Bicarb, white vinegar, pantyhose; or single-sided razor blade.**
**How to apply:** When it's cold, sprinkle the cooktop with a little bicarb followed by a little white vinegar and, while fizzing, scrub with pantyhose. Because the cooktop is made of glass, it etches easily so don't use caustic cleaners. Many come with scrapers to remove gunk. If you don't have a scraper, use a razor blade at a low angle under the caked-on muck. Don't hack into the glass surface.

## Electric

Never use strong chemicals to clean coil elements because it damages them. When cold, wipe with a pair of pantyhose wrung out in white vinegar, then follow with a clean, damp cloth.

## Gas

If you can see yellow in the flame, or if some spots have no flame at all, it means the jets are dirty. Gas jets are designed to be pulled apart and cleaned. Simply wash in warm soapy water and scrub with a nylon brush. If there's any baked-on char, sprinkle with bicarb followed by a little white vinegar and scrub with a nylon brush or a rolled up pair of pantyhose. Allow to dry.

If the jets are clogged, clear them with a needle or opened paperclip.

Knobs and dials are also designed to be removed so you can clean under them.

## SPLASHBACK

There are many types of splashback. Some common ones include:
**Glass**—clean with equal parts white vinegar and water in a spray pack applied with a pair of pantyhose.
**Tiles**—clean with bicarb and white vinegar. Scrub the grout with an old toothbrush.
**Stone and stainless steel**—clean with a damp cloth or a pair of pantyhose.

## RANGE HOOD AND EXTRACTOR FAN

The more time you leave before cleaning these workhorses, the more work you'll have to do. Most can be pulled apart and washed in warm soapy water. Get into the habit of cleaning the range hood each week—it will keep your kitchen much cleaner and use less power.

## POTS AND PANS

Instead of using scourers to clean pots and pans, use a pair of pantyhose. Simply roll the pantyhose into a ball and scrub. And as with most cleaning, the easiest way to keep your pots and pans sparkling is to clean them thoroughly after each use. If you don't, the next time you use the pot, the heat will make the charred remnants stick to it more stubbornly.

The Kitchen

## *SPOTLESS CLASSIC*
### Burnt pan

There are a couple of options when cleaning a burnt pan. One is to sprinkle with a little bicarb followed by a little white vinegar and, when the mixture fizzes, scrub with a nylon brush. If the burn is caked on, you've got quite a task ahead of you. One suggestion is to half fill the pot or pan with water and add 1 cup of white vinegar. Heat on the stove until the mixture boils. Remove, allow to cool and scrub with a scraper or nylon brush. Sprinkle with bicarb, add white vinegar and, when the mixture fizzes, scrub with a nylon brush. Another way to clean a burnt pan is to add white vinegar to a cold pan until 5 mm deep and place in the freezer. When frozen, remove the pan and allow to thaw. Sprinkle bicarb on top and, when fizzing, scrub with a nylon brush.

**Q:** 'We had Indian the other night', reports Bill, 'but I burnt the rice and it's stained the frying pan. What can I do?'

| | |
|---|---|
| **Problem:** | **Burnt rice on frying pan.** |
| **What to use:** | **White vinegar, freezer, bicarb, nylon brush.** |
| **How to apply:** | Add white vinegar to a cold pan until 5 mm deep and place in the freezer until the vinegar freezes. Remove from the freezer and allow to thaw. Sprinkle bicarb and vigorously scrub with a brush as it's fizzing. |

If the pan won't fit in the freezer, sprinkle with bicarb followed by white vinegar and scrub with a brush. Repeat until clean.

**Q:** 'I've got some cast-iron cooking pots', says Wally. 'And they've gone rusty. Can I fix them?'

|  |  |
|---|---|
| **Problem:** | **Rusty cast-iron.** |
| **What to use:** | **Cheap vegetable oil, paper towel.** |
| **How to apply:** | Add enough vegetable oil to the pot to cover the bottom and wipe around the inside with paper towel. Put the pot over low heat and when the oil starts to fume, turn off the heat and allow to cool. When it's cooled, rub with paper towel. |

# APPLIANCES

## Kettle/electric jug

One of the main problems with kettles and electric jugs is lime scale or tartar build-up. To remove, empty the kettle or jug of water and add 2 tablespoons of uncooked rice, 2 tablespoons of bicarb and 2 tablespoons of white vinegar. Cover the openings with your hands and shake for 1 minute. Rinse thoroughly. The rice gets into all the corners and acts as a scourer.

Another option is to place 2 chopped lemons inside the kettle, fill with water and bring to the boil. Pour everything out and rinse thoroughly before making your next cuppa.

Thanks to Sam for suggesting this: add 1 teaspoon of citric acid powder to the kettle and boil. She adds that citric acid is an ingredient of sherbet and is completely edible!

**TIP** Cockroaches are attracted to the heat and magnetic field of electrical appliances. Wipe with a cloth dipped in salt and water. Just make sure the appliance is switched off and you don't get water on the plugs. To protect items such as portable phone bases from cockroaches, stand them on a salt covered plate but don't allow the salt to contact metal parts. Instead, elevate with rubber stoppers or cork (slice an old wine cork).

## Sandwich makers

Sandwich makers create great snacks and light meals but cleaning them can be complicated because they can't be immersed in water. The easiest cleaning method is to half fill the inside of the sandwich maker with equal parts water and white vinegar (straight after cooking the sambo) and close the lid. If needed, turn the sandwich maker on for a short time so the steaming mixture cleans top and bottom. Wipe with a paper towel or cloth. All done!

## Espresso/coffee machines

Some espresso machines can cost thousands of dollars so it's important to care for them. Clean according to the type of material from which it's made (check the manual). Flush through with 1 tablespoon of non-iodised salt per litre of water.

SPOTLESS 2

**Q:** 'My espresso machine has white scale/calcium around the rim where the water is placed,' reports Deborah. 'Can you suggest a cleaning solution for this?'

> **Problem:** Lime scale on coffee machine.
>
> **What to use:** White vinegar, cloth, non-iodised salt, water, cheap vegetable oil, dishwashing liquid, warm water.
>
> **How to apply:** Rub the exposed surfaces with white vinegar on a cloth. To clean the steam pipes, flush through with 1 tablespoon of salt per litre of water. If smaller metallic parts are corroded (such as strainer sections), place them in a pot of vegetable oil and slowly heat until the oil starts to fume. Remove from the heat and allow to cool. Wash in a little dishwashing liquid and warm water and dry well.

## Mixers and blenders

**Q:** 'The aluminium strainer-like blade on my mixer has corroded', says Gillian. 'What can I do?'

> **Problem:** Corroded aluminium.
>
> **What to use:** Saucepan, cooking oil, dishwashing liquid, warm water.

**How to apply:** Place the corroded items in a saucepan, cover with cooking oil and heat until the oil starts to fume. Remove from the heat and allow to cool. Remove the items and wash in dishwashing liquid and warm water. Dry well.

**Prevention:** Store clean mixer parts in greaseproof paper.

## Benchtop ovens

If you don't clean benchtop ovens after each use, nasty odours can develop. Before cleaning, unplug the oven and remove the grills. Wash the racks in the sink in dishwashing liquid and wipe the interior with a damp soapy cloth. If needed, add white vinegar to the cleaning cloth. Don't use sharp implements to remove gunk or you could damage the surface.

## Barbecue grill

To clean a dirty barbecue grill, sprinkle with bicarb, splash with white vinegar and, while it's fizzing, scrub with a nylon brush. To remove rust, heat the grill, sprinkle with a little sugar and splash a little white vinegar on top. Together, the vinegar and sugar create a toffee which bonds to the old char, making it easier to remove with a scraper. While the grill is still hot, cover with cheap vegetable oil and continue heating until the oil starts to fume. Rub the grill with a handful of paper towel. The oil seasons the grill, leaving a non-stick surface that won't rust as easily.

SPOTLESS 2

## Microwave

**Q:** 'How can I remove the smell of burnt popcorn from my microwave?' asks Christina.

| | |
|---|---|
| **Problem:** | **Burnt popcorn in microwave.** |
| **What to use:** | **Bicarb, white vinegar, water, microwave-safe bowl, damp cloth.** |
| **How to apply:** | Mix 2 tablespoons of bicarb, 2 tablespoons of white vinegar and 1 cup of water in a microwave-safe bowl. Place the bowl in the microwave and heat until the water just comes to the boil and the interior is covered in steam. Wipe every surface of the microwave, including the back grille, with a cloth wrung out in the mixture. If the smell remains, you may need to wash the filter pad behind the perforated grille at the back of the microwave. If this grille has a catch for easy opening, remove the pad and rinse in bicarb and vinegar. If the grille is screwed down, have it professionally treated or you will risk losing your warranty. |

## Dishwasher

We know it's a bit annoying to have to clean the filter each time you use the dishwasher but it's necessary. If you don't, nasty smells may develop. If there's an odour, put bicarb in the wash slot and white vinegar in the rinse slot and run empty on a short cycle.

Don't forget to check and clear the jets in the arm. If needed, unblock them with a needle or opened paperclip. Clean the seals with bicarb and white vinegar on a butter knife wrapped in a tea towel. If the water in your area has a high mineral content, you're more likely to get lime scale, so fill the wash slot with bicarb and the rinse slot with white vinegar and run empty on the short cycle every 10 washes.

**TIP** Most new appliances have sticky labels on them and some are harder to remove than others. Put a drop of dishwashing liquid and a little water on some plastic wrap, mix together and place the plastic wrap over the label. Leave for 10 minutes. The label should come off when you remove the plastic wrap. For stickier labels, apply a couple of drops of tea tree oil along the top edge of the label and leave for about 15 minutes. It should peel off easily. Stronger still is eucalyptus oil applied with a cotton ball but use sparingly because it can remove paint. If none of these techniques work, run a hair dryer backwards and forwards over the label to melt the glue.

## Refrigerator

New fridges have solid shelves which are really easy to clean. Just wipe with a damp pair of panythose or cloth. For monthly cleans, remove shelves and trays and clean with bicarb and white vinegar on a pair of pantyhose or a cloth. If you have an older fridge and the plastic has come away from the wire shelves, spray the steel with heat-resistant engine paint (available from hardware stores). Leave to dry and return to the fridge.

**Q:** 'I have a stainless steel fridge with a water filter and ice-maker', says Caroline. 'But the black plastic drip tray has white stains on it. I have tried many cleaners and they won't shift. Any help?'

**Problem:** **White marks on plastic.**

**What to use:** **Glycerine, talcum powder, cloth.**

**How to apply:** The marks could be from harsh cleaning products or minerals salts from the water. Mix equal parts glycerine and talcum powder and polish with a cloth. If this doesn't work, the plastic is permanently damaged.

**Q:** 'Our power went off while we were away', reports Diana. 'And the freezer section of the fridge really smells. What can I do?'

**Problem:** **Smelly fridge.**

**What to use:** **Sugar, bicarb, white vinegar, nylon brush or pantyhose, cloth, butterknife.**

**How to apply:** Turn the fridge off and sprinkle sugar over the base of the freezer to speed up defrosting. Sprinkle with bicarb and white vinegar and, while it's fizzing, scrub with a nylon brush or pantyhose. Dip a cloth in white vinegar and wrap it over the end of a blunt butterknife to clean in all the grooves and creases in the seals.

## Water filter

When it's time to change the water filter cartridge, add ½ cup of salt to 1 litre of water, pour it into the top reservoir and allow it to work through the filter. While you're waiting, wipe the outside of the reservoir with salt and water on a cloth. Once the salt water has worked through, fill with clean water and replace the cartridge. For stand-alone water containers, add a pinch of salt and ½ teaspoon of white vinegar when refilling with water. This stops the water from becoming brackish but won't affect the taste.

## Juicer

**Q:** 'I have a stainless steel and plastic juicer and wash it after each use', reports Margaret. 'But brown stains are beginning to mark it. What can I do?'

**Problem:** **Brown stains on juicer.**

**What to use:** **Glycerine, warm water, bicarb, white vinegar, nylon brush or pantyhose, water.**

**How to apply:** When some fruit is exposed to oxygen, it goes brown (think of a cut apple). Over time, this builds up and stains. Right after using the juicer, put ½ teaspoon of glycerine in 1 cup of warm water and pour it into the juicer. Turn the machine on for 1 minute. To clean the exterior, sprinkle with bicarb, followed by white vinegar and, while it's fizzing, scrub with a nylon brush or pair of pantyhose. Rinse thoroughly with water. In some cases the staining will have penetrated into the plastic and you'll just have to live with it. It's still safe to use.

# BENCHTOPS

Benchtops can be made of laminate, Formica, quartz (such as CaesarStone, Quantum Quartz, Silestone), acrylic compounds (such as Corian), marble, granite, timber or stainless steel. When cleaning, first work out if they're sealed and with what. For marble and granite, put your eye level with the surface and shine a torch along the top. If the light shines in an uninterrupted beam, the benchtop is coated in polyurethane. If the beam has lights and dots, it's not sealed. To work out the sealant for other benchtops, see page 360. If the polyurethane is damaged, you have to reseal the entire surface, which is a big job. Seek professional help with this. To remove scratches, apply a small amount of Brasso to a cloth and polish using speed rather than pressure. This partially melts the polyurethane. It will look worse before it looks better.

The best polishing cloths for benchtops are pantyhose and they can be used on most surfaces. They're excellent for removing those ever-present fingermarks but there is a technique to using them. Have two pairs—one damp and one dry. Rub the damp pair over the surface and follow right away with the dry pair. This technique will even make stainless steel streak-free and gleaming.

The Kitchen

## Laminate/Formica

Laminate and Formica benchtops are very popular and can be cleaned with a damp cloth and the rinse water from the washing up or a sprinkle of a little bicarb followed by a little white vinegar (rub while it's fizzing). Wipe clean with a damp cloth. Avoid abrasive cleaners because they can scratch the surface.

**Q:** 'I've spilt coffee on my laminate benchtop', complains Mike. 'What's the easiest way to get it out?'

| | |
|---|---|
| **Problem:** | **Coffee on laminate.** |
| **What to use:** | **Gumption, glycerine, pantyhose, damp cloth.** |
| **How to apply:** | Mix equal parts Gumption and glycerine and polish with a pair of rolled up pantyhose. Remove with a damp cloth. |

**Q:** 'I've got a big blob of superglue on my laminate benchtop', reports Kamahl. 'Any ideas?'

| | |
|---|---|
| **Problem:** | **Superglue on laminate.** |
| **What to use:** | **Superglue remover, pantyhose, white vinegar, cloth; or steam, pantyhose.** |
| **How to apply:** | Apply superglue remover only over the superglue and it will melt. Rub off with pantyhose and neutralise the remover |

by wiping with white vinegar on a cloth. Alternatively, apply steam to the superglue and rub with a pair of pantyhose.

**TIP** To make superglue set more quickly, breathe on it (but don't inhale!). The humidity helps superglue to set more quickly.

## Q: 'The colour from a plastic bread wrapper has stuck to my laminate benchtop', reports Nigel. 'Can it be removed?'

> **Problem:** **Coloured plastic on laminate.**
> **What to use:** **Hair dryer, glycerine, talcum powder, pantyhose, damp cloth.**
> **How to apply:** Gently warm the laminate with a hair dryer. Mix equal parts glycerine and talcum powder to form a paste the consistency of runny cream, place on the mark and rub with pantyhose—it takes a bit of elbow grease. Wipe clean with a damp cloth.

## Q: 'How do you get burn marks off laminate?' asks Tom.

> **Problem:** **Burn marks on laminate.**
> **What to use:** **Cigarette ash, toothpaste, pantyhose; or Gumption, white spirits, cloth.**

**How to apply:** Mix equal parts cigarette ash and toothpaste and polish with pantyhose. Alternatively, mix equal parts Gumption and white spirits and polish with a cloth. If the burn has penetrated, it will need to be repaired professionally.

**Q:** 'I've got mould on my laminate benchtop', says George. 'Can it be removed?'

**Problem: Mould on laminate.**
**What to use: Oil of cloves, warm water, 1 litre spray pack, pantyhose.**
**How to apply:** Mix ¼ teaspoon of oil of cloves with warm water in a spray pack (the warm water makes it easier for the oil of cloves to penetrate the surface). Spray over the mould, leave for 20 minutes and scrub with pantyhose. If needed, spray the mixture again and leave for 24 hours to allow the oil of cloves to kill the mould spore.

**Q:** 'I've got a hair-dye stain on my laminate benchtop', reports Alice. 'What's the solution?'

**Problem: Hair dye on laminate.**
**What to use: Same brand hair dye, cloth, cheap shampoo, damp cloth.**
**How to apply:** Use the same brand and colour hair dye and rub a dab over the mark with a cloth until the stain begins to loosen and spread. Add a little

shampoo and continue rubbing until the stain starts to loosen even more, then wipe with a damp cloth. Repeat the shampoo step if necessary.

## CaesarStone/Quantum Quartz/Silestone

Many modern kitchens have quartz-based benchtops which are not porous, so they don't need sealants such as polyurethane. Clean with a damp cloth and remove glues or resins with a single-sided razor blade held at a low angle. Fill chips with a malleable epoxy resin.

**Q:** 'I had a new kitchen installed and chose a dark blue Silestone benchtop', says Louise. 'But it never looks clean. It shows every fingerprint, watermark and cloth mark. Can you suggest anything that would help the benchtop look clean and shiny?'

|  |  |
|---|---|
| **Problem:** | **Streaky Silestone.** |
| **What to use:** | **White vinegar, pantyhose, damp cloth.** |
| **How to apply:** | Silestone is a great benchtop but when it's brand new the high-gloss surface shows dirt, oil and dust. Clean with a little white vinegar on a rolled up pair of pantyhose and wipe with a damp cloth. Polish with a dry pair of pantyhose. |

## Marble

Marble is often coated in polyurethane to give a slick finish and provide protection. Be careful not to damage the polyurethane because it's difficult to repair. If you have unsealed marble, protect it with a good quality marble floor wax (follow the instructions on the pack).

## Q: 'I've got tea stains under my sealed marble benchtop,' says Fran. 'Can I get them out?'

**Problem:** **Tea stains on polyurethane-sealed marble.**

**What to use:** **Cloth, acetone, plastic wrap, pantyhose, warm water, plaster of Paris, glycerine, plastic scraper, marble floor wax.**

**How to apply:** This is a big job and you may decide to live with the stain rather than go through this tricky process. It's likely the tea has penetrated through a tiny hole in the polyurethane but you'll need to remove a relatively large area of polyurethane to remove the stain. Seek professional help or, if you're handy, remove the polyurethane coating by tightly wringing a cloth in acetone and placing it over the stained area. Cover the cloth with plastic wrap so the acetone doesn't evaporate and leave for 20 minutes. Remove the plastic wrap and the cloth and rub with a pair of rolled up pantyhose dampened in warm water. To remove the tea stains, mix plaster of Paris with water to form a paste the consistency of peanut butter. For each cup of mixture, add ½ teaspoon of glycerine. Apply a

1 cm thick layer of the mixture on the stain and leave to dry. When it's completely dry, remove with a plastic scraper. Have the polyurethane replaced by a professional or seal with marble floor wax.

**Prevention:** To prevent staining on marble, apply marble floor wax every month.

*(TIP)* You can repair chips in marble with crayon wax, candle wax or surfboard wax in a matching colour. Melt the wax into the chip with a hair dryer and buff with pantyhose until it's level with the surface.

## Q: 'I've got rust marks on unsealed marble', says Pat. 'What do you suggest?'

**Problem: Rust on unsealed marble.**

**What to use: Plaster of Paris, water, stiff brush; or bicarb, white vinegar, nylon brush.**

**How to apply:** Mix plaster of Paris and water to form a paste the consistency of peanut butter. Paint a 1 cm thick layer of the mixture over the stains and leave until dry. Brush off with a stiff brush. You may need to repeat this several times. If the marble is sealed, sprinkle with bicarb and white vinegar. Scrub with a nylon brush and rinse quickly because vinegar can make holes in marble.

The Kitchen

# Granite

Even though many granite benchtops are sealed, the surface is still porous so if there's a spill, wipe it up as soon as possible. For spills that have penetrated, mix plaster of Paris and water to form a paste the consistency of peanut butter. To each cup of mixture, add 1 teaspoon of dishwashing liquid (to remove oils) or 1 teaspoon of white vinegar (to remove coffee and tea stains) and place over the stain. When the plaster is completely dry, brush away. The plaster of Paris absorbs the stain.

**Q:** 'A bottle of dishwashing liquid leaked onto our granite benchtop and penetrated under the sealed surface', reports Jenny. 'How can I get it out?'

| | |
|---|---|
| **Problem:** | **Dishwashing liquid on sealed granite.** |
| **What to use:** | **Acetone, cloth, plastic wrap, plaster of Paris, water, white vinegar, stiff brush.** |
| **How to apply:** | If it is a small area, mix plaster of Paris and water to form a paste to the consistency of peanut butter. For each cup of mixture add 1 teaspoon of white vinegar. Apply a 1 cm thick layer to the stain and leave to dry. Brush away with a stiff brush. If it is a large area you may need to remove the polyurethane. This can be done by a professional or if you wish to attempt it yourself, soak a cloth in acetone and place it over the stained area. Cover with plastic and leave for 20 minutes. Clean the melted polyurethane off with a |

vinegar-soaked cloth, then rinse with clean water and leave to dry before using the plaster of Paris mix above. When the stain is clean, replace the polyurethane. This is often better done by a professional as it can be tricky to get a nice smooth finish. If you don't wish to replace the polyurethane you can use a quality marble flooring wax.

## Stainless steel

Stainless steel can discolour if left in contact with harsh chemicals, including acidic food, for extended periods so clean regularly with damp pantyhose. If it is very dirty, damp the pantyhose with white vinegar. Always rub in the direction of the grain or it will lose its shine. Never use steel wool, scourers or stainless steel wool because they will cause rust marks. And don't use baby oil because it creates a build-up that attracts dust and dirt.

**Q:** 'How do you remove a rust mark from a stainless steel benchtop?' asks Andy.

**Problem:** **Rust on stainless steel.**
**What to use:** **Non-iodised salt, lemon juice/lemon, pantyhose, damp cloth.**
**How to apply:** Place salt over the mark, add lemon juice and scrub with pantyhose. Alternatively, sprinkle salt over the top of a cut lemon and scrub. Wipe clean with a damp cloth.

## Tiles and grout

The grout between tiles is very porous and will stain, particularly in the area behind your cooktop. Clean it with equal parts bicarb, white vinegar and an old toothbrush.

**Q:** "The kitchen tiles surrounding my stovetop are stained with grease that's accumulated over the years', says Thelma. 'I've tried everything to remove it without success and have been told by experts that the grease has penetrated into the glaze of the tiles and the only solution is to replace them. As this is an expensive and messy job, and I love the colour of my wall tiles which have now gone out-of-date, it means I would need to have my whole kitchen redone. Is there any solution at all?'

**Problem:** **Grease on tiles.**

**What to use:** **Grout rake, plaster of Paris, water, dishwashing liquid, stiff brush.**

**How to apply:** Remove the grout with a grout rake (available at hardware stores). Mix plaster of Paris and water to form a paste the consistency of peanut butter. For each cup of mixture, add 1 teaspoon of dishwashing liquid. Apply a 1 cm thick layer to the entire side of the tile. Leave it to dry completely and remove with a stiff brush. If any oil or grease remains, repeat. When all the staining is removed, replace the grout.

## CHOPPING BOARDS

**Q:** 'I was chopping some raw meat on my timber chopping board and it's left blood stains', complains Natalie. 'What's the best way to get it out?'

**Problem:** **Blood on timber.**

**What to use:** **Cake of bathroom soap, cold water, white vinegar, cloth, sawdust.**

**How to apply:** Scribble over the stain with a cake of bathroom soap dipped in cold water and scrub with a dish brush. Rinse with white vinegar on a cloth, sprinkle with sawdust (available at hardware stores) and leave in the sun to dry. Brush the sawdust into the garden (it's great mulch).

## SINK

**Q:** 'How do you remove tobacco burns from a white sink?' asks Rebecca.

**Problem:** **Cigarette stain on white plastic sink.**

**What to use:** **Talcum powder, glycerine, pantyhose, damp cloth.**

**How to apply:** Mix equal parts talcum powder and glycerine, place on the stain and scrub with pantyhose. Wipe clean with a damp cloth.

The Kitchen

**TIP** To clean along silicone joins, use equal parts white vinegar and water on a cloth.

## GARBAGE DISPOSAL UNIT

The easy way to clean and freshen a garbage disposal unit is to place ½ raw potato and ½ lemon inside the unit and turn it on. Add hot water until it stops making a noise. The starch from the potato attracts dirt and the acid from the lemon helps break down grease. The lemon also leaves a clean, fresh smell.

## CUPBOARDS

Clean cupboards with equal parts white vinegar and water in a 1 litre spray pack. If you have an issue with cockroaches, spray with ½ cup of salt combined with 1 litre of water in a spray pack and wipe with a cloth. If strips of veneer are coming away from the edges of your cupboards, hold the strip in place and put a dripping wet towel on top. Iron on a cool setting and the steam will soften the adhesive and hold the strip in place. Don't add extra glue because the cupboard doors won't close properly. Specialist irons are available at electrical and plant hire.

**Q:** 'I spilt a bottle of pure cinnamon oil from India and it splashed onto the vinyl-wrap white kitchen cupboard doors,' reports Sandy. 'What should I do?'

SPOTLESS 2

| | |
|---|---|
| **Problem:** | **Cinnamon oil on vinyl wrap.** |
| **What to use:** | **Plaster of Paris, water, dishwashing liquid, stiff brush; or car polish, cloth.** |
| **How to apply:** | This is a tricky job because cinnamon oil penetrates and permanently damages surfaces. To try to remove the stain, mix plaster of Paris and water to form a paste the consistency of peanut butter. For each cup of mixture, add 1 teaspoon of dishwashing liquid and mix well. Place over the stain. When dry, brush away. Alternatively, use a dab of car polish and rub over the area. This will remove a fine layer from the vinyl. If the surface is permanently damaged, you may have to repaint, resurface or replace it. |

**Q:** 'The melamine edging on the cupboards around my stove has yellowed', says Rob. 'Can this be fixed or will I need to replace the strips with new ones?'

| | |
|---|---|
| **Problem:** | **Yellowed melamine.** |
| **What to use:** | **Glycerine, talcum powder, pantyhose; or melamine spray finish.** |
| **How to apply:** | Try to remove the yellow stain with a paste of equal parts glycerine and talcum powder and polish with pantyhose. If this doesn't work, replace or recoat the surface with a melamine spray finish (available from hardware stores and specialist paint stores) or consult a professional. |

**Q:** 'A mouse died in my kitchen cupboard', says Kate. 'That was bad enough, but there's still an awful smell. What do you suggest?'

**Problem: Dead mouse smell in cupboard.**

**What to use: Cloth, white vinegar.**

**How to apply:** The smell is probably from mouse urine. Scrub every surface with a cloth dampened with white vinegar. Don't forget to clean the tops of the cupboards as well. Mice are particularly clever at peeing on the ceiling areas of cupboards.

# CROCKERY

To keep crockery and china in top condition, don't wash in the dishwasher. Instead, hand wash in a little dishwashing liquid and warm water and rinse in clean warm water. For extra sparkle, add 1 tablespoon of white vinegar to the rinse water.

If you keep special china in a 'good cabinet', wash it every 6 months to prevent crazing or at least put a glass of water in with it. If the crockery is crazed or discoloured, add 2 denture tablets to a sinkful of warm water and soak the items overnight, then dry them in the sunshine.

SPOTLESS 2

**Q:** 'How do you get tannin stains off fine English bone china mugs?' asks Timothy.

**Problem:** **Tannin stains on china.**

**What to use:** **Methylated spirits, cotton bud, bicarb, white vinegar, pantyhose.**

**How to apply:** If the mugs have a metallic trim (including gold, white gold and platinum), wipe the trim with methylated spirits on a cotton bud. Clean the rest of the mug with ½ teaspoon of bicarb and 1 teaspoon of white vinegar and rub with pantyhose. Don't get the mixture on the trim (it's very delicate).

**Q:** 'I've got two crystal bowls that are stuck together', says Anna. 'How can I get them apart without scratching them?'

**Problem:** **Crystal bowls stuck together.**

**What to use:** **Hot water, iced water.**

**How to apply:** Run hot (but not boiling) water into your kitchen sink. Place the bowls in the water so the bottom one floats. Slowly add iced water in the top bowl. The top bowl will contract and the bottom bowl will swell and they'll pop apart.

**Q:** 'I have some stained and scratched Bessemer plates', reports Morag. 'What can I do?'

**Problem:** **Stained Bessemer plates.**
**What to use:** **Glycerine, talcum powder, pantyhose or cloth.**
**How to apply:** Bessemer is a type of melamine. To remove stains, mix equal parts glycerine and talcum powder and polish over the stain with pantyhose or a cloth. If there's extensive scratching, replace the plates because bacteria can get into the scratches. Turn the scratched ones into pot-plant saucers or paper plate supports at a picnic.

# TEAPOT

**Q:** 'How do you remove tea stains from a teapot?' asks Roland.

**Problem:** **Tea on crockery.**
**What to use:** **Bicarb, white vinegar, nylon brush or pantyhose.**
**How to apply:** Sprinkle with bicarb followed by white vinegar. When the mixture fizzes, scrub with a nylon brush or pantyhose. Wash and dry normally.

SPOTLESS 2

**TIP** To remove tannin build-up on strainers, dip pantyhose in methylated spirits and rub over the surface. Allow to dry, then rinse well.

## Q: 'How do you clean a silver teapot?' asks William.

**Problem:** Dirty silver.

**What to use:** Bicarb, white vinegar, cloth; or unprocessed wheat bran, bowl, white vinegar, pantyhose, cotton socks/gloves.

**How to apply:** To remove heavy tarnish on solid silver or silver plating, sprinkle with bicarb followed by a sprinkle of white vinegar and, while it's fizzing, polish with a clean cloth. With regular cleaning, place 1 cup of unprocessed wheat bran in a bowl and add white vinegar drop by drop, stirring as you go. It's ready when the mixture is clumpy like brown sugar. Either put the mixture into the toe of a pair of pantyhose, tie it off and scrub over the pieces. Or apply the mixture directly wearing a pair of old cotton socks on your hands to prevent sweat from your hands tarnishing the silver.

The Kitchen

# JARS

**Q:** 'What's the best way to get rid of garlic odour from a jar lid?' asks Jo.

**Problem:** **Garlic odour in jar lid.**
**What to use:** **Coarse salt, chopped fresh parsley, cloth.**
**How to apply:** Rub the lid with a mixture of 1 tablespoon of coarse salt and 1 teaspoon of finely chopped parsley. Wipe with a dry cloth.

**(TIP)** Many glass jars have plastic or rubber linings inside the lid which absorb smells and oils and can contaminate your preserves. Put a film of beeswax or paraffin wax (available at the hardware or craft store and some supermarkets) over the preserves before securing the lid. The easiest way is to place 2 tablespoons of wax into a microwave-safe dish and heat in 10-second bursts in the microwave until just melted. Hold a warm teaspoon face down over the preserve and trickle the wax over the back of the warmed spoon. This allows a thin, even layer of wax to settle over the preserve that's easy to remove.

# PLASTIC CONTAINERS

At a Stain Clinic in Perth Harold brought along a white plastic bowl with a red ring circling the middle of the inside edge. Shannon said the red mark was from reheating tomato soup in the microwave. This can be a tough stain to fix if the tomato dye has been absorbed into the plastic. The solution is to scrub the stain with a paste of equal parts glycerine and talcum powder on a nylon brush. Alternatively, sprinkle coarse salt over the cut face of half a lemon, scrub over the stain and leave in the sunshine to dry.

**Q:** 'I have a couple of old Tupperware containers that are quite sticky to touch', says Sonia. 'What can I do?'

**Problem:** **Sticky Tupperware.**
**How to apply:** Tupperware has a lifetime guarantee and the company will replace the item. It's best not to use containers that are sticky because bacteria can stick to it.

*TIP* To get rid of greasiness on plastic containers, add 1 teaspoon of white vinegar to the rinse water.

## LUNCH BAGS

**Q:** 'I've got salmon juice all over a cloth-insulated lunch bag', says Louise. 'It stinks!'

**Problem:** **Salmon juice on cotton.**
**What to use:** **Cake of bathroom soap, cold water, sunshine.**

The Kitchen

**How to apply:** Run a cake of bathroom soap under cold water and scribble over the stain. Massage the stain with your fingers, including into the creases, and rinse in plenty of cold water. Hang it in the sunshine to dry. If the stitching along the edge rots, smells or becomes rough, it's time to throw the bag away because it's vulnerable to bacteria. A plastic lunch box is sturdier.

# CUTLERY

Most cutlery is fairly robust. If it has plastic handles, it won't last as long but they're generally cheaper to buy. Buy the best quality you can afford.

**Q:** 'Is there a way I can rejuvenate our 30-year-old everyday cutlery?' asks Mary. 'It's made of stainless steel and has fine scratches on the handles and blades.'

**Problem: Scratches on stainless steel cutlery.**
**What to use: Gumption, cloth, bicarb, white vinegar, tea towel.**
**How to apply:** Stainless steel is a wonderful material because it's extremely tough and doesn't damage easily. On the downside, it's difficult to polish out scratches. To ameliorate the scratches, apply a dab of Gumption to a cloth, rub over the

scratch, sprinkle with bicarb and splash with a little white vinegar and rub as it's fizzing. Polish with dry tea towel.

## KNIVES

Hand wash your knives or you could get rust marks on them. If this happens, wipe with bicarb on a damp cloth. To help a knife retain its edge, try Shannon's trick. Keep a glass of water next to you when chopping onions and garlic and dip the knife in the water while you chop. Onion and garlic blunt knives!

## GLASSWARE

To make glasses sparkle, add 1 cup of white vinegar to a sink of warm rinse water. This removes streaking and detergent residue from glass. To dry, stand the glasses upside down on a clean tea towel.

To remove scratches in glass, make a paste of equal parts glycerine and whiting (available from leadlighting stores) and polish the scratches out. If the scratches are deep, this can take a long time. Wash in warm water and polish with a clean tea towel.

If glass is etched, wipe with sweet almond oil on a cloth. It won't clean the glass but removes the cloudy appearance.

## THE PANTRY

Keep the pantry clean by regularly wiping surfaces with a damp cloth. Get into the habit of putting newer cans and packaging at the back, rather than at the front, of the pantry. That way you'll get to things before the expiry date (hopefully!). After opening a packet of food, store the food in an airtight container or you could get moths flying about in your pantry. If this happens, place bay leaves along the shelves or wipe over them with a couple of drops of bay oil or oil of pennyroyal on a cloth. **Don't use oil of pennyroyal if anyone in the house is pregnant, including pets.**

**Problem:** **Ants.**

**What to use:** **Powdered borax, cornflour, icing sugar; or powdered borax, finely grated parmesan cheese; or boiling water.**

**How to apply:** Work out whether the ants are attracted to sweet or savoury flavours. For those with a sweet tooth, mix ½ teaspoon of borax, ½ teaspoon of cornflour and ¼ teaspoon of icing sugar and place along the ant trail. For savoury eaters, mix equal parts borax and parmesan and scatter along the ant trail. The ants will take the mixture back to the nest and die. Be careful using borax around pets and children—it is mildly toxic! Alternatively, a non-toxic option is to go nest hunting by sprinkling cornflour on an ant trail so that the ants walk it back to the nest, making a visible track for you to follow. When you find it, pour boiling water down the ant nest.

**Prevention:** Keep benchtops spotless.

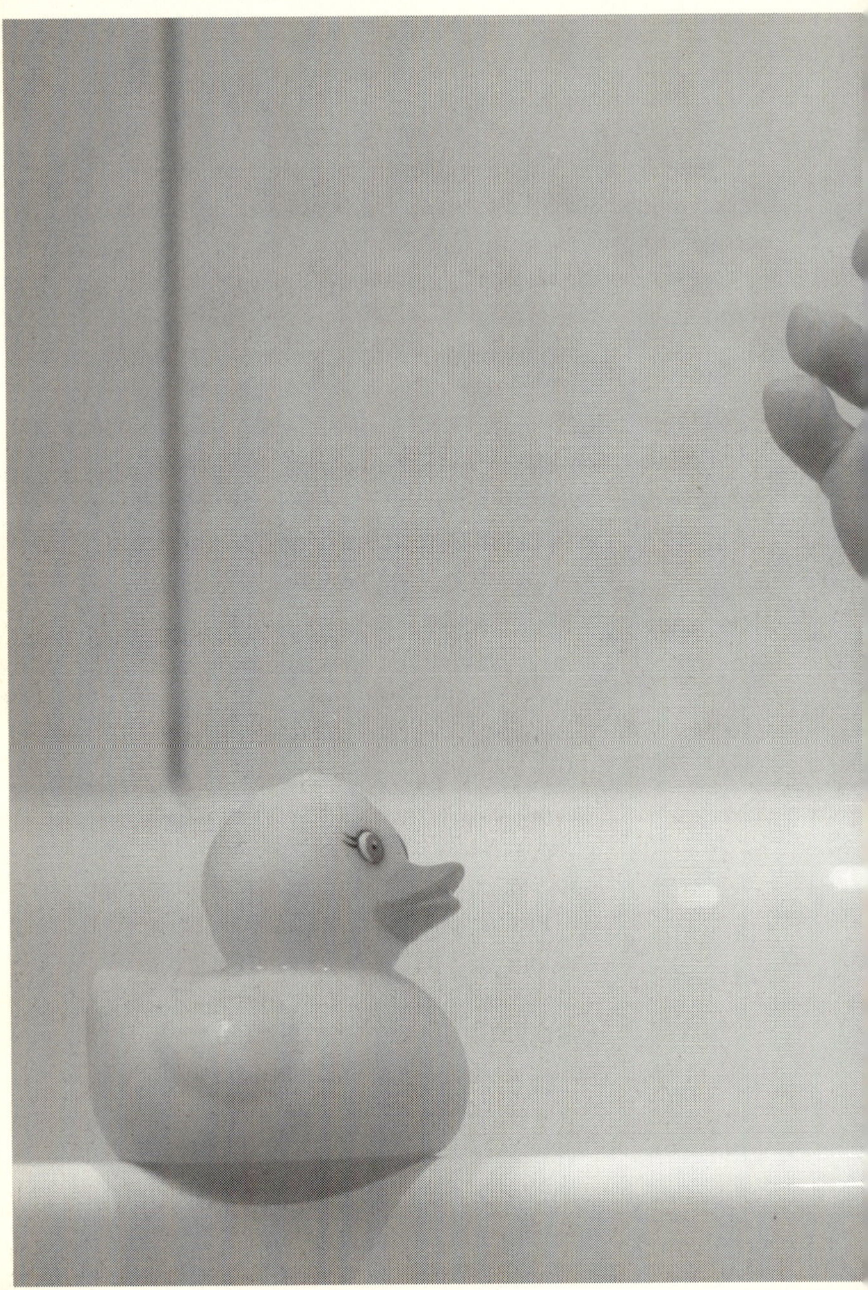

# The Bathroom

There's nothing more relaxing than sinking into a hot bath! But this blissful state can be ruined if, as you lie back, you notice mould or mildew on the walls. The green and black stuff is the bane of many a bathroom cleaner, particularly in older bathrooms, as Jennifer knows only too well. Shannon loves cleaning the bathroom because she ends up with plenty of sparkling surfaces. Grab the right cleaning items, put on a favourite CD and in no time your bathroom surfaces will be gleaming.

The Bathroom

## TACKY TIMBER: Reg's story

**INCIDENT:** 'I've got sealed timber walls in my bathroom but there are numerous toothpaste and soap stains around the vanity area. It ruins the clean Swedish image. What do you suggest?'

**SOLUTION:** Roll pantyhose into a ball, dampen with water and rub over the stains. It's likely the toothpaste will have bleached the timber. If this is the case, wipe with a damp tea bag. The tannins in the tea draw out the tannins in the timber and replace the lost colour. Always remove toothpaste marks as soon as possible.

# TOILET

Cleaning the toilet is easier if you don't allow grime to accumulate—and, besides, most toilets are easy to clean (for instructions, see *Spotless*, page 50).

One of the most common toilet stains is urine. Now, how do we put this delicately? There are often 'spray' issues that not only stain but leave a noxious smell as well. Fix by wiping the area with white vinegar or lemon juice on a cloth, making sure you also wipe the pipes at the back and the floor area around the toilet. If your floor is unsealed marble, dilute white vinegar and rinse with clean water when you have finished or the vinegar could damage the surface.

Shannon isn't keen on the 'if it's yellow, let it mellow' approach to water saving. She thinks it's okay to leave urine in the bowl for a few hours but says it can remove the surface from

SPOTLESS 2

the porcelain, leaving a rougher surface for bacteria to stick to. To neutralise acid in urine, sprinkle bicarb into the toilet bowl after peeing (½ teaspoon should do the job) and flush every 24 hours. You'll add a layer of protection to the surface of the toilet bowl if you lightly spray with a mix of 1 teaspoon of lavender oil to a 1 litre spray pack of water after cleaning.

For a super-duper clean, scoop the water out of the toilet bowl with a paper cup (you don't want to chip your good china) and lightly sprinkle the entire bowl with a little bicarb, followed by an equal amount of white vinegar and, as it's fizzing, scrub with a toilet brush. Repeat if needed. If there are very grotty stains, flush first with hot water (pour it straight from the kettle) to dissolve fats and oils that build up on the surface. And there's always the Coke solution! Many people swear that adding Coke to the toilet bowl gives a great clean; however, it can damage the ceramic glaze, leaving a greater surface area for bacteria to stick to. (If Coke does that to a toilet, imagine what it does to your stomach.)

# Q: 'We have a septic tank and live near a stream and are therefore careful about the cleaning products we use', says Melanie. 'The toilets have marks on the bottom inside the bowl (below the water level) and I'd like to remove them. What do you suggest?'

**Problem:** **Cleaning a septic toilet.**
**What to use:** **Paper cup, bicarb, white vinegar, toilet brush.**

**How to apply:** Use a paper cup (to avoid scratches) to remove the water from the toilet bowl. Sprinkle the bowl with a light dusting of bicarb followed by an equal amount of white vinegar and, as the mixture fizzes, scrub with a toilet brush. Because the quantities of bicarb and vinegar are equal, it creates salt water which isn't damaging for septic systems.

**Q:** 'I've got a pale blue stain (water stain, I think) at the back of the toilet', says Joan. 'The house is near the coast with a lot of limestone in the ground which probably affects the water quality. What do you suggest?'

**Problem: Water stain on back of toilet.**
**What to use: Talcum powder, disposable rubber gloves, CLR/Ranex.**
**How to apply:** The blue line running down the back of the toilet is likely to be from mineral deposit in the water. Flush the toilet, lightly dust the bowl with talcum powder and allow to dry. Put on rubber gloves and apply CLR or Ranex to the talcum powder. The talcum powder holds the CLR or Ranex in place, allowing it to soak in. To prevent the problem, add 1 capful of CLR or Ranex to your cistern when you do a regular clean of your toilet.

# BATH

To clean your bath, lightly dust with bicarb, add equal parts white vinegar and, while it's fizzing, give a good scrub with a cloth or soft broom. That's all your bath should need to be clean and gleaming. If you have a build-up of dirt and it's difficult to shift, try the denture tablet trick. Fill your bath with hot water, add 12 denture tablets and leave overnight. When you pull out the plug and give it a rub, the dirt will wash down the drain. If you've got seriously ingrained dirt in your bath (old ones are susceptible to this), commercial sponge products are available where you just add water and scrub over the muck. Be aware that these products actually remove the top surface of the bath. It might be necessary to try one of these if you have a century-old bath but use the sponges sparingly in other cases. An alternative method is to cut a lemon in half, sprinkle the cut surface with non-iodised salt and scrub the lemon over the surface of the bath. It's abrasive but the salt crystals break down so it's not damaging to the surface of your bath.

If the surface is badly scratched or you want an update, you can have baths professionally resurfaced for around $500.00 (depending on the size). If yours has been renovated in this way, be careful when adding hot water because the new surface will expand at a different rate to the base surface and may crack. Protect the new surface by putting a little cold water in the bath before adding hot water.

The Bathroom

**TIP** Reduce your cleaning time by wiping the bath with a rolled up pair of pantyhose immediately after using it. You won't get dirt rings and it will minimise any etching.

## Q: 'I have a fibreglass bath with stains from essential oils', reports Jodie. 'The stains look like tiny little brown marks. Can you help me?'

**Problem:** Essential oil on fibreglass.

**What to use:** Dishwashing liquid, glycerine, talcum powder, pantyhose, soft cloth.

**How to apply:** Mix 1 teaspoon of dishwashing liquid, 1 teaspoon of glycerine and 1 teaspoon of talcum powder and scrub over the stain with pantyhose. Leave for 20 minutes and polish off with a soft cloth. Repeat if necessary.

## Q: 'I've spilt liquid shoe polish onto a white enamel bath', admits Anne. 'What can I do?'

**Problem:** Liquid shoe polish on enamel.

**What to use:** Tea tree oil, cloth.

**How to apply:** Wipe the stain with a dab of tea tree oil on a cloth. It should come away easily.

**Q:** 'We have bore water', reports Frances. 'And it's left a stain on the ceramic bath. What do you suggest?'

| | |
|---|---|
| **Problem:** | **Bore water stain on ceramic.** |
| **What to use:** | **Disposable rubber gloves, water, CLR/Ranex, nylon brush.** |
| **How to apply:** | Put on rubber gloves, fill the bath with water and add 2 capfuls of CLR or Ranex. Leave for 2 hours, drain the bath and scrub with a brush. Don't get CLR or Ranex on your skin because it can cause irritation. |

## Spa bath

When you're sitting back enjoying a jet-filled soak, don't use soap because it gets into the filter and creates a cloggy mess. Instead, use shower gel or liquid soap. To clean a spa bath, put 1 cup of bicarb in a full tub of water, run the spa bath for 5 minutes and allow the bicarb to circulate. Add 2 cups of white vinegar and run for a further 5 minutes. Drain and rinse with clean water.

# SHOWER

In these water-saving times, we're encouraged to spend only 3 minutes taking a shower—and it's a lovely 3 minutes. One of the most common problems with showers is mould, particularly in the silicone. The reason mould grows is from a combination of moisture and lack of ventilation, so get into the habit of wiping

## The Bathroom

up any water in the shower area and allow air to circulate in the room. You could even leave a squeegee in the shower area and encourage users to wipe over the area after each shower. If your shower is vulnerable to mould, spray with ¼ teaspoon of oil of cloves in a 1 litre spray pack of water.

If your shower includes polymarble, clean it with a rolled up pair of pantyhose after each use. It doesn't react well to soaps or shampoos left on the surface. Don't clean with bicarb or vinegar or it will damage the polymarble.

Some modern bathrooms are designed as wet rooms that are completely open with nothing separating the water spray from the shower from the rest of the bathroom. If this is the case in your home, you'll know it's important to have a protected area for your towel!

**Problem:** **Rust marks on shower tiles.**

**What to use:** **Water, talcum powder, disposable rubber gloves, CLR/Ranex, white vinegar, cloth.**

**How to apply:** Wet the affected area with water and sprinkle with talcum powder, to help with absorption. Put on rubber gloves, apply CLR or Ranex and leave for 10 minutes. The rust should be gone. Neutralise the chemicals by wiping with white vinegar on a cloth.

**Q:** 'My shower recess has a fancy border tile along the wall which is made of marble and runs right around the bathroom', reports Kerry. 'The tiles in the shower (that get wet) are turning white-ish and have lost their shine. What can I do?'

    **Problem:** **Dull marble in shower.**

    **What to use:** **Glycerine, talcum powder, pantyhose or cloth, marble wax.**

    **How to apply:** The marble is reacting to the caustic properties in soap. Polish with a paste of equal parts glycerine and talcum powder on a pair of pantyhose or cloth. Finish by polishing with a quality marble wax, such as Cera Wax. In high-traffic areas such as the shower, marble needs to be cleaned after every use, even if it's only a wipe down. Marble should be waxed once a week if used regularly.

**Q:** 'I've had a rubber suction mat on the bathroom floor', reports Dawn. 'And it's left marks. What can I do?'

    **Problem:** **Rubber on tiles.**

    **What to use:** **Water, coarse salt, stiff scrubbing brush or broom, damp cloth.**

    **How to apply:** Damp the tiles with water and scrub salt over the marks with a brush or broom. Remove the salt with a damp cloth.

**TIP** To remove make-up and dead skin cells, place unprocessed wheat bran in the toe of a pair of pantyhose, tie to enclose, dampen with water and gently rub over your skin. It's a great exfoliator.

## Shower screen

Most shower screens can be cleaned with white vinegar or methylated spirits on a cloth. Polycarbonate shower screens can be cleaned only with white vinegar. If you clean shower screens regularly, you won't get stain build-up. To tackle mould, combine ¼ teaspoon of oil of cloves with 1 litre of water in a spray pack, lightly spray the solution over the affected area and leave for 24 hours. If mould has formed behind the silicone join, combine ¼ teaspoon of oil of cloves with 1 litre of water in a spray pack and after spraying, scrub with an old toothbrush. If the mould is ingrained in the silicone, you'll need to replace the silicone. You can replace it yourself or seek professional help.

### *SPOTLESS CLASSIC*
### Cloudy shower screen

We get many questions about how to fix streaky marks on shower screens. Sometimes it's from a build-up of soap or shampoo which can be removed with bicarb and white vinegar. But in many cases, the cloudiness is from tiny air bubbles etched into the screen (often caused by caustic cleaning products) that Shannon calls 'glass cancer' and the damage is permanent. You can alleviate the problem by wiping with sweet almond oil on a cloth or pantyhose. To prevent it, don't use caustic cleaning products and clean with bicarb and white vinegar instead.

SPOTLESS 2

## Shower curtain

Most shower curtains are made of fabric or plastic and can be washed in a washing machine, laundry tub or bucket. Whatever you do, don't clean them with bleach. The curtains will look whiter but bleach breaks down the surface and makes them more susceptible to mould and you'll find them more difficult to clean later. Instead clean with 1 teaspoon of dishwashing liquid, ¼ teaspoon of oil of cloves and 1 litre of warm water. Fabric curtains look good but wear more quickly and need to be washed each week, more if you've got a home full of footballers. Wipe plastic shower curtains after each use and hook up over the rod so they don't collect water, condensation and mould.

## Shower head

Most people don't think to clean the shower head but it's vulnerable to staining. To clean, wipe with damp pantyhose. One problem you may encounter is black prickly things coming out of the nozzles. If this is the case, see *Speedcleaning*, page 103.

**Q:** 'We have green-coloured marks on our shower head', reports Penny. 'What should we do?'

    **Problem:** **Green marks on shower head.**

**What to use:** **Disposable rubber gloves, CLR/Ranex, old plastic ice-cream container, water.**

**How to apply:** The marks are probably from mineral build-up or oxidisation. Put on rubber gloves, place CLR or Ranex and water (according to the directions on the pack) in an ice-cream container and immerse the shower head for 10 minutes. Rinse with water.

# TAPS

Most taps are chrome, gold or brass-plated and can be cleaned with bicarb and white vinegar. Don't forget to clean the back of the taps—the easy way is to wrap pantyhose around the tap and move them backwards and forwards in a sawing action. An old toothbrush also does the trick, particularly at getting into the area where the tap joins the basin or vanity top.

# TILES

Reapplying grout between your tiles is relatively easy and really gives your bathroom a great lift. To remove old grout, use a grout rake. Run this nifty tool backwards and forwards along the grout until it becomes powdery. Clean the area thoroughly and apply the new grout. Make sure you wipe off any excess grout before it dries.

One of the common complaints with tiles and grout in bathrooms is mould. The best way to deal with mould is to combine ¼ teaspoon of oil of cloves with 1 litre of water in a spray pack, lightly spray the solution over the affected area and leave for 24 hours. After that, clean the grout with bicarb and white vinegar using an old toothbrush. The visible mould should be gone. Lightly mist again with the oil of cloves mixture and repeat every 2 months. Oil of cloves is very strong and will burn plastic, so it must be diluted—once an item is burnt, it's very difficult to repair. If you have a burn stain from oil of cloves, mix equal parts glycerine and talcum powder and rub with pantyhose. It won't fix the burn but it will improve the appearance.

## Q: 'I've got a black line over my white tiles', says Bruce. 'What do you suggest?'

**Problem:** **Black line on white tiles.**
**What to use:** **Pencil eraser or biro eraser, water.**
**How to apply:** It sounds as though someone has accidentally bumped an aerosol can over the tile and left a black line. Remove it with a pencil eraser or biro eraser dipped in water.

## Q: 'The builder left silicone on the tiles', says Sarah. 'What can I do to remove it?

**Problem:** **Silicone on tiles.**
**What to use:** **Kerosene, single-sided razor blade.**
**How to apply:** Apply a little kerosene to a razor blade and use it to scrape under the silicone on the tiles. The silicone will slide off.

## Q: 'We've laid small dark tiles and a dark colour grout at the base of our shower', reports Kellie. 'But it's really hard to keep the grout looking good, especially with soap. Any ideas?'

**Problem:** **Soap scum on dark-coloured grout.**

**What to use:** **Broom, pantyhose, bicarb, white vinegar, sweet almond oil, cloth.**

**How to apply:** Force the head of a broom into the leg of a pair of pantyhose. Sprinkle the tiles with a light dusting of bicarb followed by a light spray of white vinegar and, while it's fizzing, scrub with the broom and rinse with water. If any white scum remains, polish with a couple of drops of sweet almond oil on a cloth.

# MIRROR

**Q:** 'My bathroom mirror has silicone smeared around one corner', says Sandra. 'Can I remove it? It looks streaky.'

**Problem:** **Silicone on mirror.**

**What to use:** **Single-sided razor blade, kerosene; or pantyhose, kerosene, white vinegar, paper towel.**

**How to apply:** If the silicone is quite thick, dip a razor blade in kerosene and slide it under the silicone and along the mirror to remove it. If it's only a very thin film of silicone, remove by dipping a rolled up pair of pantyhose in kerosene and rubbing over the silicone. Once the silicone has been removed, wipe with a little white vinegar on paper towel.

# HAND BASIN AND VANITY

**Q:** 'What's the best way to clean the marble on my vanity?' asks Trish. 'Water seems to have penetrated the sealant.'

**Problem:** Watermarks on sealed marble.

**What to use:** Brasso, pantyhose.

**How to apply:** In most cases, marble in a bathroom is sealed with polyurethane. If this is the case, apply a little Brasso to rolled up pantyhose and rub in a circular motion. Be fast and don't apply too much pressure. This partially melts the polyurethane and removes bubbles that appear to be watermarks. You may need to reseal the surface—seek professional help.

**Prevention:** To provide a protective coating for marble, apply a good quality marble floor wax. Renew the wax regularly.

**Q:** 'I've got a green copper mark on my plastic bathroom sink', says Cheryl. 'How do I remove it?'

**Problem:** Green copper mark on basin.

**What to use:** Glycerine, talcum powder, pantyhose.

**How to apply:** Clean with a mixture of equal parts glycerine and talcum powder. Polish on with a pair of pantyhose and leave for around half an hour then polish off.

## The Bathroom

**Q:** 'I need help to remove yellow water marks on my white basin', reports Johnny. 'It's where the water sits in the soap holders and around the plug hole.'

    **Problem:** **Yellow water marks on basin.**

  **What to use:** **Talcum powder, disposable rubber gloves, CLR/Ranex.**

  **How to apply:** It's likely to be from mineral deposit in the water. Sprinkle the affected area with talcum powder and allow to dry. Put on rubber gloves and apply CLR or Ranex to the talcum powder and allow to soak in. Rinse with water. Don't get CLR or Ranex on your skin because it can cause irritation.

**Q:** 'How do you get Tiger Balm out of hair?' asks Monique.

    **Problem:** **Tiger Balm in hair.**

  **What to use:** **Tea tree oil, dishwashing liquid, olive oil, warm water.**

  **How to apply:** Tiger Balm has an oil and wax base. Mix 1 teaspoon of tea tree oil, 1 teaspoon of dishwashing liquid and 1 teaspoon of olive oil and massage into the scalp and hair. Rinse with warm water, massaging as you rinse. You may need to repeat.

SPOTLESS 2

# TOWELS

If your towels are stiff and scratchy, see page 311.

**Q:** 'I've got liquid foundation make-up on my towels', reports Julie. 'And it won't come out in the wash. What do you suggest?'

**Problem:** **Liquid foundation on towels.**
**What to use:** **Methylated spirits, dishwashing liquid.**
**How to apply:** Mix equal parts methylated spirits and dishwashing liquid and rub into the stain with your fingers. Wash normally.

# BATHROOM WALLS

For many, the smell of bleach equates to cleanliness—and while bleach does whiten surfaces, it doesn't necessarily remove dirt and isn't great for the environment or your health. (Bleach contains dioxins that can produce the environmental pollutants trihalomethanes, which are also believed to be carcinogenic.) For a less toxic cleaning option, sprinkle bicarb on a cloth, add some white vinegar and wipe over the walls. Use ¼ teaspoon of oil of cloves in a 1 litre spray pack of water to tackle mould.

The Bathroom

# Q: 'I seem to have gunk down my bathroom drains', reports Sue. 'How can I unclog them?'

**Problem:** **Clogged drains.**

**What to use:** **Coat-hanger, pantyhose, bicarb, white vinegar, boiling water.**

**How to apply:** Some blockages occur when talcum powder or hair sticks to the inside edge of the drain. To prevent the problem, put gauze or a piece of pantyhose fabric underneath the drain grate. To clean, wrap a pair of pantyhose around the end of a straightened coathanger and knot it tightly. Use the coathanger just like a big bottle brush to scrub down inside the drain. Now put ½ cup bicarb down the drain and leave for 20 minutes, followed by ½ cup of white vinegar. Leave for half an hour and pour boiling water (from the kettle) down the drain.

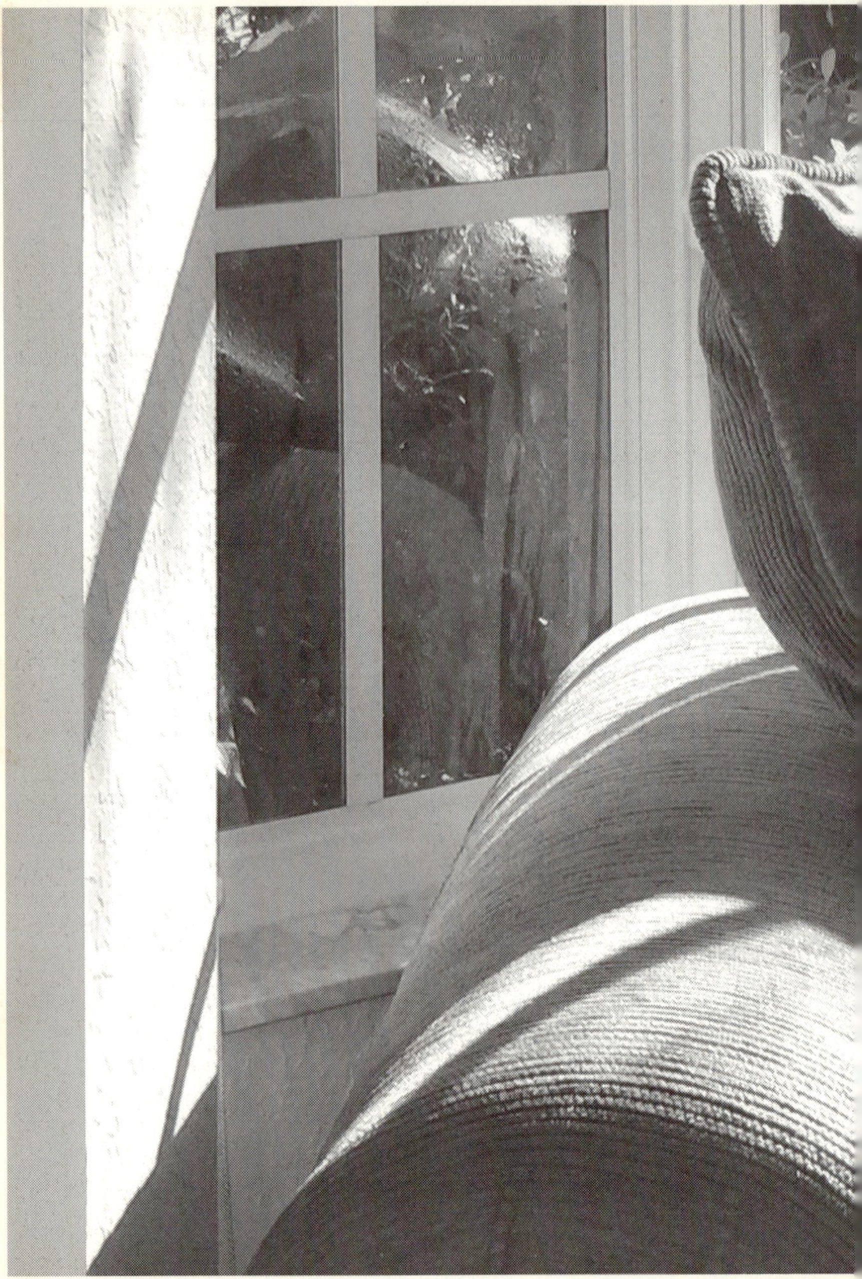

# Lounge, Dining and Family Rooms

Who doesn't love coming home after a long day, kicking off the shoes and lying back on a comfy couch? And if the remote is within reach, even better. These rooms are the social hub of the home—and in many houses they're combined in one big space. Furniture tends to get a lot of use so there's more cleaning to do, particularly if you watch TV while eating dinner (it's only a short distance between the plate and the couch). When working out how to fix a spill, think about the components of the stain and the surface it's on. Sort that out and you're on your way to a clean living area.

Lounge, Dining and Family Rooms

## FETA FALL: Sue's story

**INCIDENT:** 'I've got a gorgeous Italian couch covered in microsuede. During a recent soiree, some marinated feta cheese dropped onto the couch. I dampened it with detergent and water and there are now watermarks on the fabric. Can it be saved?'

**SOLUTION:** To remove the watermark, make a bran ball (see below). Use the bran ball as though it is an eraser and rub over the upholstery in every direction. To remove the oily part of the stain (from the marinade), place a couple of drops of dishwashing liquid on your fingertips and massage into the stain until it feels like jelly. Remove the dishwashing liquid with a damp cloth and dry immediately and thoroughly by pressing with paper towel.

# COUCHES

In some homes, the couch is the most-used piece of furniture. Deal with stains as soon as possible because they become harder to remove when they set. If you're not sure what the stain is, first do a stain diagnosis (see page 362). Since *Spotless*, Shannon has refined the technique for cleaning upholstery, and other items that can't be put in the washing machine, and uses a bran ball. To make a bran ball, put 1 cup of unprocessed wheat bran in a bowl and add white vinegar, 1 drop at a time, until the mixture resembles brown sugar—it should be clumping but not wet. Place the mixture into the toe of a pair of pantyhose and tie tightly. Rub the pantyhose across the surface as though using an eraser. The bran ball is preferable to carpet cleaner when giving the couch a spruce up because it's gentler on fabrics. After cleaning, spray with Scotchgard (around once a year) to provide the couch with a layer of protection. And if you get lots of grubby marks, consider making or buying removable slipcovers that can be put in the washing machine. Much easier!

Cushion covers generally need special care. If there's no care label attached, treat them as if they are made of silk. Wash in blood-heat water with a small amount of cheap shampoo and rinse in blood-heat water. Smooth the cover flat and place in the shade to dry. When ironing cushion covers, always use a cool setting and place a clean cloth between the iron and the cover and, if possible, iron inside out. Don't use starch because they won't mould to the shape of the cushion insert.

**TIP** Keep paper towel or a Slurpex near your couch to mop up any spills as soon as they happen.

**Q:** 'I have some lovely linen cushion covers with red silk appliqués and red silk cord around the edge,' says Megan. 'One cushion got a black (looked like grease) mark on it and so I hand washed it in cold water. The red silk wasn't colourfast and left orangey coloured splodges on the cushion. And the black mark still remains. Is there anything I can do?'

    **Problem:** **Grease and dye on linen.**
**What to use:** **Dishwashing liquid, cloth, cold water, Colour Run Remover: Coloursafe, cloth, salt, bucket.**

Lounge, Dining and Family Rooms

**How to apply:** To remove the grease mark, add a couple of drops of dishwashing liquid to your fingers and massage into the stain until it feels like jelly. Then wipe over with a cloth wrung out in cold water. To remove the dye run, mix 1 part Colour Run Remover: Coloursafe to 5 parts water, wring a cloth in the mixture and sponge over the affected area until the colour is removed. Then rinse in salt water (1 cup of salt per 9 litre bucket of cold water). Hang on the clothesline on a cool day or dry flat in the shade.

## *SPOTLESS CLASSIC*
### Pen marks on couch

Even if you don't have children, it's common to get pen marks on your couch. They can be tricky stains to tackle because different pens use different inks and each has a different solvent. As a general rule, biro pen marks are removed with rotten milk solids placed over the ink (see *Spotless*, page 66). With permanent markers, write over the stain using the same pen and quickly follow with a cotton bud dipped in white spirits. Repeat until removed. With Artline pens and whiteboard markers, wipe only over the mark with a cotton bud dipped in methylated spirits and repeat until removed. With fluorescent pens, write over the stain using the same marker quickly followed by a cotton bud dipped in white spirits. If you're not sure, do a test first using a cotton bud and the various solvents.

# COTTON/LINEN UPHOLSTERY

**Q:** 'I spilt coffee over the arm of my cotton couch', reports Louise. 'The fabric can't be removed and I don't know what to do. Can you help?'

>   **Problem:** **Coffee on cotton.**
>   **What to use:** **Glycerine, cotton ball, dishwashing liquid, damp cloth, paper towel.**
>   **How to apply:** Dab a cotton ball with a little glycerine and wipe over the stain. Leave for 20 minutes. Massage a couple of drops of dishwashing liquid into the stain using your fingers. Wipe off with a damp cloth and dry by pressing with paper towel. Don't use too much moisture. Repeat if necessary.

**Q:** 'My husband fell asleep while holding a glass of red wine and it spilled all over our pale loose linen sofa which had been Scotchgarded,' reports Megan. 'At 3am, he got out my copy of *Spotless* and, in an attempt to undo the damage, proceeded to rub the red wine into the sofa. The care instructions state the linen can only be dry-cleaned. Help, please!'

>   **Problem:** **Red wine on upholstered linen.**
>   **What to use:** **Paper towel or Slurpex, bicarb, cloth, white vinegar, vacuum cleaner.**

Lounge, Dining and Family Rooms

**How to apply:** Remove as much moisture as possible with paper towel or Slurpex. Then sprinkle a little bicarb over the area—it will turn a grey colour. Wring a cloth tightly in white vinegar and wipe over the mark. Repeat until the stain is removed. Pat dry with paper towel. If needed, vacuum using the brush attachment when it is dry.

**Q:** 'My daughter has used crayons all over our light beige cotton couch', reports Margie. 'What can I do?'

**Problem: Crayon on cotton.**

**What to use: Pencil eraser, vacuum cleaner, tea tree oil, dishwashing liquid, damp cloth, paper towel.**

**How to apply:** Crayon contains wax, so rub over the marks with a pencil eraser then vacuum. Mix 2 drops of tea tree oil with 1 teaspoon of dishwashing liquid and massage over the crayon marks with your fingers until the crayon dissolves, then wipe with a damp cloth. Use as little moisture as possible on the stains. Dry by pressing with paper towel.

**Problem: Coloured pencil on cotton.**

**What to use: Pencil eraser, methylated spirits, cotton bud, talcum powder, vacuum cleaner.**

SPOTLESS 2

**How to apply:** Rub over the pencil marks with a pencil eraser and vacuum. Wipe over the marks with methylated spirits on a cotton bud until the colour bleeds. Now cover with talcum powder. When the talcum powder dries, vacuum. Repeat if necessary.

**Problem:** **Oil on cotton.**
**What to use:** **Dishwashing liquid, damp cloth, paper towel.**
**How to apply:** Put a couple of drops of dishwashing liquid on your fingertips and massage into the oil until it feels like jelly. Wipe repeatedly with a damp cloth and dry by pressing with paper towel.

**Problem:** **Steam cleaning didn't remove tea stains on cotton.**
**What to use:** **Glycerine, cloth, white vinegar.**
**How to apply:** When you steam clean tea stains, it sets them into the fabric. To unset them, put a couple of drops of glycerine on a cloth and wipe over the stain. Leave for 20 minutes. Tightly wring out a cloth in white vinegar and wipe over the glycerine. Repeat until the stain is gone and wipe with a cold damp cloth before drying thoroughly.

**Q:** 'I've got ear drop stains on my fabric chair', reports Pat. 'What should I do?'

    **Problem:** **Eardrops on cotton.**

**What to use:** **Bran ball.**

**How to apply:** Wipe a bran ball (see page 85) over the ear drops.

# MICROSUEDE, MACROSUEDE, SUPERSUEDE AND NUBUCK

These popular coverings are usually treated to repel spills and stains. Whatever you do, don't use upholstery cleaner on these fabrics or it will leave a watermark and cause warping. Instead, clean with a bran ball (see page 85).

**Q:** 'My budding artist left a mural on the microsuede lounge with a child's Texta pen', says Jayne. 'The colour is mid-green. Can you help me?'

    **Problem:** **Texta on microsuede.**

**What to use:** **Cotton bud, methylated spirits, paper towel, cotton ball.**

**How to apply:** Dip a cotton bud in methylated spirits, wipe over the Texta mark and press with paper towel. The Texta will transfer to the paper towel. Repeat until removed. If you can, place a cotton ball behind the stain to stop it spreading through the fabric.

|            |                                                        |
|------------|--------------------------------------------------------|
| **Problem:** | **Felt tip pen on nubuck.** |
| **What to use:** | **White spirits, cotton bud, talcum powder, vacuum cleaner; or methylated spirits, cotton bud, paper towel.** |
| **How to apply:** | What to use will depend on the type of ink. First, try white spirits on a cotton bud and wipe over the mark. Then apply talcum powder over the white spirits. Leave to dry and vacuum. If this doesn't work, use methylated spirits on a cotton bud and wipe over the mark. Press with paper towel until dry. |

**Q:** 'I was eating melted cheese on toast', reports Larry. 'And some of the hot melted cheese landed on my microsuede lounge. What can I do?'

|            |                                                        |
|------------|--------------------------------------------------------|
| **Problem:** | **Melted cheese on microsuede.** |
| **What to use:** | **Ice-cubes, zip-lock bag, plastic knife, dishwashing liquid, damp cloth, paper towel.** |
| **How to apply:** | Put an ice-cube in a zip-lock bag and place over the cheese. When the cheese is hard, remove the ice and scrape off the cheese with a plastic knife. To remove the oily smear, put a couple of drops of dishwashing liquid on your fingers and massage into the stain until it feels like jelly. Wipe over with a damp cloth and dry by pressing with paper towel. |

Lounge, Dining and Family Rooms

**Q:** 'How do you remove crayon from microsuede fabric?'

> **Problem:** **Crayon on microsuede.**
>
> **What to use:** **Brown bread, tea tree oil, pantyhose.**
>
> **How to apply:** Crayon has wax in it so rub the mark with brown bread. If any crayon remains, wipe with a couple of drops of tea tree oil on pantyhose.

**Q:** 'I've got 10 years' worth of sweat and body oil on a nubuck lounge', says Mike. 'Is it time to recover it or can you save my beloved lounge/recliner?'

> **Problem:** **Sweat/body oil on nubuck.**
>
> **What to use:** **Bran ball, dishwashing liquid, damp cloth, paper towel.**
>
> **How to apply:** Rub a bran ball (see page 85) over the affected area until it's clean. For any oily spots, massage in a little dishwashing liquid using your fingers until it feels like jelly, then wipe with a damp cloth. Dry by pressing with paper towel.

**Q:** 'I spilt nail polish on a microsuede couch', says Margaret. 'What can I do?'

> **Problem:** **Nail polish on microsuede.**
>
> **What to use:** **Acetone, cotton bud, methylated spirits or white vinegar, cloth.**

**How to apply:** Rub a little acetone (not nail polish remover) on a cotton bud over the nail polish. Once the polish has been removed, wipe over the spot with a little methylated spirits or white vinegar on a cloth to remove the acetone. This must be done quickly or the acetone could damage the fibres in the fabric.

# JACQUARD

**Q:** 'A recent visitor was breastfeeding her baby on my jacquard chair and the baby regurgitated milk on it', says Karen. 'It has a dark stain that I can't seem to get out. What do you suggest?'

**Problem:** **Baby milk vomit on jacquard.**

**What to use:** **Cake of bathroom soap, cold water, damp cloth, bran ball.**

**How to apply:** If the stain has a dark edging, it's a protein stain. To remove, run a cake of bathroom soap under cold water and using it like a big crayon, scribble over the stain and wipe with a damp cloth. Press with paper towel to absorb moisture. If there's a watermark, rub a bran ball (see page 85) over the stain until removed.

Lounge, Dining and Family Rooms

# TAPESTRY

Tapestry can be delicate so take care when cleaning it. Rub a bran ball (see page 85) over upholstery. For smaller items, such as cushion covers, put 1 cup of unprocessed wheat bran inside a pillowcase. Place the tapestry in the pillowcase, close the top and shake vigorously—the bran acts as a scourer. Remove the tapestry (over a bin or outside) and shake away the bran.

# WOOL

The best way to clean a woollen lounge is with a bran ball (see page 85). If there's staining, put a small amount of cheap shampoo on your fingertips and massage into the stain. Wipe with a damp cloth and dry by pressing with paper towel. Don't use a hair dryer to dry wool because it will cause puckering.

# LEATHER

If you think about it, leather is just toughened skin and like any skin it needs to be kept moist. To keep it looking good, use a good quality leather conditioner but don't apply too much; 1 teaspoon impregnated in a cloth is enough for an entire couch. Deal with any scratches first with shoe cream (not shoe polish) in a matching colour (available from shoe repair shops). After applying the shoe cream, rub the scratches with the back of a warmed stainless steel spoon to set the shoe cream and prevent it getting on your clothes. Now use a good quality leather conditioner and cleaner—it should feel like a moisturiser

# SPOTLESS 2

you'd be happy to put on your own skin. Place a small amount (again, don't overuse the product) onto a cloth and warm in the microwave in 10-second bursts so the conditioner melts into the cloth. When you've finished conditioning the couch, put the cloth into a zip-lock bag and seal it ready to use at the next cleaning session.

Leather reacts differently if it's been waxed, plasticised or oiled so work this out before tackling any stains. To do this, place a single bead of water on an inconspicuous part of the leather. If the water rolls off, the leather coating is plasticised. If the water soaks into the leather, it's not sealed. If the water soaks in slowly, it's waxed.

**Q:** 'I'm so cranky', says Lynne. 'The kids sat on my dark brown leather lounge in their swimming costumes and the chlorine has faded the leather. Is there anything I can do?'

**Problem:** **Bleached brown leather.**

**What to use:** **Walnuts, leather conditioner; or shoe cream, warm stainless steel spoon.**

**How to apply:** This only works with brown leather. Break a fresh walnut in half and rub the nut over the faded area. Now apply a good quality leather conditioner to bring back the sheen of the leather. For lighter coloured leather, use shoe cream in a matching colour and wipe over the stain. To set the colour, rub with the back of a warm stainless steel spoon.

Lounge, Dining and Family Rooms

**Q:** 'What's the best way to remove nail polish from a leather lounge?' asks Claire.

**Problem:** **Nail polish on leather.**

**What to use:** **Talcum powder, acetone, cotton bud, white vinegar, cloth, vacuum cleaner, leather conditioner.**

**How to apply:** Make a ring of talcum powder around the nail polish mark to protect the leather around the stain. Dip a cotton bud in acetone and wipe over the nail polish, then wipe straight away with a clean cotton bud. Repeat this process until the nail polish is removed. To neutralise the acetone, wipe with white vinegar on a cotton bud and sprinkle on talcum powder. When it dries, brush away with the back of your hand or vacuum. To finish, apply a small amount of quality leather conditioner.

**Q:** 'I've got blue biro on a leather sofa', reports Margaret. 'I did a test using methylated spirits and found some of the maroon colour came off on my white cloth. What should I do?'

**Problem:** **Biro on leather.**

**What to use:** **Cotton bud, white spirits, talcum powder, leather conditioner.**

**How to apply:** It was a good idea to do a test first. It's best not to use methylated spirits on leather unless it's been plasticised. Instead, dip a cotton bud in white spirits and write over the biro. Sprinkle on talcum powder and brush away with the back of your hand when dry. Apply leather conditioner.

**Q:** 'Can you tell me how to remove the dye from blue denim on my white leather couch and cream leather car seats please?' asks Monica.

**Problem: Dye on leather.**

**What to use: Colour Run Remover: Whites, water, cloth, talcum powder, leather conditioner.**

**How to apply:** To remove dye, use Colour Run Remover: Whites, which is available in the laundry aisle at the supermarket. Mix 1 part Colour Run Remover to 20 parts water and wipe over the stain with a cloth. Have a dry cloth in your other hand and wipe hand over hand. Sprinkle with talcum powder and brush away when dry. When finished, apply a little quality leather conditioner.

***TIP*** To prevent dye from running in fabric clothes (not leather or suede), wash in a heavy salt solution (1 kg of non-iodised salt per 9 litres of water).

Lounge, Dining and Family Rooms

**Q:** 'My daughter splashed some paint on our leather barstools', reports Erin. 'I didn't notice for a couple of days and have tried to remove the stains with soap and water and then methylated spirits. But all I have done is make an ugly mark from the methylated spirits and the paint spots are still there. Can you help?'

**Problem:** **Paint on leather.**

**What to use:** **Tea tree oil, white vinegar, pantyhose, white spirits, cotton ball, walnut or shoe cream, warm stainless steel spoon, leather conditioner.**

**How to apply:** The leather on barstools is high in wax so wipe with equal parts tea tree oil and white vinegar on pantyhose. Follow with a cotton ball dipped in white spirits. If the barstool is brown and colour comes away, break a walnut in half and rub the inside over the mark. For barstools in other colours, use shoe cream in a matching colour and apply with the back of a warmed spoon. When clean, rub on a small amount of quality leather conditioner.

## THE UNEXPECTED

**Q:** 'Our lounge room ceiling recently collapsed. Now fine plaster powder and insulating rockwool material have become ingrained in the black leather of the lounge chairs.

SPOTLESS 2

I have vacuumed and cleaned three times with leather cream but the chairs still retain the powder and look a dirty grey in parts. Any ideas?'

**A:** The leather cream has actually made the powder stick to the leather. To remove the dust, put an old sheet on the ground and turn your lounge upside down over it. Then shake the couch until all the plaster is removed. To remove the leather cream, use a good quality saddle soap. Each saddle soap uses a different technique, so follow the manufacturer's directions. Resurface the leather by rubbing with a matching tinted leather cream using the back of a warm stainless steel spoon.

## VINYL

**Q:** 'What's the best way to get rid of cigarette smoke smell in a vinyl-covered chair?' asks Samuel.

| | |
|---|---|
| **Problem:** | **Cigarette smoke smell in vinyl.** |
| **What to use:** | **Bicarb, disposable rubber gloves, white vinegar, cigarette ash, cloth.** |
| **How to apply:** | Take the chair outside and turn it upside down. Sprinkle bicarb inside the chair and shake so the bicarb spreads throughout the chair. Leave |

for 20 minutes, turn the chair upright and shake out the bicarb. Put on rubber gloves and clean the vinyl surface with equal parts bicarb, white vinegar and cigarette ash on a cloth (be careful because the mixture can burn your skin). Follow by wiping thoroughly with a damp cloth.

# THROWS

Throws—or 'threws', as Trude and Prue call them—are a great way to change the look of a couch and keep you warm in winter. Mohair is a popular choice but it sheds and leaves hairs over your couch. The best way to minimise shedding is to wash the throw in a little cheap shampoo and blood-heat water. Then rinse in a little cheap hair conditioner and blood-heat water. The water temperature must be the same. Dry in the shade. When dry, place in a plastic bag and put into the freezer for half an hour. Cold fibres don't frizz or shed as easily.

# CANE, BAMBOO, WICKER AND WATER HYACINTH

Clean with a salt solution (1 cup of non-iodised salt per 9 litre bucket of water) on a cloth and remove any residual water by wiping with a towel. Don't use soap or detergents because they can swell the cane and dry it out, making it vulnerable to splitting.

SPOTLESS 2

# METAL-FRAMED FURNITURE

To clean aluminium, use cold black tea on a cloth. To remove rust from painted wrought iron, use steel wool and turpentine.

# TIMBER FURNITURE

When cleaning timber, it is important to remember that you are cleaning the surface not the core. Timber can be sealed in polyurethane, varnish, shellac or beeswax. To identify the surface and use the appropriate solution, see page 360 for instructions. To remove scratches in polyurethane, use Brasso on a cloth and rub along the grain using speed, not pressure. It will look worse before it looks better.

**Q:** 'I have an unsealed timber coffee table', says Sandy. 'And there are many water stains on it from glasses and cups. How can I remove the staining?'

| | |
|---:|:---|
| **Problem:** | Watermarks on timber. |
| **What to use:** | Pantyhose, cold strong black tea, beeswax or carnauba wax. |
| **How to apply:** | To replace the tannins in the bleached area and clean away fat and grime, scrub with a pair of pantyhose dipped in cold black tea. Polish with a fine coating of beeswax or carnauba wax. |
| **Prevention:** | Protect timber surfaces with coasters. |

Lounge, Dining and Family Rooms

**Q:** 'My son ate greasy takeaway fish and chips at the coffee table', explains Julie. 'And it's left a white cloudy stain on the timber. Can you suggest a solution?'

**Problem:** **Cloudy stain on timber.**

**What to use:** **Brasso, cloth; or beeswax, lemon peel.**

**How to apply:** The heat has created tiny bubbles on the surface of the coffee table. To repair the timber, first work out what the table is sealed with (see page 360). If it's sealed with polyurethane, rub a small amount of Brasso on a cloth in the direction of the grain. It will look worse before it looks better. Just keep rubbing but don't add any more Brasso. If the surface is sealed in varnish, shellac or wax, apply warmed beeswax with the yellow side of a piece of lemon peel, rubbing in the direction of the grain. Work quickly.

# ORNAMENTS

Ornaments are lovely to look at but a challenge to clean with dust easily finding its way into every nook and cranny. For an easy clean, add a tiny amount of sweet almond oil to a paintbrush and wipe over the dusty area. The dust will stick to the oil. If it's stubborn dust, aim a hair dryer over the dust and use sweet almond oil on a brush. (See pages 81–82 of *Spotless* for more information.)

# ORIENTAL FURNITURE

Oriental and Asian lacquered furniture can be difficult to clean. Never use heavy polishes because they can react with the lacquer and cause a bloom. If the surface is sticky, clean with pantyhose and a little skim milk and polish with a soft dry cloth. Use a little carnauba wax and beeswax on a cloth and polish over the whole surface. You can remove a build-up of wax with warmed pantyhose (put in the microwave for 10 seconds—no longer or they will melt). Polish in circles using speed, not pressure. Put potted plants near the furniture to provide humidity. If the plants start to die, the air is too dry and they need additional watering. You'll save the plant and be able to monitor the room's humidity.

***TIP*** Use skim milk to polish lacquered timber.

# FIREPLACES

To work out when it's time to call the chimney sweep, scrape a fingernail on the inside of a cold chimney. If soot flakes off, rather than smears off, it's time for a clean. Other clues are excess smoke from the fire (see pages 84–85 of *Spotless* for details on how to deal with this) and soot falling down the chimney into the fireplace. Bronze, copper, brass, white metal, tin and iron are best cleaned with bicarb and white vinegar. Prevent further tarnishing by wiping with a little sweet almond oil on a cloth. This will also make future cleaning easier.

Lounge, Dining and Family Rooms

**Q:** 'We've got a copper chimney above our slow combustion heater', reports Matthew. 'The copper has gone black at the bottom. How do we fix it?'

    **Problem:** **Blackened copper.**

**What to use:** **Bicarb, cloth, white vinegar, pantyhose, bamboo skewer, copper coating, sweet almond oil.**

**How to apply:** Put bicarb on a cloth and wipe over the blackened areas. Now spray with white vinegar. While it's fizzing, scrub with a rolled up pair of pantyhose. Sometimes copper is coated in a clear varnish which can become pitted and look like small black spots. To determine if the copper has been coated, scratch an inconspicuous part using a bamboo skewer. If the copper is coated, prevent tarnish by respraying the surface with a copper coating. Or slow the corrosion by rubbing with a dab of sweet almond oil on a cloth.

**Q:** 'How do I clean a bronze fire screen?' asks Robyn.

    **Problem:** **Dirty bronze fire screen.**

**What to use:** **Sweet almond oil, pantyhose.**

**How to apply:** Rub on sweet almond oil with a pair of rolled up pantyhose. It will give a great sheen without destroying the patina.

## MANTLEPIECES

Clean mantlepieces according to what they're made of.

**Marble**—if stained, mix plaster of Paris and water to form a paste the consistency of peanut butter. Apply to the stain, allow to dry, then brush away. Seal with marble flooring wax. If you can't get marble flooring wax, use milk.

**Granite**—if stained, mix plaster of Paris and water to the consistency of runny cream. Apply the mixture and leave to dry. Rub off with pantyhose.

**Sandstone, brick**—if stained, mix equal parts cigarette ash, bicarb and white vinegar. Apply to the stain and scrub well with a brush. Rinse with a damp cloth. Don't use on limestone or marble because this mixture is too acidic.

**Timber**—can be easily damaged with smoke. If finished in plaster or paint, clean with a paste of bicarb and water. Polish on with a cloth, allow to dry and polish off with a cloth.

## HEATERS

Don't forget to clean your heater during the weekly clean because dust can affect its operation. Of course, don't clean when it's on or still warm. If finished in enamel, wipe with pantyhose dipped in equal parts white vinegar and water. If made of chrome, sprinkle with bicarb, wipe with white vinegar on a cloth and wipe clean with a damp cloth.

**Q:** 'I've got melted polyester on the glass of my gas heater', says Natalia. 'Can it be removed?'

Lounge, Dining and Family Rooms

**Problem:** **Melted polyester on glass.**
**What to use:** **Glycerine, talcum powder, pantyhose, damp cloth.**
**How to apply:** Make a paste of glycerine and talcum powder. When the glass is cold, apply the paste with pantyhose and scrub. Leave to dry and polish off with a damp cloth.

**Q:** 'Our wood-burning fire has a glass door', reports Gerry. 'And over the years, it's been badly stained brown-black which makes it difficult to see the flames and condition of the fire. Can you help?'

**Problem:** **Burnt/stained glass.**
**What to use:** **Cigarette ash, bicarb, white vinegar, pantyhose, water.**
**How to apply:** Mix equal parts cigarette ash, bicarb and white vinegar. Apply to the glass with a pair of pantyhose and leave for about an hour. When dry, polish off with damp pantyhose.

**Q:** 'My column oil heater blew up and oil spilt everywhere', says Paul. 'I soaked the oil up with towels but the problem is getting the smell out of my towels. Can you help?'

**Problem:** **Heater oil on towels.**
**What to use:** **Dishwashing liquid.**

**How to apply:** Because the oil has bonded to the towels, place a couple of drops of dishwashing liquid on your fingers and massage into the oil until it feels like jelly. After this treatment, wash normally. Don't forget to clean the area around the heater with dishwashing liquid on your fingers followed by a damp cloth.

# ENTERTAINMENT SYSTEMS

## TVs

Having a massive plasma TV screen with multiple speakers means you can almost have the cinema experience at home—with much cheaper popcorn. To clean plasma TVs, consult the manufacturer's manual. Never use detergent or caustic cleaners because they could damage the screen. Most marks can be removed with a soft damp cloth.

During a Stain Clinic, Tom recommended Plexus plastic cleaner to clean LCD screens but said you must apply it with a cloth over the entire screen. We've since learned that Plexus is used to clean aircraft windshields and plastic in cars.

## Stereos

Most stereos are made with aluminium-coated plastic or chrome-plated plastic. Expensive ones are made of metal. Use a non-abrasive cleaner, such as pantyhose, and be careful cleaning around electrics. You don't want to get any moisture or chemicals in them. Remove fingermarks with damp pantyhose.

Lounge, Dining and Family Rooms

Clean inside a CD player regularly with a puffer brush (available from department and electronic stores) or the dust will clog the mechanism. Vacuum the cloth front of your speakers using the brush attachment. You'll know there's too much dust when there's a buzz in your speakers.

**Q:** 'I've got black rubber foot marks on a wooden cabinet from my stereo speakers', says Mick. 'How do you remove them?'

**Problem:** **Rubber marks on timber.**
**What to use:** **Damp salt, cloth.**
**How to apply:** Rub the marks with a small quantity of damp salt on a cloth.
**Prevention:** To stop rubber from perishing, rub with talcum powder.

**Q:** 'What's the best way to remove sticky tape residue from vinyl records?' asks Michelle. 'We've got some old Golden Book records we'd like to play to the kids.'

**Problem:** **Sticky tape residue on vinyl records.**
**What to use:** **Tea tree oil, warm water, pantyhose.**
**How to apply:** Add ½ teaspoon of tea tree oil to 2 cups of warm water. Roll up a pair of pantyhose, dip into the solution and rub over the record in the direction of the grooves until the residue is removed. Allow to air dry.

SPOTLESS 2

# PIANOS

**Q:** 'I own a piano that's french polished', says Tim. 'But it's got white candle wax on it. How can I get it off?'

    **Problem:** **Wax on timber.**
**What to use:** **Ice-cubes, zip-lock bag, talcum powder, damp silk.**
**How to apply:** Put ice-cubes in a zip-lock bag and place over the wax. When the wax is cold, remove the ice and sprinkle talcum powder over the wax. Rub with a piece of damp silk in the direction of the grain. This cuts through the wax without damaging the surface.

# GUITARS

**Q:** 'How can I clean my high tensile guitar strings to make them last longer?' asks Wayne.

    **Problem:** **Cleaning guitar strings.**
**What to use:** **Sweet almond oil, lint-free cloth.**
**How to apply:** Place a little sweet almond oil on a lint-free cloth (such as an old T-shirt) and wipe over the strings. Sweet almond oil prevents corrosion and helps keep metal in good condition.

Lounge, Dining and Family Rooms

# BILLIARDS

**Q:** 'How do you repair discoloured billiard balls?' asks Lesley.

**Problem:** **Discoloured billiard balls.**

**What to use:** **Glycerine, talcum powder, cloth (plastic); sweet almond oil, cloth (ivory); or toothpaste, water, cloth.**

**How to apply:** If they're made of plastic, mix equal parts glycerine and talcum powder to form a paste and polish with a cloth. If made of ivory, clean with sweet almond oil on a cloth. If plastic or ivory are very dirty, use equal parts toothpaste and water on a cloth before applying the methods described above.

# BAR

**Q:** 'I've got a red wine stain in my decanter', says Judith. 'And it just won't budge. What do you suggest?'

**Problem:** **Red wine stain in decanter.**

**What to use:** **Bicarb, white vinegar, uncooked rice, water, sweet almond oil, thin paintbrush.**

**How to apply:** Empty the decanter. Put 1 tablespoon of bicarb, 1 tablespoon of white vinegar and 1 tablespoon of uncooked rice inside and shake. This will

SPOTLESS 2

remove the red pigment. Rinse with water and allow to dry. Put sweet almond oil on a thin paintbrush and run along the etched mark. Be aware the oil will affect the taste of the wine so use sparingly and rinse with water before reusing. Never leave wine in a decanter because it will etch into the glass.

# DINING TABLES

Shannon loves hosting big family gatherings around her dining table, which has special significance because it was her mother-in-law's. Jennifer's dining table is a converted shed door made by her father and it's been the location of many happy dinner parties.

The most common dining table problems raised at Stain Clinics involve heat and water. Both can be tricky to fix so always put some form of protection, such as mats, over a table if there are hot dishes, full glasses or vases. Before tackling any stain, you'll need to know the product used to seal the dining table. To find out, see page 360.

**Q:** 'How do I clean heat/water marks from an antique french polished table?' asks Lynn.

**Problem:** **Heat/water marks on french polish.**
**What to use:** **Beeswax, microwave, lemon peel.**
**How to apply:** Warm beeswax in the microwave until it's just softened. Put it on the outer part (skin side) of

Lounge, Dining and Family Rooms

a piece of lemon peel and rub quickly over the mark using speed rather than pressure. The wax and oil from the lemon will fill the heat and watermarks.

**Q:** 'On remarriage, I gained a 14-seater french polished timber veneer dining table', reports Pamela. 'I was able to convince my husband we should enjoy the table and have had numerous dinner parties. Sadly, condensation from a jug ran under a large coaster and has left a slightly puckered semi-raised surface. Can it be fixed?'

**Problem:** **Water mark on french polish.**
**What to use:** **Professional.**
**How to apply:** Because the surface has puckered it will need to be repaired by a professional. Some restorers make things look brand new which devalues the piece. Instead, choose a 'sympathetic' restorer to repair the table in keeping with its age and condition.

*TIP* To clean french polish, make your own polishing cloth. Mix 1 tablespoon of beeswax, 2 drops of lavender oil and 2 drops of lemon oil in a microwave-safe bowl. Place a 100 per cent white cotton cloth over the top and put the bowl inside the microwave. Heat in 10-second bursts until the beeswax melts. Store the cloth in a zip-lock bag. To remove sticky fingerprints, polish the

SPOTLESS 2

table with a pair of rolled up pantyhose. If the fingerprints are particularly greasy, sprinkle the table with a little cornflour before polishing with pantyhose.

## WHAT NOT TO DO...

**Q:** 'I have accidentally spilt craft glue on our wooden dining table. I tried to remove the glue with a damp cloth and hot water which seems to have left a bleach mark. What can I do?'

**A:** Moisture is bad news for timber because it makes it swell. Reduce bleaching by rubbing with a damp tea bag. Depending on the extent of the damage, the table may have to be sanded and resurfaced. In future, remove glue with damp pantyhose heated in the microwave for 10 seconds (no longer or the pantyhose will melt). Rub over the glue in the direction of the grain using speed, not pressure. Dry thoroughly with a cotton cloth.

**Q:** 'I have a marble-covered dining table', says Maria. 'And the marble is beginning to show fingerprints and other marks, such as glass rims. Any ideas?'

**Problem:** Marking on marble.
**What to use:** Brasso, cloth; or cake of bathroom soap, water, soft cloth, marble milk wax or skim milk.

Lounge, Dining and Family Rooms

**How to apply:** If the marble is coated in polyurethane, rub with a little Brasso applied with a cloth using speed, not pressure. This partially melts the polyurethane. It will look worse before it looks better. If it's machine polished, rub with a soft cloth that's been rubbed with a cake of bathroom soap and water. Then apply a good quality marble milk wax or skim milk. To work out what the sealant is, see page 360.

# Q: 'When our son was a baby, he used to shove his peas under the table protector (unbeknown to us)', says Tyson. 'So now we have all these green stains over our polished wooden dining table. What can we do?'

**Problem:** **Peas on timber.**

**What to use:** **Glycerine, talcum powder, cloth; or beeswax; sunlight or ultraviolet light.**

**How to apply:** Firstly, work out what the table is sealed with (see page 360). If the table has a polyurethane finish, polish with a paste of equal parts glycerine and talcum powder on a cloth. If the table has a shellac finish, use beeswax on a cloth. To remove any residual green, expose the stains to sunlight or an ultraviolet light.

SPOTLESS 2

**Q:** 'The green dye from my bamboo table mat has leached onto my varnished veneer dining table', says Charmaine. 'What can I do?'

| | |
|---|---|
| **Problem:** | **Green dye on timber.** |
| **What to use:** | **Brasso, cloth, soft cloth; or Colour Run Remover: Coloursafe, cotton ball, silicone-free furniture polish.** |
| **How to apply:** | Firstly, work out what the table has been sealed with (see page 360). If it's a polyurethane finish, use a little Brasso on a cloth, rub in the direction of the grain and polish with a soft cloth. It will look worse before it looks better. This removes a little of the finish and the dye. If finished in shellac, use a small amount of Colour Run Remover: Coloursafe. Apply with a cotton ball and rub in the direction of the grain until the colour is removed then wipe with a damp cloth. Use a silicone-free furniture polish. |

# TABLECLOTHS

**Q:** 'I've got a damask tablecloth with mildew on it', complains Lee. 'What can I do?'

| | |
|---|---|
| **Problem:** | **Mouldy cotton.** |
| **What to use:** | **Bucket, non-iodised salt, water, soft brush.** |

Lounge, Dining and Family Rooms

**How to apply:** Soak the tablecloth in a bucket of salt water solution (1 kg of salt per 9 litres of water) overnight. Remove, gently squeeze but don't wring before hanging on the clothesline in the sun. Leave to dry and a salt crust will form. Remove the crust with a brush and the mould/mildew will come away.

**Q:** 'I had stains from a pot-plant seep through to my white tablecloth cover', reports Susie. 'How do I get rid of them?'

**Problem:** **Soil and mould on cotton.**
**What to use:** **Oil of cloves, 1 litre spray pack, water, non-iodised salt, lemon juice, sunshine.**
**How to apply:** Mix ¼ teaspoon of oil of cloves in a spray pack of water. Lightly spray onto the tablecloth and leave for 24 hours. Place a little mountain of salt over the marks and squeeze on a little lemon juice to moisten the salt. Leave in the sunshine to dry, then wash and dry normally.

**Q:** 'I was given a table with a vinyl top that's been slightly water damaged', reports June. 'The vinyl looks bumpy in some spots. Is there any way to flatten this out?'

**Problem:** **Buckled vinyl.**
**What to use:** **PVA glue, water, syringe, plastic wrap, heavy object (such as a book).**

**How to apply:** Mix equal parts PVA glue and water and load into a syringe. Inject the glue under the buckled vinyl and rub with your fingers to flatten. Cover in plastic wrap and place a heavy object on top until it dries.

# SILVER

You can clean silver with a little bicarb followed by a little white vinegar. Rub it with a cloth while it's fizzing. Wear a pair of old cotton socks on your hands to prevent the acid from your skin transferring to the silver and causing it to tarnish. To prevent future tarnish, rub with a couple of drops of sweet almond oil on a cloth to seal.

## WHAT NOT TO DO...

**Q:** 'My solid silver teapot set was heavily tarnished and blackened. So I washed it in warm detergent. Then I wrapped it in aluminium foil and added a solution of bicarb and water to the inside of the pot and brought it to the boil for 3 minutes. The result is AWFUL. The silver appears to have undergone a chemical change. Please help!'

**A:** This technique not only removes tarnish but removes a layer of silver. If you want to restore the silver, you'll need to have it professionally replated. To clean silver, sprinkle with bicarb, add white vinegar and, while fizzing, rub with a soft cloth. To slow tarnishing, once it's clean, rub with a couple of drops of sweet almond oil on a cloth.

Lounge, Dining and Family Rooms

# COMPUTERS

If you share a computer with someone else, here's some alarming information. Research by the University of Arizona found the average office desktop harboured 400 times more bacteria than the average office toilet seat! To clean your computer, turn it off, turn the keyboard upside down and gently shake to remove any crumbs.

Never spray anything directly onto a computer or keyboard because moisture is bad for electrics. Instead, spray white vinegar or methylated spirits on a soft cloth and wipe the screen and keyboard. Jennifer thinks white vinegar is the best cleaner. To clean between the keys on your keyboard, use a little white vinegar or methylated spirits on a cotton bud. It's fine to use your vacuum cleaner to remove dirt outside the computer but never use it inside the computer because it creates static electricity and could ruin it.

To deter bugs, spray surface insecticide (not any of the lure and kill varieties) on a cloth and wipe over the back of the computer.

## Mouse and mouse mat

You know it's time to clean the mouse when it becomes sticky and hard to manoeuvre. The latest ones are optical and can't be pulled apart but you can clean the case by wiping with a cloth dampened with white vinegar or methylated spirits. Make sure you clean the track wheel. To clean the underside of the mouse, dip a cotton bud in methylated spirits, wipe the slide points that make contact with the mat and dry upside down. Remove skin cells and sweat from the mouse mat and cord by wiping with methylated spirits on a pair of pantyhose.

## FAX MACHINES

Clean the outside of the fax with a damp cloth. Clean rubber rollers with a little methylated spirits on a cotton bud. To remove cotton bud fibres, wipe again with a damp lint-free cloth.

## SCANNERS/PHOTOCOPIERS/PRINTERS

Clean the outside as described for the fax. Clean the glass with a little methylated spirits on a lint-free cloth. Clean the buttons with methylated spirits on a cotton bud.

## DESKS

**Q:** 'I wonder if you have tips on how to successfully remove ink stains from an old leather desk top?' asks Mark. 'I'd appreciate it!'

**Problem:** **Ink stain on leather.**

**What to use:** **Rotten milk, white spirits, cloth, talcum powder, leather conditioner.**

**How to apply:** If it's ink from an inkwell, rot some milk in the sun until it becomes lumpy. Strain the solids and place over the stain until the ink bleeds into the milk solids. Remove the solids and wipe the remaining stain with white spirits on a cloth. Sprinkle with talcum powder, leave to dry and brush clean. Treat with leather conditioner.

# BOOKS AND BOOKSHELVES

Shannon says she can't bear to part with books because they're like friends to her. Jennifer is also a keen reader but unless she wants to read a book again, she generally passes them on to family and friends. Don't forget to vacuum bookshelves and over the books while you're at it and always store books away from direct sunlight and moisture. To preserve old leather-bound books, rub the leather with a little sweet almond oil.

**Q:** 'My document safe has a very musty smell and all the documents stink', says Jack. 'What can I do?'

**Problem: Musty paper.**

**What to use: White chalk, loose-leaf tea.**

**How to apply:** Put 6 sticks of white chalk inside the safe to absorb the moisture. Leave an opened packet of loose-leaf tea inside the safe to get rid of the smell. Close the door and leave for a week.

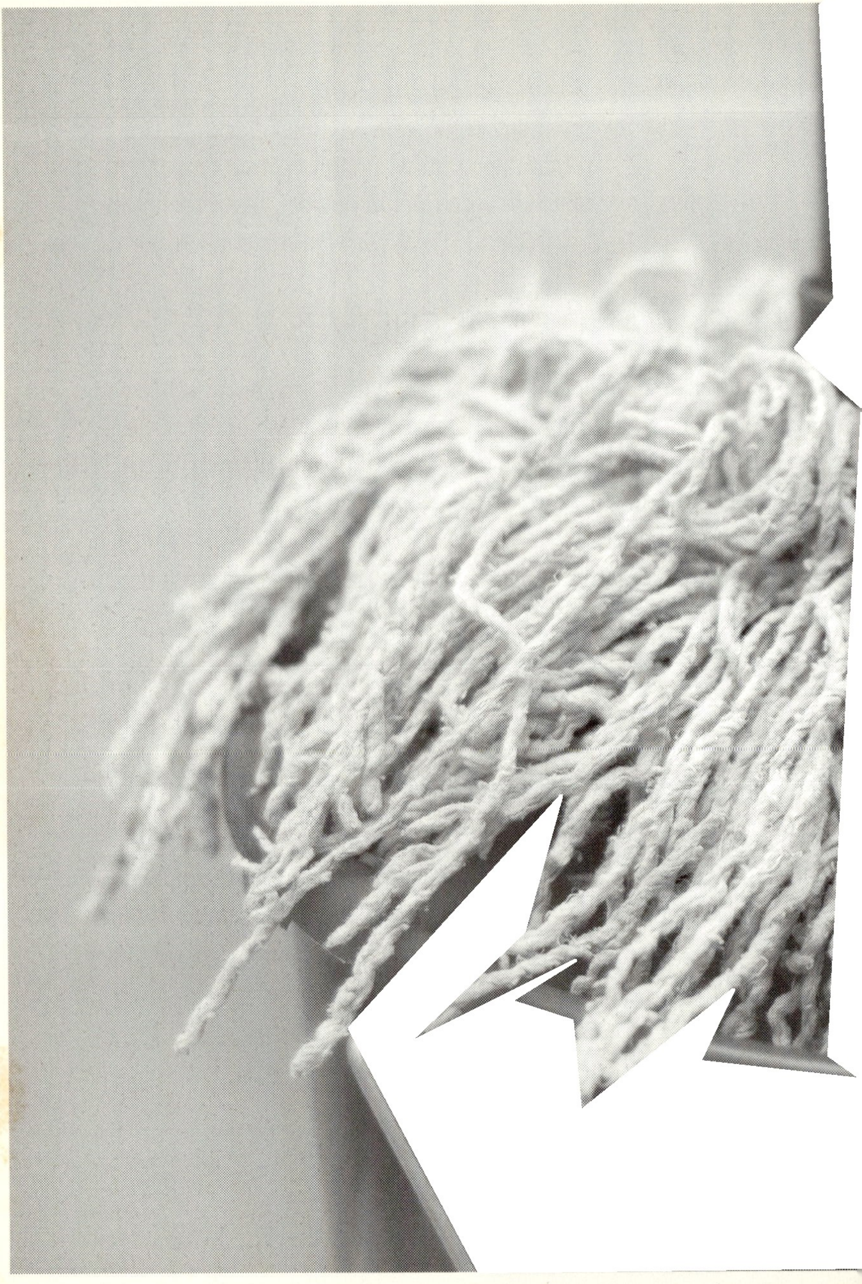

# Floors, Walls and Windows

Shannon likes having carpet in bedrooms because it's a soft landing for your feet when you get out of bed but she prefers floorboards, cork or self-levelling vinyls elsewhere in the home (except in the bathroom where tiles are the best surface). Jennifer loves floorboards because they look good and are easy to clean. Choose what works for you. And don't stress about stains on floors; thanks to gravity, a spill is almost inevitable. You're less likely to get stains on walls, although grubby hands may leave an imprint. And don't forget to clean windows and coverings.

Floors, Walls and Windows

## PEANUT BUTTER PANIC: Suzanne's story

**INCIDENT:** 'We've got lovely new timber stairs. But sadly, before we sealed them, my son got peanut butter all over them. Can you help?'

**SOLUTION:** Mix plaster of Paris and water to form a paste the consistency of peanut butter (sorry!). For every cup of mixture add 1 teaspoon of dishwashing liquid and 2 teaspoons of white vinegar. Place a 1 cm thick layer of paste over the stain. Leave to completely dry and brush off with a broom.

# FLOORS

The next time you're about to sweep your floor, take an up-close look at the broom head. No doubt there's some dirt and grime on the bristles which will be added to the floors you're supposed to be cleaning. Before using, wash the broom head with a little dishwashing liquid and water, rinse under water and set aside in the sunshine, handle-end down, to dry.

## Timber and cork

Sealed timber and cork floors are easy to clean and last longer than unsealed ones. Most are sealed in polyurethane, tung-oil, varnish or wax. For timber and cork sealed in polyurethane, clean with 1 cup of white vinegar in a 9 litre bucket of warm (not hot) water. The warm water helps cut through grease. Apply with a broom head covered in pantyhose or an old T-shirt and dry and polish as you go by standing on a towel (shuffle forward).

SPOTLESS 2

By doing this, you don't leave excess water on the polyurethane. If you leave excess water, you can get white bloom marks. For timber and cork floors finished in tung-oil, varnish or wax, clean with cold black tea and warm water (1 cup of tea or 3 tea bags in a 9 litre bucket of water). Tea raises the tannin levels in timber and cork, helping retain the colour and quality.

**TIP** To fix a dent in timber, place a hot, wet, used tea bag over the indentation and leave until the timber has expanded.

## Blood/meat juice

**Q:** 'When I brought the shopping home, meat juice leaked through the plastic and left blood over the timber floor', reports Anne. 'It's soaked through!'

|  |  |
| --- | --- |
| **Problem:** | **Blood/meat juice on timber.** |
| **What to use:** | **Plaster of Paris, water, white vinegar, broom.** |
| **How to apply:** | Mix plaster of Paris and water to form a paste the consistency of peanut butter. For every cup of mixture, add 2 teaspoons of white vinegar. Apply a 1 cm thick layer of paste over the stain. Leave until completely dry and sweep away with a broom. Repeat if needed. |

Floors, Walls and Windows

## Cigarette burn

**Q:** 'I have polished floorboards with a slight cigarette burn on the surface', admits Brian. 'It looks like lightly burnt toast. How can I get it out?'

**Problem:** **Cigarette burn on timber.**

**What to use:** **3 per cent hydrogen peroxide, cloth, Brasso.**

**How to apply:** If the burn is on the surface and hasn't penetrated the polyurethane, immerse a cloth in 3 per cent hydrogen peroxide, tightly wring out, place over the stained area only and leave for 20 minutes. The burn will come away when you remove the cloth. If the burn has penetrated the surface, use the technique described above, then rub with a little Brasso on a cloth. For a burn the size of a 5 cent piece, use 1 drop of Brasso on a cloth and rub lightly and quickly in the direction of the grain. In the first couple of seconds, the mark will look worse before it looks better.

## Dye

**Q:** 'I have a blob of dark hair dye on a timber floor—found an hour later', reports Sally. 'The floor is finished with wax and polyurethane. Help!'

**Problem:** **Hair dye on timber.**

**What to use:** **Disposable rubber gloves, same brand and colour hair dye, cloth, anti-dandruff shampoo, warm water.**

**How to apply:** Put on rubber gloves to protect your skin. Apply the same hair dye to the stain with a cloth, rubbing in circles until the stain loosens. Follow immediately with a little anti-dandruff shampoo on a cloth and rub into the stain to loosen further. Continue rubbing until the entire stain has lifted, then wipe with a cloth dampened with warm water. This technique works on all surfaces.

## Engine oil/grease

**Q:** 'My new unsealed timber floor has a car oil stain on it', reports Sam. 'The stain is greasy black and I need to remove it before sealing the floor. What do you suggest?'

**Problem:** **Engine oil on unsealed timber.**

**What to use:** **Baby oil, cotton ball, disposable rubber gloves, dishwashing liquid, cloth, warm water.**

**How to apply:** Place a little baby oil on a cotton ball and rub on the stain until it looks muddy. Put on rubber gloves, place a couple of drops of dishwashing liquid on your fingertips and massage into the stain until it changes texture and feels like jelly.

Wipe with a cloth dampened with warm water. If any oil remains, apply dishwashing liquid again. Leave the floor to dry for at least 2 days before sealing.

## Fat/oil (cooking)

**Q:** 'I have light-coloured floating floors', says Richard. 'And the area around the stove has splatterings of fat from cooking. Would you be able to help me fix this? It looks like I have a dirty floor!'

| | |
|---|---|
| **Problem:** | **Fat/cooking oil on timber.** |
| **What to use:** | **Dishwashing liquid, pantyhose, Brasso, cloth.** |
| **How to apply:** | The floor is likely to be coated in polyurethane. Place a couple of drops of dishwashing liquid on pantyhose and rub over the stain. Then wipe with another pair of damp pantyhose. You can even put the pantyhose on your feet so you don't have to bend over. For any remaining marks, apply a little Brasso with a cloth and rub in the direction of the grain, using speed not pressure. |
| **Prevention:** | Constant exposure to oil can damage polyurethane so protect the area by placing a mat in front of the stove. |

## Nail polish

Q: 'My daughter spilt nail polish on a wooden floor', says Chris. 'What can I do?'

>**Problem:** **Nail polish on timber.**
>
>**What to use:** **Acetone, cotton bud, pantyhose, white vinegar, cloth, Brasso; or beeswax.**
>
>**How to apply:** For a polyurethane finish, use a little acetone applied with a cotton bud but work quickly using as little pressure and acetone as possible. Only rub over the nail polish, not the surrounding floor. When the colour is removed, neutralise with white vinegar on a cloth. If the surface is dulled, polish with a little Brasso on a cloth. For oil-based varnish, shellac or wax-based surfaces, use the same technique as polyurethane but polish with a little beeswax rather than Brasso. Acetone can affect acrylic surfaces so you may need to reapply the acrylic after removing the nail polish.

## Urine

Q: 'How do I get rid of the smell of cat urine from floorboards in my house?' asks Elizabeth.

>**Problem:** **Cat urine on timber.**
>
>**What to use:** **Ultraviolet light, white chalk, white vinegar, cloth, plaster of Paris, broom.**

Floors, Walls and Windows

**How to apply:** The first task is to find where the urine is. In a darkened room, turn on an ultraviolet light and the urine stains will show up yellow. Mark around the yellow stains with a piece of white chalk so you know where the offending areas are when the light is on. Wipe inside the chalk marks with a cloth wrung out in white vinegar. If the urine has soaked through the grooves of your floorboards, make a paste of plaster of Paris and water to the consistency of peanut butter. For every cup of paste, add 2 teaspoons of white vinegar. Paint a 1 cm thick layer of paste over the floorboards. When completely dry, brush off with a broom. You need to remove every bit of urine or the smell will remain.

## Wax

**Q:** 'I have a large red candle wax stain on our hardwood floor', reports Ricky. 'The stain has probably been there for about a month. What's the best way to remove it without scratching the floor or removing the varnish? I normally clean the floors with warm water and a well-wrung mop.'

**Problem:** **Red wax on timber.**

**What to use:** **Ice-cubes, zip-lock bag, plastic spatula, tea tree oil, cloth, ultraviolet light, cardboard.**

**How to apply:** Put a couple of ice-cubes in a zip-lock bag and place on top of the wax. Once the wax is chilled, flake it off with a plastic spatula. If a greasy stain remains, rub with a little tea tree oil on a cloth. In some cases, the red dye from the candle will penetrate the varnish and leave a stain. To remove it, aim ultraviolet light at the area (cover areas around the wax with cardboard or they'll lighten as well) checking every 2 hours until removed.

## Bamboo, cane and palm

Newer types of flooring can be made from bamboo, cane and palm. Be aware that long-cut bamboo is sturdier than short-cut bamboo and both types need to be sealed to make it easier to clean. Only clean bamboo, cane and palm with 1 cup of white vinegar per 9 litre bucket of water. If the floor is exposed to sunshine, add 1 cup of black tea to the mixture. Don't use bicarb on it because it's too abrasive.

## Tiles

To clean tiles, sprinkle a little bicarb over them, add a little white vinegar and when the mixture fizzes, sweep with a broom. To finish, wipe with a damp cloth. Most tiles are sealed with a glaze so that they're not porous. If tiles are not sealed, they'll stain easily (it's best to seal them). Don't clean glazed tiles with detergent because it makes them slippery and affects the surface.

Floors, Walls and Windows

**TIP**  If it looks as though someone has written on your tiles with a lead pencil, don't panic. These marks, called 'tile marks', are caused by metal touching the tiles. Remove by rubbing over the marks with a pencil eraser (for tiles with a smooth finish) or biro eraser (for tiles with a rougher finish) that's been dipped in water.

**Q:** 'We have a tiled floor and our dog, on a few occasions, has not woken us up to go out to the bathroom', says Jim. 'Consequently, the grout has become dark and discoloured from urine and poo. How can I get the stain out of the grout and stop him from returning to the same area?'

**Problem:** **Dog urine/poo on tile grout.**

**What to use:** **White vinegar, cloth, lavender oil (urine); cake of bathroom soap, cold water, old toothbrush, white vinegar, lavender oil (poo).**

**How to apply:** The grout between tiles is very absorbent and stains easily. Remove the urine by rubbing with a cloth dampened with white vinegar. To remove the poo stains, rub a cake of bathroom soap over an old toothbrush, run it under cold water and scrub over the stain. Rinse clean by wiping with a cloth wrung out in white vinegar. Dogs don't like the smell of lavender oil so add a couple of teaspoons to a 1 litre spray pack of water and lightly mist over the area. They'll stay away.

## Concrete

Polished concrete has become popular in some modern homes but it needs to be cleaned regularly with bicarb and white vinegar because dirt and grit remove its sheen. For a comprehensive clean, sprinkle with bicarb, then spray on white vinegar and scrub with a broom. Rinse with water, allow to dry, then wax with carnauba wax using a polishing machine (available from hire companies or vacuum cleaner shops). Don't use beeswax because it's too soft and leaves a build-up.

## Marble/limestone

This flooring is porous and alkaline based, so don't use vinegar to clean it because it can damage the surface. Instead, clean with Ph neutral soap. Grate 1 teaspoon of soap into a 9 litre bucket of warm water, stir and wipe over the surface. To seal (do this when the surface has dulled), coat with a thin layer of good quality marble flooring wax.

## Rammed earth floors

If you have rammed earth floors, maintain the polish by mixing 2 cups of powdered milk into a 9 litre bucket of water. Rub over the earth with a wet river stone (bought at nurseries). Drill a hole through your river stone and pull it around the floor. When drilling into stone, use a masonry bit, work on the slowest speed and fill the hole with a little water to keep the masonry bit cool.

## Carpet

You'll have to deal with stains on your carpet at some stage. To clean carpet, vacuum regularly. Scatter a light dusting of bicarb but don't create a ski field or you'll damage your vacuum cleaner.

Floors, Walls and Windows

Your carpet will last longer if you steam-clean it at least once a year. Do it more often if you have heavy traffic—kids, pets, heavy boots. When removing stains, be very sparing with water and other types of moisture. If you use too much liquid, you'll get jute staining from the back of the carpet. More is not better. After removing the stain, remove as much moisture as possible with paper towels or a Slurpex.

## DIY steam-cleaning

You've probably walked past a stand of carpet cleaners as you've left the supermarket. These can be hired and are easy to use. They come with a bottle of chemicals but only use half as much as the manufacturer recommends and top up with 2 tablespoons of bicarb, 2 tablespoons of white vinegar, 2 tablespoons of methylated spirits and 2 teaspoons of eucalyptus oil. If you have mystery stains on your carpet, add 2 teaspoons of glycerine. This recipe is also a great multi-purpose spot cleaner so leave it in a spray bottle and use when needed.

### WHAT TO DO

Prepare the room by moving all the furniture to the centre. Clean the outside edges of the room first. Spot clean any stains, then vacuum. Then use the carpet steamer. Begin by working parallel to the wall (create stripes), then perpendicular to the wall (create checks) so you clean in all four directions. This means each side of the carpet fibre is cleaned. When you finish cleaning, run the steam-cleaner over the carpet without water in it (do not push the steam button). This will suck excess moisture out of the carpet and help it to dry faster. Allow the carpet to dry (about 3 hours), then vacuum. Always clean the head of your vacuum cleaner with a damp cloth so you don't transfer dirt to your clean carpet. Move the furniture back into place, placing clear plastic under any legs so they won't mark the carpet. Clean the middle of the room in the same way (stripes and checks). Allow to dry and vacuum.

### TIPS

Start early in the morning to allow time to dry.

- Make sure windows are open for ventilation. Fresh air will also speed the drying time.
- Work slowly, if you work too quickly, the water suction won't work.
- Use attachments to get right into corners.
- If the carpet is very dirty, you may need to steam twice.
- Put a note on the front and back door asking people to remove their shoes before stepping on your freshly steam-cleaned carpet. Always place a towel inside the front and back doors for people to wipe their feet.
- Spray Scotchgard over high traffic areas to add a layer of protection.
- Once cleaned and dried, keep a rug over the carpet in high traffic areas.

## If you use professional steam-cleaners...

There are many chemicals used in steam-cleaning, including chlorine. If you've had your carpet professionally steam-cleaned and you get a fresh stain on it, before doing any spot cleaning, sponge the stain with a cloth that's been tightly wrung out in white vinegar. This will neutralise the chemicals. Don't worry, it's easy to do.

Many new carpet cleaning mixtures contain orange oil which can leave, surprise surprise, orange spots on your carpet. The residue is the problem. And while orange-based cleaning products can be good at removing stains, it must be rinsed and dried thoroughly. The thing is, some spots don't appear until about 6 months later. Yikes! This is what happened to Elsa.

**Q:** 'Last year, I had our grey berber carpet professionally cleaned. The cleaner showed me some 'new' orange-based solution which he sprayed on the walk areas. After cleaning, the carpet took about 4-5 hours to dry, whereupon I found slight orangey stains where he had sprayed the mixture. The other areas were fine. Just recently, another cleaner did our floors and this time it took about 12 hours to dry. The orange colour came to the surface and spread. I am now left with this orangey brown surface stain over a larger area. What can I do to remove it?'

**A:** You can remove the stains but it takes a bit of work. Place a couple of drops of glycerine on an old toothbrush and comb through the bristles of the carpet. Hire a carpet cleaning machine and follow the technique described in DIY steam-cleaning, above. Use the cleaner again without water (and without pushing the steam button) so it sucks up excess moisture from the carpet. If there's good airflow, your carpet will dry quickly.

## Barbecue sauce

**Q:** 'I was eating dinner in front of the TV', says Sam. 'And managed to get barbecue sauce on the carpet. What can I do?'

|  |  |
|---|---|
| **Problem:** | **Barbecue sauce on carpet.** |
| **What to use:** | **Damp cloth, white vinegar, paper towel, ultraviolet light, cardboard.** |
| **How to apply:** | Remove the bulk of the stain with a damp cloth, then wipe with a cloth wrung out in white vinegar. Place paper towel over the top and stand on it to remove excess moisture. Aim ultraviolet light at the stain, protecting the surrounding carpet with cardboard. Check every 2 hours until the stain is removed. |

## Beetroot

|  |  |
|---|---|
| **Problem:** | **Beetroot on carpet.** |
| **What to use:** | **White vinegar, cloth, paper towel.** |
| **How to apply:** | Immerse a cloth in white vinegar, tightly wring out and sponge over the stain until removed. Press with paper towel until dry. |

# Betadine

**Q:** 'Some time ago, I managed to spill some Betadine on pink wool carpet', reports Marjorie. 'Can I get it out?'

|              |                                                                                                                                                                                                 |
| ------------ | ----------------------------------------------------------------------------------------------------------------------------------------------------------------------------------------------- |
| **Problem:** | **Old Betadine spots on carpet.**                                                                                                                                                               |
| **What to use:** | **Lavender oil, cloth, white vinegar; or glycerine, old toothbrush, white vinegar, paper towel, dishwashing liquid, water, cloth.** |
| **How to apply:** | Put a couple of drops of lavender oil on a cloth and wipe over the stain. Then wipe with a cloth wrung out in white vinegar. Alternatively, put a couple of drops of glycerine on an old toothbrush and apply to the stain working north–south and east–west across the carpet fibres. Leave overnight because it's an old stain. The next day, wipe over the stain with a little dishwashing liquid on a cloth, place paper towel over the top and stand on it to remove moisture. Wipe with a cloth wrung out in white vinegar, allow to dry and repeat until clean. |

SPOTLESS 2

## Bleach

**Q:** 'How do I remove a bleach mark from a dark carpet?' asks Phil.

**Problem:** **Bleach mark on carpet.**

**What to use:** **Folk art paint, toothbrush, hair dryer.**

**How to apply:** Replace the colour with folk art paint (available from art suppliers or craft stores) that matches the colour of your carpet. You may need to create your own mix from a couple of tubes. Test the paint on an inconspicuous corner of the carpet to make sure it's an exact match and allow each test section of paint to dry because many change colour. Don't use a hair dryer to speed up the drying process or you'll set the colour. Once you've got the right colour, use a toothbrush to brush the paint into the bleached spot on the carpet (use the toothbrush as though you were brushing your hair), feathering the edges so you don't get an obvious line. Then move a hair dryer backwards and forwards across the paint to set it.

Floors, Walls and Windows

## Blood

**Q:** 'What's the best way to remove blood from carpet?' asks Joan.

>**Problem:** **Blood on carpet.**
>**What to use:** **Cake of bathroom soap, cold water, old toothbrush, damp cloth, paper towel, white vinegar, glycerine.**
>**How to apply:** Blood is a protein stain. Dampen a cake of bathroom soap in cold water and scribble over the stain as though using a big crayon. Scrub with a toothbrush making sure you rub in every direction across the carpet fibre (north, south, east and west). Wipe with a damp cloth, place paper towel on top and stand on it to remove moisture. If you've applied any other product to the blood, neutralise it first by wiping with a cloth wrung out in white vinegar. Put a couple of drops of glycerine on a toothbrush, scrub over the stain and leave for 20 minutes. Then use soap and cold water technique described above.

## Butter/margarine

>**Problem:** **Butter/margarine on carpet.**
>**What to use:** **Dishwashing liquid, damp cloth, paper towel.**

SPOTLESS 2

**How to apply:** Put a couple of drops of dishwashing liquid on your fingertips and massage into the stain until it changes texture and feels like jelly. Wipe with a cold damp cloth. Place paper towel over the stain and press down to remove excess moisture.

## Chocolate

**Q:** 'I managed to get chocolate on my light-coloured pure wool carpet', reports Karen. 'How do I get it out?'

**Problem:** **Chocolate on carpet.**
**What to use:** **Cheap shampoo, cold water, paper towel.**
**How to apply:** Put a couple of drops of cheap shampoo on your fingers and massage gently into the carpet until the stain begins to loosen. If it starts to dry out, add a little cold water to your fingers and keep on massaging. Place paper towel over the stain and stand on it. Repeat until the stain is removed.

## Coffee

**Problem:** **Coffee stain on carpet.**
**What to use:** **Glycerine, old toothbrush, white vinegar, cloth, paper towel.**

Floors, Walls and Windows

**How to apply:** Put a couple of drops of glycerine on a toothbrush and work from the outside to the inside of the stain. Leave for 20 minutes. Wipe with a cloth wrung out in white vinegar. Place paper towel over the stain and press down to remove excess moisture.

## Cordial

**Problem:** **Red cordial on carpet.**
**What to use:** **White vinegar, cloth, ultraviolet light, cardboard, paper towel; glycerine.**
**How to apply:** Wipe with a cloth wrung out in white vinegar. Aim ultraviolet light at the stain until it begins to fade (check every 2 hours). Cover around the stain with cardboard if the carpet is coloured. Again, wipe with a cloth wrung out in white vinegar. Place paper towel over the stain and press down to remove excess moisture. For old stains, wipe a couple of drops of glycerine over the stain first and leave for 20 minutes. Then use the above technique.

## Cough medicine

**Q:** 'I dropped a bottle of very sticky cough medicine on the berber carpet in our bedroom', reports Sally. 'I've mopped and sponged it to no avail. Please don't tell me we will have to replace the carpet!'

**Problem:** **Cough mixture on carpet.**

**What to use:** **White vinegar, warm water, pantyhose, paper towel.**

**How to apply:** Cough mixture is very high in sugar and requires extra persistence when removing it. Mix equal parts white vinegar and warm water. Dip a pair of rolled up pantyhose into the solution and wring out tightly. Scrub the stain in all directions (north, south, east and west) until removed. Place paper towel over the stain and stand on it. When the carpet appears to be almost dry, repeat the entire process. If a shadow returns in a couple of weeks, repeat. Sugar stains can be very stubborn because sugar crystallises in the carpet fibres and continues to resurface. Fortunately, you don't have to rub too vigorously—just repeatedly.

## Crayon

**Problem:** **Crayon on carpet.**

**What to use:** **Pantyhose, tea tree oil.**

**How to apply:** Place a couple of drops of tea tree oil on a pair of pantyhose and roll over the crayon mark in a circle. Don't forget to clean your pantyhose before using again or you'll transfer coloured crayon to the next job!

Floors, Walls and Windows

## Curry

**Q:** 'Help!' exclaims Garry. 'I've got green chicken curry on my carpet. It looks awful.'

| | |
|---|---|
| **Problem:** | **Green chicken curry on carpet.** |
| **What to use:** | **Dishwashing liquid, white vinegar, cloth, paper towel, ultraviolet light, cardboard; or lavender oil, water, spray pack, pantyhose.** |
| **How to apply:** | To remove the oils, place a little dishwashing liquid on your fingers and massage into the stain. Wipe with a cloth wrung out in white vinegar. Place paper towel over the stain and press down to remove excess moisture. Aim ultraviolet light at the stain, protecting the carpet around the stain with cardboard, until it begins to fade (check every 2 hours). If the curry has any yellow colouring, combine 1 teaspoon of lavender oil and 1 litre of water in a spray pack, lightly spray over the area and scrub with pantyhose. Repeat until removed. |

## Dog poo

**Q:** 'How do I remove dog diarrhoea from light bone-coloured carpet?' asks Joan. 'I've tried bicarb and white vinegar but a light yellow stain was left behind.'

SPOTLESS 2

**Problem:** **Dog poo on carpet.**
**What to use:** **Comb, toilet paper, cake of bathroom soap, cold water, old toothbrush, paper towel, bicarb, white vinegar, cloth, vacuum cleaner.**
**How to apply:** The yellow stain could be from colouring used in some dog food or a tannin stain from using too much moisture on the carpet. To remove the diarrhoea, slide a comb underneath and lift as much as you can from the carpet. Place toilet paper on top to absorb it. Dip a cake of bathroom soap in cold water and scribble over the stain as though using a crayon. Don't use too much water. Then scrub the area with a toothbrush. Place several sheets of paper towel on top and stand on them to remove moisture. Repeat until the stain is removed. For regular dog poo, remove as much as possible and apply the above technique. For any remaining stain, sprinkle with a little bicarb and wipe with a cloth wrung out in white vinegar. Leave to dry completely before vacuuming.

## Dye

**Q:** 'I had a mishap with a hot water bottle', admits Trish. 'It burst, spilled hot water onto a cushion and the dye from the cushion then soaked through to a pure wool cream-coloured rug. What can I do?'

Floors, Walls and Windows

>**Problem:** **Dye on carpet.**
>**What to use:** **Colour Run Remover: Whites, cloth, blood-heat water, paper towel.**
>**How to apply:** Mix 1 part Colour Run Remover: Whites to 5 parts water. Place a cloth into the mixture, wring it out tightly and wipe until the stain is removed. Then wipe with a cloth wrung out in blood-heat water. Apply paper towel to remove moisture. With white or pale cream carpet, use Colour Run Remover: Whites. With other carpet, use Colour Run Remover: Coloursafe.

# Egg

>**Problem:** **Egg on carpet.**
>**What to use:** **Combs, tissue, cold water, cake of bathroom soap, damp cloth, cloth, cold water.**
>**How to apply:** If it's raw egg, wrap two combs in a tissue so the teeth stick out. Slide the combs toward each other and lift the egg. Dip a cake of bathroom soap in cold water, scribble on the stain, then sponge with a damp cloth. If it's scrambled or cooked, scribble a cake of bathroom soap on the stain and sponge with a cloth wrung out in cold water.

SPOTLESS 2

## Fanta

Q: 'My child spilled some of her Fanta soft drink on our wool beige carpet', reports Steve. 'The carpet has been professionally cleaned and they said the stain can't be removed. Can you help?'

|  |  |
|---|---|
| **Problem:** | **Fanta stain on carpet.** |
| **What to use:** | **White vinegar, cloth, ultraviolet light, cardboard, paper towel.** |
| **How to apply:** | Fanta contains vegetable dye and sugar. Remove the vegetable dye by wiping over the stain with a cloth wrung out in white vinegar. Then aim ultraviolet light at the stain, protecting the carpet around the stain with cardboard. Check every 2 hours until the stain is gone. Fanta is high in sugar so you may get a shadow stain a couple of weeks later. If so, wipe with a cloth wrung out in white vinegar. Apply paper towel and stand on it to absorb moisture. |

## Fluorescent pen

Q: 'I've got pink fluorescent pen on my carpet', reports Richard. 'What can I do?'

|  |  |
|---|---|
| **Problem:** | **Fluorescent pen on carpet.** |
| **What to use:** | **Ice-cubes, zip-lock bag, water, non-iodised salt, damp cloth, paper towel.** |

Floors, Walls and Windows

**How to apply:** Place ice-cubes in a zip-lock bag. Slightly damp the stain with water and sprinkle a generous amount of non-iodised salt over the stain. Place the ice on top and leave until it melts. Remove the zip-lock bag and sponge the stain with a damp cloth. Apply paper towel to absorb all the moisture.

## Fruit (non-tannin based)

**Q:** 'I had some friends over the other evening', reports Sally. 'And one of the strawberry daiquiris went spilling onto the carpet. Any suggestions?'

**Problem:** **Strawberry daiquiri stain on carpet.**
**What to use:** **Cloth, white vinegar, ultraviolet light, cardboard.**
**How to apply:** Wring out a cloth in white vinegar and wipe over the stain. Aim ultraviolet light at the area, protecting the rest of the carpet with cardboard, and check every 2 hours until the stain fades.

## Glycerine

**Q:** 'I used glycerine to remove a coffee stain on my carpet', reports Veronica. 'But now I'm left with what looks to be a wet mark. Can it be removed?'

**Problem:** **Glycerine on carpet.**
**What to use:** **Cloth, white vinegar.**

**How to apply:** Wring out a cloth in white vinegar and wipe over the stain. Don't overuse glycerine. A couple of drops should be enough for an area 30 cm in diametre.

## Glue

What to do will depend on the type of glue. To remove superglue, use superglue remover (available from hardware stores) or acetone. Craft and PVA glues (which go on white and dry clear) are removed with steam and rubbing with pantyhose. To generate steam, fill a watering can with boiling water and aim the steamy spout over the stain (don't get any water on the carpet). When the glue softens, rub with pantyhose. Two-part epoxy glues (Araldite) are removed with acetone (see 'Nail polish' on page 130 for instructions). Gums and paper glues are removed with a warm damp cloth. For contact adhesives (sticky tape, double-sided tape or shoe repair kits), use tea tree oil. A single drop will remove a large piece of tape. Put 1 drop on the top edge of the tape and allow to soak for 20 minutes. For sticky tape and masking tape residue, put 1 drop of tea tree oil on pantyhose and wipe over the glue.

## Graphite powder

**Q:** 'My husband was lubricating the baby's bedroom door hinges with graphite powder and spilt it over the sisal wool-blend carpet in that corner of the room', says Simone. 'I have only tried vacuuming with no luck. Any suggestions?'

Floors, Walls and Windows

**Problem:** **Graphite powder on carpet.**

**What to use:** **Cake of bathroom soap, cold water, 9 litre bucket, damp cloth, paper towel.**

**How to apply:** Graphite and other fine powders are often left behind when vacuuming. To pick up fine matter, dampen a cake of bathroom soap with a little cold water and dab it up and down over the graphite spots on the carpet. The graphite will stick to the soap. For a large spill, keep a bucket of cold water next to you and dip as you go. Remove excess soap with a damp cloth. Apply paper towel to remove moisture. Alternatively, cut the soap into a sausage shape by cutting lengthways and trimming the corners with a warm knife. Roll backwards and forwards over the carpet. Use sewing machine oil or baby oil rather than graphite powder to lubricate hinges in a baby's room (graphite powder isn't great for a baby's lungs).

**Prevention:** Put a covering, such as newspaper, underneath the door when applying graphite powder or any other substances that may spill.

## Grass

**Problem:** **Grass on carpet.**

**What to use:** **White spirits, cloth, white vinegar, paper towel.**

**How to apply:** Dab white spirits on a cloth and wipe over the grass stain. Immerse another cloth in white vinegar, wring out tightly and wipe the area. Apply paper towel to absorb all the moisture.

## Gravy

**Problem:** **Gravy on carpet.**

**What to use:** **Cake of bathroom soap, cold water, old toothbrush, damp cloth, dishwashing liquid, paper towel.**

**How to apply:** This is a protein and oil stain. Dip a cake of bathroom soap in cold water and scribble over the stain as though you are using a crayon. Scrub over the stain with a toothbrush and wipe with a cold damp cloth. Put a couple of drops of dishwashing liquid on your fingers and massage into the stain until it feels like jelly. Then sponge with a damp cloth. Apply paper towel to absorb all the moisture.

## Grease

There was confusion in *Spotless* about how to remove different types of grease. The treatment to use depends on whether the grease is dark or light coloured. As a general guide, dark-coloured grease is removed with baby oil followed by dishwashing liquid rubbed in with your fingers. Light-coloured grease is removed with dishwashing liquid rubbed in with your fingers. If you've used baby oil on a light-coloured grease stain, put dishwashing liquid on your fingers and rub into the baby oil until it feels like jelly and wipe with a damp cloth. Absorb moisture with paper towel.

**Q:** 'I've got car grease stains on wool carpeted stairs', says Trish. 'How do I get rid of them?'

| | |
|---|---|
| **Problem:** | **Car grease on carpet.** |
| **What to use:** | **Tissue, metal comb, disposable rubber gloves, dishwashing liquid, damp cloth, paper towel.** |
| **How to apply:** | Wrap a tissue around a metal comb, wedge it under the grease and comb out as much as possible. If it's a large amount of grease, you may need to repeat this with clean tissues. Put on rubber gloves and rub dishwashing liquid into the stain with your fingers until it changes texture and feels like jelly. Remove the dishwashing liquid by wiping with a clean damp cloth. Apply paper towel to dry. |

## Hair gel

**Q:** 'I've got hair gel on my carpet', reports Sue. 'What can I do?'

**Problem: Hair gel on carpet.**

**What to use:** **Dishwashing liquid, damp cloth, tea tree oil, paper towel.**

**How to apply:** Rub a couple of drops of dishwashing liquid into the gel with your fingers until it feels like jelly and wipe with a warm damp cloth. If the gel contains wax, mix ½ teaspoon of tea tree oil with ½ teaspoon of dishwashing liquid and rub into the carpet using your fingers. Wipe with a damp cloth. Apply paper towel to absorb moisture.

## Hair serum

**Q:** 'My daughter emptied my anti-frizz hair serum onto our bedroom carpet', reports Susie. 'It's a rental home and I'm pretty sure the carpet is wool.'

**Problem:** **Anti-frizz hair serum on carpet.**

**What to use:** **Glycerine, cloth, dishwashing liquid, old toothbrush, damp cloth, paper towel.**

**How to apply:** If the stain is brown in colour, wipe with a couple of drops of glycerine on a toothbrush. Then put a couple of drops of dishwashing liquid onto the toothbrush and scrub over the stain. Two drops of each is enough for a 30 cm circle. Wipe over with a damp cloth. Apply paper towel with pressure to absorb moisture. If it is grey in colour, use dishwashing liquid as described above.

Floors, Walls and Windows

## Ice-cream

**Problem:** **Ice-cream on carpet.**

**What to use:** **Cake of bathroom soap, cold water, cloth, dishwashing liquid, damp cloth, white vinegar, dry cloth, paper towel.**

**How to apply:** Ice-cream is high in protein, fat and sugar and each element will have to be removed separately but in this order. First, remove protein by dipping a cake of bathroom soap in cold water and scribble over the stain as though using a crayon. Scrub with a toothbrush and sponge with a damp cloth. Second, remove fats by putting a couple of drops of dishwashing liquid onto your fingers and massaging into the stain until it feels like jelly. Wipe with a damp cloth. Third, remove sugar by wringing out a cloth in white vinegar. Place the vinegar cloth out in one hand and a dry cloth in the other and wipe over the stain, hand over hand as though you're stroking a cat. Apply paper towel with pressure to absorb all the moisture.

## Ink

There are many different types of ink and to complicate matters each requires a different solution. If you don't know what's been used, test with methylated spirits on a cotton bud. If this doesn't work, use white spirits.

SPOTLESS 2

**Biros**—place rotten milk solids over the stain. You will see the ink absorbing into the milk solids. When the ink has visibly soaked into the milk solids, slide a comb under the solids to lift without squashing. Remove any residue by washing with a little soap on a damp cloth.

**Gel pens**—place methylated spirits on a cotton bud and wipe over the stain until removed. Rub off with paper towel.

**Fine-point liners**—dip a cotton bud in methylated spirits and wipe over the liner. For stronger grade liners, use white spirits in the same way.

**Permanent markers**—contain their own solvent so use the same permanent marker and draw over the mark. Then dip a cotton bud in white spirits and wipe over the mark. Sprinkle with talcum powder and vacuum. Repeat the white spirits step if necessary.

## Insects

**Q:** 'I think I have an insect stain on our beige wool carpet', queries Jill. 'And it's been there for some time. What should I do?'

| | |
|---|---|
| **Problem:** | **Insect stain on wool carpet.** |
| **What to use:** | **Glycerine, cloth, dishwashing liquid, old toothbrush, damp cloth, paper towel.** |
| **How to apply:** | Wipe over the stain with a couple of drops of glycerine on an old toothbrush. Then dip a cake of bathroom soap in cold water and scrub over the stain. Rub a toothbrush in all four directions—north, south, east, west—over the top. Wipe with a cold damp cloth, apply paper |

Floors, Walls and Windows

towel and stand on it to dry it thoroughly. If it's insect faeces (looks like an orange splash), dip a cake of bathroom soap in cold water and scribble over the stain. Wipe with a cold damp cloth, apply paper towel and stand on it to dry thoroughly.

## Jam

**Problem:** **Plum jam spilt on wool carpet.**

**What to use:** **Cloth, white vinegar, water, glycerine, old toothbrush, paper towel.**

**How to apply:** Wring a cloth out in white vinegar and wipe over the stain. Wipe straight away with a dry cloth. Repeat hand over hand, as though you're stroking a cat. If there's a light brown stain, use a couple of drops of glycerine on a toothbrush and brush over the top of the carpet fibres. Leave for 20 minutes and use the vinegar solution. Apply paper towel with pressure to absorb moisture.

## Jelly beans

**Q:** 'I've got jelly beans on my white carpet', says Margaret. 'They've been mashed into it.'

**Problem:** **Jelly beans on carpet.**

**What to use:** **Comb, dishwashing liquid, old toothbrush, damp cloth, paper towel.**

**How to apply:** Wedge a comb beneath the mashed jelly bean and remove as much as possible. Put a couple of drops of dishwashing liquid on a toothbrush and brush over the carpet fibres in each direction. Remove the dishwashing liquid with a warm damp cloth. Repeat until the stain is removed. Apply paper towel with pressure to absorb moisture.

## Lubricant (personal)

**Problem:** **Lube on carpet.**

**What to use:** **Cake of bathroom soap, cold water, paper towel; or dishwashing liquid, damp cloth, paper towel.**

**How to apply:** There are two varieties of personal lubricant. One is gelatine-based and is high in protein. The other is oil-based. It is quite easy to work out which type of lube it is. Gelatine-based lube has a stain with a dark outer edge and oil-based is even in colour. For gelatine-based stains, use a cake of bathroom soap, dip it in cold water and scribble over the mark. Scrub with an old toothbrush before applying paper towel to absorb moisture. For oil-based stains, put a couple of drops of dishwashing liquid on your fingers and massage into the area until it's jelly-like. Wipe with a damp cloth. Apply paper towel to absorb moisture.

## Mayonnaise

**Problem:** **Mayonnaise on carpet.**

**What to use:** **Dishwashing liquid, damp cloth, paper towel; or cake of bathroom soap, cold water.**

**How to apply:** Mayonnaise contains a lot of oil. Put dishwashing liquid on your fingertips and massage into the stain until it feels like jelly. Remove the residue with a damp cloth and apply paper towel to absorb moisture. If it's whole egg mayonnaise, use a cake of bathroom soap and cold water first. Then massage in dishwashing liquid with your fingers. Wipe with a damp cloth and apply paper towel to remove moisture.

## Mould

**Problem:** **Mould on carpet.**

**What to use:** **Oil of cloves, water, 1 litre spray pack, vacuum cleaner, non-iodised salt, stiff broom.**

**How to apply:** If the mould is from condensation, combine ¼ teaspoon of oil of cloves with 1 litre of water in a spray pack, lightly mist over the carpet and leave for 24 hours. Vacuum the next day. If the mould remains, repeat. If the mould is from chronic damp over a large area, use the oil of cloves and water mixture first and leave for 24 hours. Scatter non-iodised coarse salt over the affected area and sweep with a broom before vacuuming. If you can still smell the mould, it's best to remove the carpet and install floorboards. **WARNING:** Don't use more oil of cloves than suggested. Oil of cloves is a volatile oil and can cause damage if used in large quantities or incorrectly.

People often complain about mouldy smelling homes at Stain Clinics. Mould can be harmful to your health, so it's best to deal with it promptly! The first step is to determine the areas of highest mould concentration. If it's in the walls, you might need to have a damp course put under the house (you'll need professional help with this). To alleviate the problem, mix ¼ teaspoon of oil of cloves with 1 litre of water in a spray pack and lightly mist over the mouldy surfaces. If you have floorboards, spray over them or under them if you possibly can. Regularly spray through vents under the house.

## Milk

> **Problem:** **Milk on carpet.**
> **What to use:** **Bathroom soap, cold water, old toothbrush, paper towel.**

Floors, Walls and Windows

**How to apply:** Dampen a cake of bathroom soap in cold water and scribble over the stain as though using a big crayon. Use an old toothbrush and rub in every direction over the carpet fibres. Rub with a damp cloth and place paper towel over the stain and stand on it to absorb all the moisture. Yes, the smell is awful but once you remove the stain, the smell will go too!

## Mud

**Q:** 'Fresh mud has been tramped through the house', complains Vicky. 'What do you suggest?'

**Problem:** **Black mud on carpet.**
**What to use:** **Stiff brush, vacuum cleaner, cake of bathroom soap, cold water, paper towel.**
**How to apply:** Allow the mud to dry or it will smear. Once it is dry, rub with a brush and vacuum. If it was rubbed when wet, dampen a cake of bathroom soap in cold water and scribble over the area. Rub with a damp cloth and apply paper towel to remove moisture. Allow to dry and brush vigorously before vacuuming.

## Nappy rash cream

**Q:** 'How can I get lanolin-based nappy rash cream out of our new carpet?' asks Donna.

SPOTLESS 2

> **Problem:** **Nappy rash cream on carpet.**
> **What to use:** **Dishwashing liquid, tea tree oil, cold water, damp cloth, paper towel, talcum powder, pantyhose.**
> **How to apply:** Massage a couple of drops of dishwashing liquid into the stain with your fingers. Mix 1 teaspoon of tea tree oil with 1 cup of cold water and wipe the mixture over the area with a well-wrung cloth. Apply paper towel to absorb the moisture. For zinc-based nappy rash creams, remove as much as possible by sprinkling with talcum powder and scrubbing with pantyhose. Then use the above technique.

## Orange juice

This solution has been updated since *Spotless* because the carpet cleaner Shannon prefers to use is no longer available.

> **Problem:** **Orange juice on carpet.**
> **What to use:** **Paper towel, white vinegar, cloth, ultraviolet light, cardboard, glycerine, old toothbrush.**
> **How to apply:** Remove as much orange juice as possible with paper towel. Wipe with a little white vinegar on a cloth. Apply more paper towel. Aim an ultraviolet light at the stain, protecting the carpet around the stain with cardboard, until it

Floors, Walls and Windows

fades. Check the UV light every 2 hours. For an old stain, wipe over the area with a couple of drops of glycerine on a toothbrush before using the above technique.

## Pot-plant mark

**Q:** 'My pot-plant has marked the carpet with a big brown mark', says Linley. 'How can I fix it?'

**Problem:** **Pot plant mark on carpet.**
**What to use:** **Glycerine, old toothbrush, cloth, white vinegar, paper towel.**
**How to apply:** This is a tannin stain. Put a couple of drops of glycerine on a toothbrush and scrub over the stain. Leave for 20 minutes. Wring a cloth in white vinegar, rub over the area, then apply paper towel to absorb moisture. Repeat until the stain is removed.

## *SPOTLESS CLASSIC*
### Red wine stain

This is one of the most common carpet stains. Don't throw salt or soda water over the red puddle. Instead, use bicarb and white vinegar, ensuring you don't use too much moisture or you'll get staining from the jute backing of the carpet, which releases a brown tannin stain if it gets wet. Remove jute stains with ½ teaspoon of glycerine and ½ teaspoon of dishwashing liquid on an old toothbrush, working from the outside to the inside of the stain. Wipe with a damp cloth and apply paper towel to remove moisture.

Absorb as much of the red wine spill as possible with paper towel. Sprinkle with a little bicarb and the stain will change from red to pale grey. Don't use too much bicarb or it will whiten the carpet around the stain. Wring a cloth out in white vinegar, wipe and leave to dry completely, then vacuum. Repeat if needed. For old stains, apply a little glycerine with an old toothbrush. Then use the above technique.

# Rubber

**Problem:** **Rubber mark on carpet.**
**What to use:** **Damp cloth, non-iodised salt, pantyhose, vacuum.**
**How to apply:** Wipe the mark with a damp cloth, sprinkle it with non-iodised salt and scrub with pantyhose. Wipe again with a damp cloth and vacuum.

*Floors, Walls and Windows*

**TIP** If you've pulled up old carpet and there are rubber marks on the concrete underneath, dampen the area with a little water. Sprinkle with coarse salt and sweep with a stiff broom. Allow to dry and vacuum. Repeat if necessary.

## Rust

**Q:** 'My office chair didn't have stoppers', says Mark. 'And has left rust stains on the carpet. Can they be removed?'

**Problem:** Rust stains on carpet.

**What to use:** Talcum powder, disposable rubber gloves, CLR/Ranex, water, cloth, damp cloth, white vinegar.

**How to apply:** Make a circle of talcum powder around the stain to prevent the solution spreading into other parts of the carpet. Put on rubber gloves, mix 1 part CLR or Ranex to 20 parts water and wipe the stain with a cloth. Immediately wipe with a damp cloth. Then wring a cloth in white vinegar and wipe. Rust removal products are quite harsh and can damage the glue at the back of the carpet so you need to work quickly. Repeat in this order: wipe with the mixture, wipe with a damp cloth, wipe with white vinegar then absorb excess moisture with paper towel.

SPOTLESS 2

**DID YOU KNOW?** Carpet beetles eat woollen carpets, leaving a black mark near the wall or doorframes. To remove the black marks, brush with non-iodised salt and vacuum. To deter them, stab 1 whole clove into a bay leaf and place at 1.5 m intervals along the walls.

## WHAT NOT TO DO...

**Q:** 'About 6 months ago, I spilt a cup of black tea on my cream carpet. I mopped it up and everything seemed okay. Shortly afterwards I had the carpet professionally cleaned. Since then I've noticed a darker patch where the tea spilt. I applied a large amount of glycerine, white vinegar and bicarb. It is now worse than ever. It's like the stain has grabbed the glycerine and turned it oily brown. I've just used a commercial carpet spot cleaner on it but there's only a slight improvement. Help!'

**A:** Before tackling a stain, think about what's been used on it already. In this case, the stain was affected by chemicals used by the commercial cleaner combined with the tea residue. Neutralise the chemicals by wiping with a cloth wrung in white vinegar, then apply paper towel to remove moisture. When using glycerine, or any moisture on carpet, use only a small amount. Don't wet the carpet because you'll cause stains from the jute underlay. If you do get a jute stain from the back of the carpet, mix ½ teaspoon of glycerine and

½ teaspoon of dishwashing liquid on an old toothbrush and brush onto the surface of the stain, working from the outside to the inside. Wipe with a damp cloth and apply paper towel to remove moisture. Repeat if necessary.

## Silicone

**Q:** 'My husband is a plumber and tracked blue silicone on the carpet', complains Judy. 'Can it be removed?'

**Problem:** **Blue plumber's silicone on carpet.**

**What to use:** **Metal comb, kerosene, pantyhose, dishwashing liquid, disposable rubber gloves, paper towel.**

**How to apply:** Dip a metal comb in a little kerosene and comb the silicone out of the carpet, removing as much as possible. Dip pantyhose in a little kerosene and scrub vigorously to remove the stains. This will require quite a bit of elbow grease—kerosene doesn't dissolve silicone but makes it easier to remove and you'll have to rub hard. To remove the kerosene, put on rubber gloves and massage dishwashing liquid into the spots. Wipe with a damp cloth before applying paper towel and stand on it to absorb moisture. Tell your husband to leave his dirty shoes outside!

SPOTLESS 2

## Sugar

Sugar stains are tricky to remove because sugar crystallises and sticks to carpet fibres. If you don't remove all the sugar, the stain goes darker. For details, see 'Fanta' on page 148.

## Shoe polish/scuff marks

If you get boot polish on carpet, wipe with a little methylated spirits. If the stain is from liquid shoe polish, which contains wax, use methylated spirits followed by a little tea tree oil.

## Soot

**Q:** 'How can I remove black soot from carpet?' asks Tom. 'We have a gas fireplace and fake coals and often get sooty bits on the carpet.'

**Problem:** **Soot on carpet.**

**What to use:** **Vacuum cleaner, cake of bathroom soap, water, pantyhose, paper towel.**

**How to apply:** Vacuum as much of the soot as possible. Dampen a cake of bathroom soap in water and roll it over the sooty carpet—the soot marks will stick to the soap. Repeat until removed. Wipe with damp pantyhose to remove excess soap. Apply paper towel to remove moisture.
**WARNING:** If a gas heater places soot in the room, the jets could be blocked or there may be something wrong with your heater. Consult a professional.

Floors, Walls and Windows

## Sorbolene cream

**Q:** 'I dropped some sorbolene cream on the carpet', says Wayne. 'What do you suggest?'

    **Problem:** **Sorbolene cream on carpet.**
    **What to use:** **Dishwashing liquid, damp cloth, paper towel.**
    **How to apply:** Put a couple of drops of dishwashing liquid on your fingers and massage into the stain until it feels like jelly. Wipe with a damp cloth. Apply paper towel to remove moisture.

## Soup

**Q:** 'I've spilt a cup of thick pea soup on my carpet', reports Christina. 'How can I get it out?'

    **Problem:** **Soup on carpet.**
    **What to use:** **White vinegar, cloth, pantyhose; cake of bathroom soap, cold water (removes protein); white vinegar, cloth, ultraviolet light, cardboard (removes vegetable dye); dishwashing liquid, damp cloth (removes fats and oils); white vinegar, cloth, ultraviolet light, cardboard (red colourant).**
    **How to apply:** Remove as much of the soup as possible. Wipe with a dab of white vinegar on a cloth and rub with pantyhose. For soup that's high in protein, damp a cake of bathroom soap with cold water

SPOTLESS 2

and scribble over the stain, then wipe with a damp cloth. If high in vegetable dye (tomato, pumpkin), wipe with a dab of white vinegar on a cloth, then apply ultraviolet light to the stain, checking every 2 hours until the dye fades. Protect the carpet around the stain with cardboard or it will lighten as well. If high in fats and oil, massage dishwashing liquid into the stain with your fingers and wipe with a damp cloth. If there's any chilli or red colourant, sponge with white vinegar on a cloth before applying ultaviolet light (protect surrounding carpet with cardboard).

## Suntan lotion

**Q:** 'I have a couple of stains on my daughter's bedroom carpet', reports Tracey. 'The stain that's most difficult to shift is tanning moisturiser. There are now two blotches of yellow in the middle of the beige carpet.'

| | |
|---|---|
| **Problem:** | **Suntan lotion on carpet.** |
| **What to use:** | **Dishwashing liquid, damp cloth (oil); glycerine, old toothbrush, white vinegar, cloth, paper towel (tannin).** |
| **How to apply:** | This is an oil and tannin stain. To remove the oil, put a couple of drops of dishwashing liquid on your fingertips and massage into the stain |

until it's viscous and jelly-like. Wipe with a damp cloth. To remove the tannin stain, apply a couple of drops of glycerine to a toothbrush and rub over the stain. Leave for around 20 minutes. Wipe with a dab of white vinegar on a cloth. Apply paper towel to remove moisture. Repeat if necessary.

## Timber stain

**Q:** 'There was a leak on the floor in our dining area and the carpet got very wet', reports Sally. 'The dining table legs have leached colour into the carpet, which is now badly stained where the legs stood. What can I do?'

| | |
|---:|:---|
| **Problem:** | **Timber stains on carpet.** |
| **What to use:** | **Glycerine, old toothbrush, cloth, white vinegar, paper towel.** |
| **How to apply:** | This is a tannin stain. Put a couple of drops of glycerine on a toothbrush and comb over the fibres. Leave for 20 minutes. Wipe with a cloth wrung out in white vinegar. Apply paper towel to remove moisture. Don't place the table on the carpet until completely dry. |
| **Prevention:** | Put stoppers or clear plastic under the table legs. |

SPOTLESS 2

## Tomato Sauce

**Problem:** **Tomato sauce on carpet.**
**What to use:** **Cloth, white vinegar, ultraviolet light, cardboard.**
**How to apply:** Tomato sauce contains a vegetable dye. Remove as much as possible before wiping with a cloth wrung out in white vinegar. Then aim ultraviolet light over the area, protecting the surrounding carpet with cardboard. Check every 2 hours until the dye is removed.

## Toner

**Q:** 'I've spilled bubble-jet ink on the carpet', reports Jean. 'Help!'

**Problem:** **Toner on carpet.**
**What to use:** **Rotten milk, comb, cold water, cloth, paper towel.**
**How to apply:** To remove the ink, rot some milk in the sun until it forms lumps. Strain the lumps and place them over the stain to absorb the ink. When the ink has been absorbed, lift the rotten milk lumps off the carpet with a comb. Clean the remainder by scribbing with a cake of bathroom soap and cold water. Apply paper towel to remove moisture.

Floors, Walls and Windows

## Tree sap

Q: 'I've got tree sap on my carpet', says Joanne.

**Problem:** **Tree sap on carpet.**
**What to use:** **Tea tree oil, old toothbrush, damp cloth, paper towel.**
**How to apply:** Apply a couple of drops of tea tree oil to a toothbrush and scrub. Wipe with a damp cloth. Apply paper towel to absorb moisture.

## Urine

**Problem:** **Urine on carpet.**
**What to use:** **Ultraviolet light, white chalk, cloth, white vinegar, paper towel.**
**How to apply:** If you don't know where the stain is, use ultraviolet light in a darkened room and the urine will glow yellow. Mark around the stains with white chalk so you know where they are when the light is turned back on. Wipe with a cloth dampened with white vinegar. Apply paper towel to remove moisture. Repeat if necessary.

## Vegemite

Q: 'How can I get Vegemite and butter out of my wool-blend carpet?' asks Ben. 'It's been trodden in.'

**Problem:** **Vegemite and butter on carpet.**

SPOTLESS 2

**What to use:** **Dishwashing liquid, damp cloth, paper towel.**

**How to apply:** Vegemite and butter toast always lands buttered side down! Put a little dishwashing liquid on your fingertips and massage into the carpet. Wipe with a damp cloth. Apply paper towel to remove moisture. Repeat until the mark is removed.

## Vomit

**Problem:** **Vomit on carpet.**

**What to use:** **Stain diagnosis.**

**How to apply:** It depends what's been vomited up. Consult the Stain Diagnosis on page 362. If the vomit contains bile, wipe with a cloth wrung out in white vinegar.

## Water

**Q:** 'I spilled a bottle of water on the carpet', says Christine. 'It's left a watermark. What can I do?'

**Problem:** **Watermark on carpet.**

**What to use:** **Talcum powder, vacuum cleaner, glycerine, toothbrush, white vinegar, cloth, paper towel.**

*Floors, Walls and Windows*

**How to apply:** If the carpet is still wet, cover with a sprinkling of talcum powder and leave for around 20 minutes or until dry. Then vacuum. When the mark has dried, wipe the top of the carpet fibres with a couple of drops of glycerine on an old toothbrush. Leave for 20 minutes. Then wipe with a cloth wrung out in white vinegar. Apply paper towel to remove moisture.

## Zinc cream

**Q:** 'How do you get zinc out of carpet?' asks Tom.

**Problem:** **Zinc cream on carpet.**

**What to use:** **Talcum powder, pantyhose, baby oil, dish-washing liquid, damp cloth, paper towel.**

**How to apply:** Sprinkle a little talcum powder on the stain and scrub with pantyhose. Place a couple of drops of baby oil on a cloth and rub into the stain. For any remaining stains, massage in a little dishwashing liquid using your fingertips until it feels like jelly. Wipe with a damp cloth. Apply paper towel to remove moisture.

# General cleaning guide for floors

| Surface | What to use | How to clean | How often |
| --- | --- | --- | --- |
| Wool, nylon and blend carpet | Bicarb | Lightly sprinkle the bicarb over the floor and leave for half an hour before vacuuming | Once a week. More if there's lots of traffic |
| Sisal, seagrass, plant fibre or copra | Mix 1 cup unprocessed wheat bran and ½ teaspoon white vinegar | Sprinkle the mixture over the floor and firmly sweep with a stiff broom, leave for half an hour before vacuuming | Once a week. This flooring soils easily |
| Sealed timber floorboards, parquetry, floating floors, particle board, bamboo, cork | Mix ½ cup black tea, 1 cup white vinegar and 9 litres tepid water in a bucket | Sweep/mop the solution over the floor with a clean broom covered with a pair of pantyhose. Dry with an old towel under your feet as you go | At least once a week depending on the amount of traffic |

## Floors, Walls and Windows

| Surface | What to use | How to clean | How often |
|---|---|---|---|
| Glazed tiles (terracotta, ceramic or porcelain), terrazzo | Bicarb. Combine 1 cup white vinegar with 9 litres tepid water in a bucket | If dirty, sprinkle first with a light scattering of bicarb. Sweep/mop the solution over the floor with a clean broom covered with a pair of pantyhose. Dry with an old towel under your feet as you go | At least once a week depending on the amount of traffic |
| Unglazed tiles (terracotta, ceramic or porcelain), cement, brick, slate | Bicarb. Combine 1 cup white vinegar with 9 litres tepid water in a bucket | If dirty, sprinkle first with a light scattering of bicarb. Sweep/mop the solution over the floor with a clean broom covered with a pair of pantyhose. Dry thoroughly with an old towel under your feet as you go | At least once a week depending on the amount of traffic |

SPOTLESS 2

| Surface | What to use | How to clean | How often |
|---|---|---|---|
| Marble/ limestone | Grate 1 teaspoon of pH neutral soap into a 9 litre bucket of warm water. To seal (when the surface is dull), coat with a thin layer of marble flooring wax or limestone milk | Sweep/mop the solution with a clean broom covered in pantyhouse. Dry with an old towel under your feet as you clean. When dry, apply a small quantity of quality marble flooring wax or limestone milk | At least once a week depending on the amount of traffic |
| Linoleum | Combine 2 teaspoons kerosene, 2 teaspoons dishwashing liquid and ½ cup white vinegar with 9 litres tepid water in a bucket | Sweep/mop the solution over the floor with a clean broom covered with a pair of pantyhose. Dry with an old towel under your feet as you go | At least once a week depending on the amount of traffic |
| Vinyl | Bicarb. Add 1 cup white vinegar, 2 teaspoons glycerine with 9 litres tepid water in a bucket | If dirty, sprinkle first with a light scattering of bicarb. Sweep/ mop with a clean broom covered with a pair of pantyhose. Dry with an old towel under your feet as you go | At least once a week depending on the amount of traffic |

# WHAT TO DO WHEN CARPET GETS WET

Water-soaked carpets smell awful. To dry the carpet out, hire an air blower (available from plant hire companies and councils). Follow the directions—each operates slightly differently. If the carpet is drenched, remove the batons from doorways and place a roll of paper towel under the edge of the carpet to lift it. This absorbs moisture near the doors and allows airflow under the carpet, helping it to dry faster. Once it has dried, sprinkle the carpet with bicarb and either stomp on the carpet or sweep with a stiff broom. Leave the bicarb for half an hour to an hour and then vacuum. Next, kill the mould spores by putting a ¼ teaspoon of oil of cloves into a 1 litre spray pack of water and lightly mist over the carpet. If you can't get hold of an air blower, use a combination of towels and pressure. Place the towels on the carpet and walk on them to absorb moisture. If there's brown staining once the carpet has dried, it means the jute backing has released tannin. Remove with ½ teaspoon of glycerine and ½ teaspoon of dishwashing liquid on an old toothbrush, working from the outside to the inside of the stain. Wipe with a damp cloth and apply paper towel (or towel for large areas) to remove moisture.

## Rugs and mats

**Q:** 'I have a large dirty flokati rug to wash', says Bonnie. 'What do you suggest?'

    **Problem:** **Dirty flokati rug.**
  **What to use:** **Unprocessed wheat bran, white vinegar, broom, vacuum cleaner; or bath,**

SPOTLESS 2

**blood-heat water, cheap shampoo and conditioner.**

**How to apply:** For regular cleaning, mix 1 kg of unprocessed wheat bran with drops of white vinegar (one at a time) and stir until it forms clumps that resemble brown sugar. Sprinkle over the rug, sweep with a stiff broom and vacuum. If very dirty, wash in the bath using blood-heat water and a little shampoo and conditioner. Walk up and down the rug in the bath and remove as much dirt as possible. Then rinse in blood-heat water and dry in the shade. Shake the rug occasionally to fluff up the fibres. You don't want flat flokati!

**Q:** 'I've got a Turkish wool rug', reports Pip. 'But the cotton fringing is no longer white. What can I do?'

**Problem:** **Dirty cotton fringing.**

**What to use:** **Paper towel, cheap shampoo, old toothbrush, damp cloth; or dry shampoo for blonde hair, hairbrush.**

**How to apply:** Roll up paper towel and place it under the fringe. Then apply 1 teaspoon of shampoo to every 30 cm of fringe with a toothbrush, being careful not to get it on the rug itself. Remove the shampoo with a damp cloth. Dry with paper towel. Alternatively, spray with dry shampoo and brush with a hairbrush.

# Sisal

Sisal is a type of weave and can be made of plant fibres or horse hair. Many people love the look of sisal but it can be a bit tough on bare feet and it soils easily.

**Q:** 'My daughter's cat drank green food colouring and peed on my oatmeal-coloured sisal carpet', says Maggie. 'I've already used white vinegar but now have two orange-coloured stains that get darker in rainy weather. What can I do?'

| | |
|---|---|
| **Problem:** | **Green food colouring and vinegar on sisal.** |
| **What to use:** | **Glycerine, old toothbrush, white vinegar, cloth, ultraviolet light, cardboard.** |
| **How to apply:** | The orange-coloured spots are likely to be a tannin stain from using too much vinegar. Put a couple of drops of glycerine on a toothbrush and scrub over the marks. Leave for 20 minutes. Then sponge with a cloth wrung out in white vinegar. To remove the green food colouring dye, wipe with a cloth wrung out in white vinegar. Aim ultraviolet light at the stain, protecting the carpet around the stain with cardboard, until the green is gone. |

# SPOTLESS 2

**Q:** 'I have a sisal carpet and managed to stain it with (I think) water from a Damp Rid container', says Tony. 'What do you suggest?

**Problem:** **Damp Rid on sisal.**

**What to use:** **Unprocessed wheat bran, white vinegar, vacuum cleaner, dishwashing liquid, old toothbrush, oil of cloves, 1 litre spray pack, coarse non-iodised salt, pantyhose.**

**How to apply:** This is difficult to remove because Damp Rid contains silicone. Mix 1 kg of unprocessed wheat bran with drops of white vinegar (one at a time) and stir until it becomes clumpy and resembles brown sugar. Sprinkle over the area and brush it back and forward. Leave for half an hour and vacuum. Place dishwashing liquid on a toothbrush and scrub over the stain. Put ¼ teaspoon of oil of cloves into a 1 litre spray pack of water and mist over the stain. Then lightly sprinkle a little salt (2 teaspoons of salt per 30-cm diameter) and rub with pantyhose. Allow to dry and vacuum. If this doesn't work, you'll need to patch the sisal. For details, see page 120 in *Spotless*. The good thing about patching sisal is the ribs hide the joins so you won't notice the patch job.

Floors, Walls and Windows

# Coir

This is made of coconut fibre.

**Q:** 'I warmed a tub of Vicks VapoRub and managed to spill it onto my coir carpet', says Kate. 'What can I do?'

>**Problem:** **Vicks VapoRub on coir.**
>
>**What to use:** **Unprocessed wheat bran, stiff broom, dishwashing liquid, old toothbrush, damp cloth, paper towel.**
>
>**How to apply:** This is a tricky one. Sprinkle lots of unprocessed wheat bran and sweep it back and forth over the stain with a stiff broom. Keep replacing the bran until it stops sticking to the coir. Place a couple of drops of dishwashing liquid on a toothbrush and scrub with the grain over the coir. Once it feels like jelly, wipe with a damp cloth. Put some paper towel over the top and stand on it to absorb moisture.

# Linoleum, vinyl and self-levelling plastics

**Q:** 'I have cushion vinyl on my kitchen floor', reports Pat. 'And there are a number of stiletto heel indentations. Can I remove these marks?'

>**Problem:** **Indentations on vinyl.**
>
>**What to use:** **Commercial steamer, glycerine, water.**

**How to apply:** Hire a commercial steamer (from plant and equipment hire) and add 2 teaspoons of glycerine to the water reservoir (around 9 litres). Clean the floor on the highest temperature.

**Prevention:** Stiletto heels place a huge amount of pressure on vinyl (and other) floors, so ask visitors to remove them. Have some slippers or thongs available for the guest to wear.

# Q: 'How do you get purple crepe paper stain off cream vinyl?' asks Frank.

**Problem:** **Purple crepe paper on vinyl.**
**What to use:** **Lavender oil, glycerine, pantyhose.**
**How to apply:** This is tricky because the chemical formula to make dye can be similar to the chemical formula to colour lino, so removing one will remove the other. Make a paste of equal parts lavender oil and glycerine and apply to the stain with pantyhose. Polish it out with clean pantyhose.

# Q: 'We've got scuff marks on our vinyl floors from shoes', reports Robyn. 'How can we get them off?'

**Problem:** **Rubber scuff marks on vinyl.**
**What to use:** **Biro eraser, coarse salt, broom or vacuum cleaner.**

Floors, Walls and Windows

**How to apply:** The marks are likely to be from rubber on shoes. Rub over with a biro eraser or coarse salt and sweep or vacuum.

## Q: 'What's the best way to remove rust from lino?' asks Betty.

**Problem: Rust on lino.**

**What to use: Lemon, non-iodised salt, damp cloth.**

**How to apply:** Cut a lemon in half, sprinkle with salt and scrub over the rust stains. Wipe with a damp cloth. Repeat if necessary

## Q: 'The blue wording from a plastic bag has sweated itself onto the lino of our new caravan', reports Rachael. 'We live in the Top End where temperatures get rather high and humid. What can you suggest?'

**Problem: Ink on lino.**

**What to use: Rotten milk, coarse salt, glycerine, pantyhose.**

**How to apply:** Rot some milk in the sun (the time taken will vary). Mix 2 tablespoons of rotten milk solids, 1 tablespoon of salt and 1 teaspoon of glycerine and place the smelly mixture over the stain. Leave for around 20 minutes. Polish off with pantyhose.

SPOTLESS 2

**Q:** 'How do I clean a sticky vinyl floor in the kitchen?' asks Jim.

**Problem:** **Sticky vinyl floor.**
**What to use:** **Coarse salt, 9 litre bucket, cloth, water, stiff broom.**
**How to apply:** To remove the stickiness, put 1 kg of salt into a bucket of water, stir until it dissolves, wipe the solution over the floor with a cloth and leave to dry and form a salt crust. Sweep off with a broom.

**Q:** 'How can I remove a build-up of hairspray from my embossed lino floor?' asks Raine.

**Problem:** **Hairspray on lino.**
**What to use:** **Hairspray, pantyhose, anti-dandruff shampoo, cloth, water.**
**How to apply:** Spray the floor with hairspray (it contains its own solvent). While the hairspray is still wet, wipe with pantyhose. Alternatively, spray a rolled up ball of pantyhose with hairspray and wipe over the floor. Another option is to wipe the area with a little anti-dandruff shampoo on a cloth, then rinse with water.
**Prevention:** Apply your hairspray outside.

Floors, Walls and Windows

# DOORS

Doors are often neglected during a cleaning routine but it's easy to wipe over them with a damp cloth. Clean doorknobs with a bran ball (see page 85). Grab some lavender oil—which strips through grease without damaging paint and leaves a fresh, clean smell—sprinkle a few drops on a cloth and wipe over doors and doorjambs. To remove dirty fingerprints, put 1 teaspoon of lavender oil in a 1 litre spray pack of water, spray onto pantyhose and wipe over the fingermarks.

Hinges operate more smoothly and are protected from rust if wiped with a smear of petroleum jelly (Vaseline) or sewing machine oil. Wipe across the horizontal lines of the hinge. To prevent further cleaning, put newspaper or other covering over the floor when puffing graphite powder into a lock.

*TIP* Hinges feel cold and damp when you touch them because metal attracts condensation, which makes them more susceptible to rust.

*TIP* Remove rust from screws by sprinkling salt over a cut lemon and wipe over the screws. To prevent screws from further rusting, paint the heads with clear nail polish. If you need to remove the screws, wipe over the nail polish with acetone.

## Easy soundproofing

- Use a brush strip seal on your front door; it reduces noise and keeps dust and dirt out of your home.

SPOTLESS 2

- Pin a cloth panel on the back of the door to baffle sound.
- Add another layer of curtains.
- To reduce noise from stereos, televisions, pianos, etc, place soft rubber stoppers underneath to minimise vibrations.
- To stop doors from rattling, put a felt strip on the doorjamb.

# LAMPS AND LIGHT SHADES

At the flick of a switch, you can get light but electricity contains positive ions that attract dust. Clean soft and hard lampshades every week with a bran ball (see page 85). To clean metal lamp bases, use bicarb and white vinegar on a cloth. For glass lamp bases, use white vinegar on a cloth. For timber lamp bases, use black tea on a cloth. For plastic lamp bases, use a paste of equal parts glycerine and talcum powder on a cloth. For ceramic lamp bases, use white vinegar on a cloth.

Each week, wipe a damp cloth over cold light bulbs and, if there are bugs, remove the lightbulb and vacuum the light socket (make sure it's switched off at the powerpoint). The combination of heat and dead insects can make the fitting brittle. If, like Shannon, you have lights positioned at the top of a high stairwell, put a sponge over the hook of an extendable plastic broom handle to reach. Dip the sponge in a bucket of 1 teaspoon of lavender oil per litre of water.

To remove fly speck, mix equal parts tea tree oil and water, dip in a cotton bud and spin the cotton bud over each bit of speck to remove it.

Floors, Walls and Windows

**Q:** 'Some pieces of our glass chandelier have rust stains from the internal metal rod', says Dan. 'Do you have any suggestions on how to remove them?'

    **Problem:** **Rust on metal.**

    **What to use:** **Methylated spirits, pantyhose.**

    **How to apply:** It's likely the rust was caused by a chlorine-based cleaner. To remove, rub the metal with methylated spirits and pantyhose. See pages 124–5 of *Spotless* for details on how to clean a chandelier.

# WALLS

It may sound a little odd, but Shannon cleans her walls with a vacuum cleaner. She covers the head in an old T-shirt and runs it over the walls. Remove dirty marks with a light spray of lavender oil and water on a cloth. If the walls are very dirty, mix bicarb and white vinegar on a cloth and rinse with a clean, damp cloth. Some people use sugar soap but Shannon doesn't recommend it because it leaves a residue that dirt can stick to. If you have wallpaper, clean it with a slice of brown bread. For large areas, cut a loaf of brown bread lengthways and leave overnight so it goes a little stale on the cut edge, then wipe directly on the wallpaper. Don't forget to vacuum the crumbs!

**Q:** 'I have lots of stick-on plastic hooks on the wall left from the previous owners', reports Eloise. 'I've pulled the hook bits off but can't remove the thick, tacky glue behind. What do you suggest?'

> **Problem:** **Glue on walls.**
>
> **What to use:** **Tea tree oil, plastic wrap, plastic knife.**
>
> **How to apply:** Place a drop of tea tree oil on the top edge of the glue patch and cover with plastic wrap. Leave for 20 minutes. Remove the plastic wrap and slide a plastic knife behind the glue. If it doesn't come away, replace the plastic wrap and leave for another 20 minutes, then try again.

**Q:** 'I have an oil-based fly spray unit that dispenses on a timed basis', reports Brian. 'It's left a mark on the wall. What can I do?'

> **Problem:** **Fly spray unit mark on wall.**
>
> **What to use:** **Dishwashing liquid, pantyhose, damp cloth (painted walls); or brown bread (wallpaper).**
>
> **How to apply:** If the wall is painted, place a little dishwashing liquid on pantyhose and rub over the area, then wipe with a damp cloth. For wallpaper, use a slice of brown bread and rub gently over the stain.
>
> **Prevention:** Put flyscreens on your windows. All commercial fly sprays are toxic.

Floors, Walls and Windows

## Q: 'I've got mouldy wallpaper', complains Lesley. 'What should I do?'

**Problem:** Mouldy wallpaper.

**What to use:** 9 litre bucket, warm water, non-iodised salt, cloth, soft broom.

**How to apply:** Fill a bucket with warm water, add 1 kg of salt and mix. Wring a cloth in the mixture and wipe over the walls. Leave to dry and form a salt crust. Brush the crust away with a clean, soft broom and the mould will come away with it.

### *SPOTLESS CLASSIC*
### How to deter spiders

Many people hate spiders and spider webs. The kind way to keep spiders away from your home is with lemon oil. You can buy lemon oil (lemon essence doesn't work) or use the oil from lemon skin. Rub some lemon skin or sprinkle 1–2 drops of lemon oil along the bristles of your broom (clean, of course) and wipe the broom over the areas where spiders are likely to set up home—you'll collect the old webs as you go. If you're not able to use a broom, mix 5 drops of lemon oil with 1 drop of dishwashing liquid in a 1 litre spray pack of water and lightly spray over the area. This mixture doesn't kill spiders or remove cobwebs, it simply deters them. You'll need to reapply every 3 months.

SPOTLESS 2

# LIGHT SWITCHES

Remove greasy fingermarks around light switches with 1 teaspoon of lavender oil in a 1 litre spray pack of water. Spray a small amount onto a cloth and wipe away the greasy fingermarks (do not spray the mixture directly onto the light switch or you could short the electrics).

**Q:** 'I've had a macramé wall hanging for many years', reports Jenny. 'I have vacuumed it regularly but I'm concerned that if I hand wash it, not only will the colour from the beads run, it would lose its shape. Can you help?'

| | |
|---|---|
| **Problem:** | **Dirty macramé wall hanging.** |
| **What to use:** | **Unprocessed wheat bran, bowl, white vinegar, pillowcase, bowl, vacuum cleaner.** |
| **How to apply:** | The macramé wall hanging is likely to be raw cotton twine and is easy to clean. Place 2 cups of unprocessed wheat bran in a bowl and gradually stir in drops of white vinegar until the bran clumps together and resembles brown sugar. It shouldn't be wet. Place the mixture in a pillowcase, add the wall hanging, secure the top and shake thoroughly. Gently remove the wall hanging (outside or over a bin) and shake out the excess bran. If needed, lightly vacuum to remove any remaining bits of bran. |

Floors, Walls and Windows

**Q:** 'We have columns inside and outside our home that have rust stains on them', says Bill. 'I tried to remove the rust with diluted hydrochloric acid but used an orange-coloured sponge which dissolved from the acid. So now I have rust that is stained orange. What should I do?'

**Problem:** **Rust and orange dye on sandstone composite.**

**What to use:** **Cake of bathroom soap, water, scrubbing brush, glycerine.**

**How to apply:** To remove the acid and rust, run a cake of bathroom soap under water and scribble over the stain. Then scrub with a scrubbing brush. Rinse with water. If the orange colour doesn't come away, add 1 teaspoon of glycerine to the rinse water.

**TIP** When painting a room, open the windows for ventilation. Leave a saucer of milk in the room or cut an onion and place it in a saucepan of water. The water is absorbent and attracts the fumes.

# WINDOWS

In *Spotless*, we described the cross-hatch technique for cleaning windows. In addition to methylated spirits and water, you can also clean windows with equal parts white vinegar and water in a 1 litre spray pack. If your windows are exposed to bore water or

SPOTLESS 2

fertiliser, clean them as often as possible or you could get glass cancer. Have a squeegee dedicated for the task.

If you have painted window frames and sills, clean them regularly because exposure to the sun breaks down the surface of the paint and allows dust to stick. To clean, mix 1 teaspoon of tea tree oil, 1 teaspoon of lavender oil and ½ teaspoon of dishwashing liquid in a 1 litre spray pack of water. Wipe over the windowsills with pantyhose. If you do this task every week, you'll only need to do a wipe over each time.

**Q:** 'When cleaning around the painted wooden frames of my glass doors, the sugar soap dribbled onto a number of window panes', says Ben. 'How can I get this off?'

| | |
|---|---|
| **Problem:** | **Sugar soap on glass.** |
| **What to use:** | **White vinegar, cloth; or sweet almond oil, cloth.** |
| **How to apply:** | Sugar soap is caustic and has eaten into the glass. Wipe with white vinegar on a cloth. If this doesn't work, wipe with sweet almond oil on a cloth. Reapply as needed, usually every 3 months. |
| **Prevention:** | If using sugar soap, neutralise immediately with white vinegar and water. |

**Q:** 'My husband has been making leadlight windows for our house', says Charmaine. 'It involves using leadlight cement to glue the glass in place,

Floors, Walls and Windows

whiting to remove the excess cement and stove black to make the lead black. But the stove black has become stuck to the cement remnants and is difficult to clean. Any suggestions?'

**Problem: Leadlight cement on glass.**
**What to use: Flat-bladed scalpel.**
**How to apply:** Use a flat-bladed scalpel (or leadlight knife) to cut the cement off. Tell your husband to use blacking rather than stove black when leadlighting. Blacking is a tar-like substance and can be removed with whiting (both are available from leadlighting and some hardware stores).

**Q:** 'Can you advise how to clean anodised aluminium window frames?' asks Simon. 'It's more than just dirt. There are spots of corrosion.'

**Problem: Corrosion on aluminium.**
**What to use: Damp black tea bag, pantyhose, cloth.**
**How to apply:** Place a damp black tea bag into the toe of a pair of pantyhose and rub directly over the corrosion. Alternatively, dip pantyhose into a cup of black tea and wipe over the corrosion. The tannins in tea react with aluminium oxide and dissolve it.

SPOTLESS 2

## Q: 'How can I get old tint film off windows?' asks Brett.

| | |
|---|---|
| **Problem:** | **Old tint film on windows.** |
| **What to use:** | **Dishwashing liquid, water, 1 litre spray pack, plastic wrap, credit card.** |
| **How to apply:** | Put 2 teaspoons of dishwashing liquid in a spray pack of water and spray over the tint-side of the window. Place plastic wrap the same size as the windows over the glass. Leave for around 20 minutes, then run a credit card along the edge of the tint and peel tint and the plastic wrap away. The tint should come away easily. If it doesn't, lay the plastic wrap back over the tint and leave for longer. Don't do this in direct sunlight. |

## Q: 'How can I remove scratches on window glass?' asks Sam.

| | |
|---|---|
| **Problem:** | **Scratches on glass.** |
| **What to use:** | **Sweet almond oil, cloth, whiting, glycerine, cloth.** |
| **How to apply:** | For light scratches, dab sweet almond oil on a cloth and wipe over the scratched area. For deep scratches, apply equal parts whiting (available from leadlighting and some hardware stores) and glycerine with a cloth and polish the scratches out. |

Floors, Walls and Windows

**Q:** 'There's gloss paint on my aluminium window frames', reports Brenda. 'How can I get it off?'

> **Problem:** **Gloss paint on aluminium.**
> **What to use:** **A helper, cardboard, paint scraper, pantyhose, heat gun.**
> **How to apply:** You'll need assistance with this job so enlist a helper. Cover the glass in cardboard to protect it. Put some pantyhose over a paint scraper and have one person apply the heat gun to the area in quick, even strokes. Be careful not to get heat near the silicone or glass. While the paint is still warm, the other person removes the paint with the scraper.

**Q:** 'How can I remove obstinate masking tape from my windows and aluminium frames?' asks Virginia.

> **Problem:** **Old masking tape on glass.**
> **What to use:** **Tea tree oil, pantyhose.**
> **How to apply:** When masking tape adhesive ages or warms, it becomes very hard to remove. Apply a few drops of tea tree oil to a rolled up pair of pantyhose and scrub over the adhesive. If it doesn't come off straight away, let the tea tree oil sit on it for around 20 minutes. Scrub again. Don't do this when the sun is shining on the window or the adhesive will smear.

SPOTLESS 2

**Q:** 'The previous tenants of my rental property had a dog that sat with its nose pressed to the window looking in', says Don. 'There's a mark on the window that I can't shift. I've tried methylated spirits, a scraper and steel wool without success. Can you help please?'

    **Problem:** **Saliva on glass.**

    **What to use:** **Sweet almond oil, cloth.**

    **How to apply:** Saliva contains acid and other chemicals that have etched the glass and caused glass cancer. Polish with a couple of drops of sweet almond oil on a cloth.

## Blinds

    **Problem:** **Dirty fabric/upholstered blinds.**

    **What to use:** **Unprocessed wheat bran, white vinegar, pantyhose**

    **How to apply:** Make a bran ball (see page 85) and rub along the blinds.

**Q:** 'My very creative 2-year-old son used my good friend's white polyester roman blinds as a canvas', says Jacqui. 'They're now covered in blue biro. And although my friend isn't too bothered by the biro, I am! Can you help?'

    **Problem:** **Blue biro on blinds.**

Floors, Walls and Windows

**What to use:** **Methylated spirits, cotton bud; or white spirits, cotton bud.**

**How to apply:** What to use will depend on the type of biro. To find out, wipe over the mark with methylated spirits on a cotton bud. If the colour comes away, continue to wipe with methylated spirits on the cotton bud. If not, use white spirits on a cotton bud.

## Curtains

Wash your curtains in a bath (if you have one). Fill the tub with blood-heat water and add a little cheap shampoo. Immerse the curtains and give them a good swish around. Then rinse in blood-heat water. To deter cockroaches and inhibit mould, add 1 cup of non-iodised salt to the rinse water. Dry in the shade so the fabric doesn't wrinkle and buckle but before they dry completely, hang them back in position so you don't need to iron them. You can spot-clean curtains with a bran ball (see page 85). If you have velvet curtains, fold them so the nap (hairy sides) face each other and iron the back. If you get an iron mark, wring a cloth in white vinegar and place it over the nap. Fold the velvet over the cloth to create a white vinegar sandwich and press with a cool iron.

**Q:** 'I've just moved into a house and the kitchen plastic blind has food and fat stains all over it', says Natalie. 'How do I clean it?'

**Problem:** **Food stains on plastic blind.**
**What to use:** **Dishwashing liquid, damp pantyhose.**

SPOTLESS 2

**How to apply:** Put a couple of drops of dishwashing liquid onto damp pantyhose and scrub. Wipe with damp pantyhose.

**Q:** 'I have silk curtains with light brown stains on them', reports Sally. 'I put one curtain in the washing machine and added a colourfast bleach. I put the other curtain in a strong bleach mixture. It's a disaster! They went a murky yellow/light brown colour! Are they ruined forever?'

**Problem:** **Stained silk.**

**What to use:** **3 per cent hydrogen peroxide, washing soda, 9 litre bucket, warm water, white vinegar, plate.**

**How to apply:** The bleach has burnt the silk fibres but try this option. Mix 2 cups of 3 per cent hydrogen peroxide and 8 tablespoons of washing soda in a bucket of warm water. Immerse the curtains and put a plate on top, to keep them fully in the solution. Leave for 6 hours. Remove the curtains from the bucket and place in a tub of warm water with 1 cup of white vinegar. Rinse thoroughly and hang in the sunshine to dry. If the fabric is too fragile to attempt this, you could dye the curtains with a quality silk dye. Next time, bleach silk in 2 tablespoons of washing soda and 4 tablespoons of 3 per cent hydrogen peroxide in 9 litres of water.

Floors, Walls and Windows

**Q:** 'I have rubber-lined curtains that have been stained very badly by cockroaches', reports Jane. 'They have obviously been hiding in the folds. What can I do?'

**Problem:** **Cockroach poo on rubber-lined curtains.**
**What to use:** **Damp cloth, non-iodised salt, glycerine, cloth, soapy water.**
**How to apply:** Wipe over the rubber backing with a damp cloth. Sprinkle salt on a damp cloth and scrub over the rubber. Remove the stain from the fabric side of the curtain by wiping with a dab of glycerine on a cloth. Leave for 20 minutes, then wash in soapy water. Dry in the shade so the backing doesn't buckle. Add 1 cup of salt to the rinse water to deter cockroaches.

**Q:** 'I've got mildew on my blinds', says Rose. 'Any solutions?'

**Problem:** **Mildew on blinds.**
**What to use:** **Oil of cloves, 1 litre spray pack, stiff brush.**
**How to apply:** Put ¼ teaspoon of oil of cloves into a spray pack of water and lightly spray over the blinds. Leave to dry. After 24 hours, brush the dead mildew spores away with a stiff brush.

**Q:** 'How can we remove the smell of dry-cleaning fluid from our curtains?' asks Bobbie.

| | |
|---|---|
| **Problem:** | **Dry cleaning fluid smell in curtains.** |
| **What to use:** | **Bathtub, blood-heat water, white vinegar, sunshine.** |
| **How to apply:** | Fill a bath (or large tub) with blood-heat water and add 1 cup of white vinegar. Place the curtains in the bath and swish about. Rinse in blood-heat water and hang the curtains on the clothesline to dry. When they are almost dry, hang them back in position and you won't need to iron them. |

*TIP* If there are bushfires or lots of smoke, dampen some sheets and hang them over the top of your curtains against the glass. The sheets will protect your curtains from smoke damage and are easier to clean.

## Roman blinds

The best way to clean blinds is with a bran ball (see page 85).

# CEILING

If there's fly speck on the ceiling, put a pair of pantyhose over the head of a broom and dampen with a little water. Sprinkle a little bicarb on the broom and sweep across the ceiling—the speck will attach to the pantyhose. If there are smoke stains, apply

Floors, Walls and Windows

the same technique but dampen the broom with white vinegar, then sprinkle with bicarb and sweep while the mixture is fizzing. Leave to dry, then sweep with a clean dry broom. Remove mould by covering the broom head with pantyhose and spraying with ¼ teaspoon oil of cloves in a 1 litre spray pack of water. Sweep in parallel stripes over the area. Repeat after 24 hours. The second clean removes the staining. If the mould continues to appear, you could have a problem with drainage, poor flashing in the gutter or a broken tile. Find the source of the problem and have it repaired.

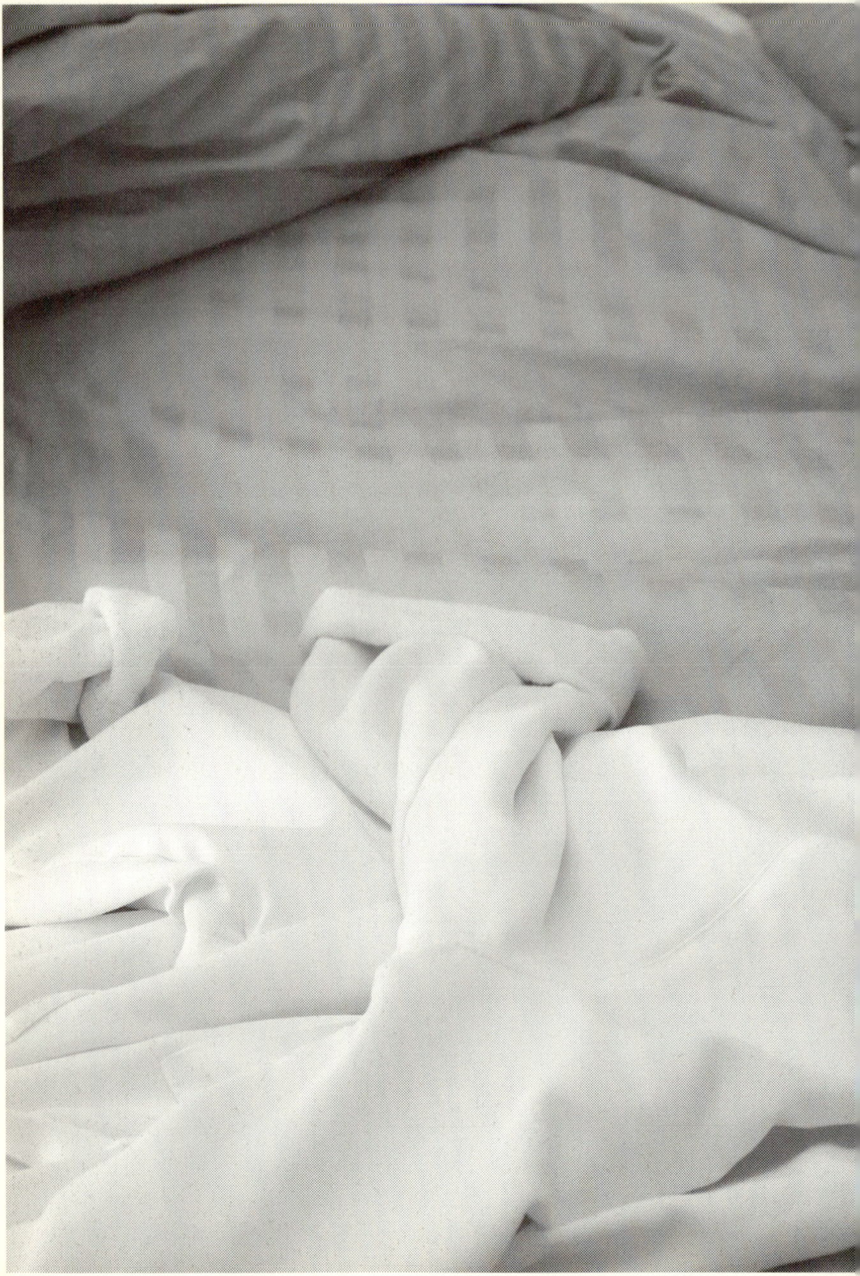

# The Bedroom

There's no good reason why you should trip over a pile of dirty clothes in the middle of the night or breathe in musty fumes from a damp bath towel: the solution is obvious. But what should you do if you accidentally spill your morning cup of tea all over the doona or mark your sheets with biro after writing a report in bed? A clean and stain-free bedroom isn't hard to achieve and you'll sleep so much more sweetly.

The Bedroom

## PERISH PANIC: Jill's story

**INCIDENT:** 'My granddaughter is devastated. I didn't notice a small hole in a hot-water bottle and during the night, it slowly leaked. The problem wasn't so much the watermark but the rubber which transferred to her brand new white quilt cover. What can I do?'

**SOLUTION:** Stretch the stained part of the quilt cover over the edge of a table or ironing board until it's taut. Sprinkle a little non-iodised salt over the rubber, roll a pair of damp pantyhose into a ball and vigorously rub over the salt. The salt will stick to the rubber and remove it without damaging the quilt. As for the hot-water bottle, you could patch the hole but it's only worth it if the rest of the bottle isn't perishing.

# BED

A bed has many functions. In addition to sleep, it's somewhere to recuperate when you're ill, a snuggly place to read a good book or, when the kids pile into it, an adventure land of mountains and valleys. As we described in *Spotless*, your bed will last longer if you use a mattress protector, air your mattress regularly and deal with stains as quickly as possible as they become more difficult to remove once they set. For a quick clean, sprinkle bicarb on the mattress, leave for 20 minutes and vacuum using the brush attachment.

SPOTLESS 2

**Q:** 'My cream valance has a rust stain from an old wire bed base', says Ian. 'How can I get it off?'

**Problem:** Rust on cotton.

**What to use:** Disposable rubber gloves, CLR/Ranex, cloth, cold water; or non-iodised salt, lemon juice, sunshine or ultraviolet light.

**How to apply:** Put on rubber gloves, place a little CLR or Ranex on a cloth and wipe over the rust. As soon as the rust starts to bleed into the rest of the fabric, rinse in cold water. If needed, repeat. If you don't want to use harsh chemicals, put a little mountain of salt over each rust spot and squeeze drops of lemon juice on top – enough to moisten the salt but not collapse it. Leave in the sunshine or under ultraviolet light. Repeat if needed. Dense rust stains can take quite a while to fade.

**Q:** 'I've got a 30-year-old cherry-stained bed head', reports Joan. 'Is there an easy way to remove scratches from it?'

**Problem:** Scratches in timber.

**What to use:** Tinted beeswax, cloth; or crayon, hair dryer, pantyhose.

**How to apply:** Wipe the scratches with tinted beeswax (available at hardware stores) on a cloth. Another option is to scribble over the scratch

The Bedroom

with a crayon in a matching colour. Aim a hair dryer over the top to gently melt the crayon into the scratch and buff with a rolled up pair of pantyhose.

**Q:** 'My parents are about to visit and I wanted to freshen up a mattress used by my teenage son', says Helen. 'Any ideas?'

**Problem:** **Freshening up a mattress.**

**What to use:** **Damp cake of bathroom soap, stiff scrubbing brush, damp cloth, bicarb, tennis racquet/cricket bat, vacuum cleaner.**

**How to apply:** This method has been updated since *Spotless*. You'll need to start preparing at least 2 days before you want to use the mattress. Most mattress stains can be removed by rubbing with a damp cake of bathroom soap and scrubbing with a brush. Once the stains are removed, wipe with a damp cloth and then the fun part begins! Sprinkle the mattress with a light dusting of bicarb and use a tennis racquet or cricket bat to whack the mattress—Shannon points out this is a good way for you to release any pent-up anger you may be feeling. Leave the bicarb on the mattress overnight and vacuum using the brush attachment. Flip the mattress and repeat on the other side.

**Q:** 'I've got mould in a futon mattress', reports Bronwyn. 'How can I get it out?'

    **Problem:** **Mould in mattress.**
    **What to use:** **Salt, water, 9 litre bucket, water, old sheet, sunshine, stiff broom.**
    **How to apply:** Add 1 kg of salt to a 9 litre bucket of water and stir until the salt dissolves. On a sunny day, take the mattress outside and rest it on an old sheet. Dip a clean broom in the salt solution and scrub into both sides of the mattress. Allow to dry and a salt crust to form. Brush away the salt crust with a broom and the mould will come away as well.

**TIP**: If there's lots of clutter in your bedroom, get a 'clutter bucket'. Place anything that doesn't belong in the room in the bucket and sort through it when you have finished cleaning.

## Sheets

Wash sheets each week and dry in sunshine. *Spotless* and *Speedcleaning* give instructions on how to remove many common stains on sheets and the chapter on Clothing and Shoes offers further guidance. If you don't know what a stain is, do a stain diagnosis (see page 362).

The Bedroom

**Q:** 'How can I whiten sheets that have yellowed?' asks Dave.

> **Problem:** **Yellowed sheets (poly-cotton and cotton).**
> **What to use:** **Methylated spirits; or NapiSan Plus, water.**
> **How to apply:** If the sheets are poly-cotton, dip in methylated spirits and wring out tightly. Wash normally in the washing machine. For 100 per cent cotton sheets, soak overnight in NapiSan Plus and warm to hot water. Wash normally and dry in sunshine.

---

### *SPOTLESS CLASSIC*
### Tea stains on sheets

It's easy to spill a cuppa in bed. Fortunately, it's also easy to whip off the sheets and remove the stain. If you get to the spill right away, wipe with a little glycerine on a cotton ball and wash the sheets on a cold setting in the washing machine. For an old stain, wipe with a little glycerine on a cotton ball followed by a little white spirits on a cotton ball and leave for 10–15 minutes. Wash on a cold setting in the washing machine and dry in sunshine.

---

**Q:** 'What's the best way to remove bore water stains on sheets?' asks Jean.

> **Problem:** **Bore water stains on sheets.**

**What to use:** **White vinegar, warm to hot water.**

**How to apply:** Soak the stained areas in white vinegar overnight. Wash normally and dry in sunshine.

**Q:** 'Help me!' pleads Sheree. 'I've got ointment stains on my sheets. How do I get them out?'

**Problem:** **Ointment on sheets.**

**What to use:** **Dishwashing liquid, warm water; or tea tree oil, cloth.**

**How to apply:** Most ointments are made with 80 per cent oil and 20 per cent water. To remove oil, put a couple of drops of dishwashing liquid onto your fingers and rub into the stain until it feels like jelly. Rinse in warm water. If this doesn't work, rub the stain with tea tree oil on a cloth. Wash normally and dry in sunshine.

## Doonas/bedcovers

Doonas and bedcovers play a big role in a bedroom's decoration and there are many varieties and styles to choose from. Don't forget to wash your doona cover and bedcovers regularly and while you're washing them, hang the doona on the clothesline or out the window to air. (For details on how to wash a doona, see *Spotless*.)

## WHAT NOT TO DO...

**Q:** 'My 2 year old has put a large amount of liquid foundation on my 100 per cent cotton quilt', says Erica. 'I've washed it in NapiSan and that didn't work. What can I do?'

**Problem:** **Liquid foundation and NapiSan on cotton.**
**What to use:** **Water, white spirits, cloth, dishwashing liquid.**
**How to apply:** NapiSan isn't the correct solvent and you'll need to remove that first by rinsing the entire quilt in water before tackling the stain. To remove the colour, wipe over the stained areas with a little white spirits on a cloth until the colour is removed. To remove the oil, put a couple of drops of dishwashing liquid on your fingers and massage into the stain until it feels like jelly. Wash normally and dry in sunshine.

**Q:** 'Our silk doona cover was accidentally washed in the washing machine and has lost its nice feel and softness', reports Julie. 'Can we do anything about it?'

**Problem:** **Silk in washing machine.**
**What to use:** **Blood-heat water, cheap shampoo, cheap hair conditioner.**

SPOTLESS 2

**How to apply:** Hand wash in blood-heat water and 1 teaspoon of shampoo (for a single-size cover). Rinse in blood-heat water and 1 teaspoon of hair conditioner. Rinse again in blood-heat water and dry flat in the shade.

**Prevention:** Always hand wash delicate items. To put the least amount of stress on fibres and dyes, ensure the rinse water is the same temperature as the wash water.

# Q: 'I've managed to get red Tiger Balm on my new cotton bedspread', says Sue. 'Help!'

**Problem:** **Red Tiger Balm on cotton.**
**What to use:** **Cake of bathroom soap, warm water, tea tree oil, cotton ball.**
**How to apply:** Red Tiger Balm contains beeswax and chilli oil. Dip a cake of bathroom soap in warm water and scrub over the stain. Rinse in water. Wipe with a little tea tree oil on a cotton ball and wash normally.

# Q: 'My husband has sleep apnoea and uses a special machine to help him sleep', reports Lucy. 'What's the best way to clean the respirator mask and the straps?'

**Problem:** **Dirty respirator mask and straps.**

**What to use:** **White vinegar, cold water, solution for contact lenses.**

**How to apply:** Respirator masks are made of a polycarbonate/silicon compound. Clean with 2 teaspoons of white vinegar and 1 litre of cold water. Soak for 20 minutes and rinse with contact lense solution (used to clean contact lenses and available at the chemist). The straps are made of wetsuit material. Clean with 2 teaspoons of white vinegar per 1 litre of cold water and leave for 1 hour. Massage the straps with your hands in cold water. Dry in the shade.

## Pillows

It's a good idea to use pillow protectors for your pillows. In *Spotless* we go into detail on how to wash pillows by hand; however, if you have a top loading washing machine, this is another option. Place two pillows in the washing machine so they sit flat around the drum and meet end to end. Allow water to fill the washing machine and rinse right away. Add 1 tablespoon of cheap shampoo and repeat. Rinse again with clean water. Dry pillows flat on a drying rack or on top of the clothesline. If using the clothesline, spread a towel over the top of the clothesline, peg in place and put the pillow on top. To prevent the pillow fibres matting, turn every 2 hours until the centre of the pillow is completely dry.

**Q:** 'What's the easiest way to remove mascara from pillowcases?' asks Thelma.

SPOTLESS 2

> **Problem:** **Mascara on cotton.**
> **What to use:** **Methylated spirits, cotton ball; or white spirits, cotton ball.**
> **How to apply:** It depends on the type of chemicals in the mascara. First try treating the stain by wiping with methylated spirits on a cotton ball. If that doesn't work, apply white spirits to a cotton ball and wipe over and into the stain. Wash normally and dry in sunshine.

## Blankets/throws

Blankets and throws are handy because they're light, portable and cosy. It's a good idea to have a variety on hand to choose from, including woollens for the cooler months and cottons the warmer. Wash in cheap shampoo and blood-heat water. If you're cleaning several at once, fill a bath (if you have one) with 1 teaspoon of cheap shampoo and blood-heat water and stomp up and down over the blankets with your feet. After draining the wash water, rinse in clean blood-heat water. Don't wring the water from the blankets but press on them with your feet. To prevent wear marks and to help them dry faster, hang them in a U shape across two lines on the clothesline. To prevent water dripping on the floor when going to the clothesline, line a clothes basket with a big plastic garbage bag before adding your just-washed blankets. Once they're dry, your blankets will be lovely, clean and soft.

**Q:** 'Do you have any advice on how to remove cat hair from woollen blankets?' asks Joan. 'Mine are covered.'

The Bedroom

|  |  |
|---|---|
| **Problem:** | **Cat hair on blankets.** |
| **What to use:** | **Disposable rubber gloves, cake of bathroom soap, water.** |
| **How to apply:** | Put on disposable rubber gloves and wash your gloved hands with a cake of bathroom soap and water. Shake dry (don't use a towel). Stroke the blanket with your gloved hands and the cat hair will attach to the rubber gloves. |
| **Prevention:** | To deter cats, put some camphorated oil, naphthalene or Vicks VapoRub near the bedroom door and the cat won't enter the room. Reapply every 6 months or so. |

## Sheepskin underlay

**Q:** 'In winter, I have sheepskin under my sheets', reports Andy. 'How should I wash it?'

|  |  |
|---|---|
| **Problem:** | **Washing sheepskin underlay.** |
| **What to use:** | **Cheap shampoo, blood-heat water, hairbrush.** |
| **How to apply:** | Place 1 teaspoon of shampoo in a tub of blood-heat water and immerse the sheepskin. Gently massage the sheepskin with your hands as though you were washing your hair. Rinse in blood-heat water. To prevent stiffening, dry slowly in the shade and brush regularly with a hairbrush. |

# CHESTS OF DRAWERS AND WARDROBES

Chests of drawers and wardrobes come in a range of finishes including french polish, beeswax, polyurethane, laminate, veneer and varnish. Consult *Spotless* for the best way to clean and care for the different surfaces. Protect the surfaces on chests of drawers with drink coasters. And don't forget to regularly vacuum inside drawers. To keep moths, silverfish and other nasties away, make a wardrobe sachet (see page 364).

**Q:** 'I've just bought a second-hand chest of drawers made of oak', says Susan. 'But there's a really strong smell of incense. Can I get rid of it?

**Problem:** Incense smell in drawers.

**What to use:** Bicarb, tea leaves.

**How to apply:** Leave 1 opened packet of bicarb and 1 opened packet of regular black tea leaves in each closed drawer for 1 week (you can reuse the same packets for each drawer). The bicarb absorbs smells and the tea releases smells. The smell should take about 1 week to clear. If it doesn't, repeat.

*TIP* If there's damp in your wardrobe, tie 6 sticks of white chalk together with string or ribbon and leave inside the wardrobe to absorb moisture. When the chalk sticks are wet, place them in the sun until they dry out.

The Bedroom

You can use them over and over again. For serious continuous damp, seek professional advice.

**Q:** 'A glass of water spilled on my bedside table', reports Veronica. 'The water dripped down to the felt pads under the feet of the table and stained the carpet. What do you suggest?'

**Problem:** **Felt pad staining on carpet.**

**What to use:** **Colour Run Remover: Coloursafe, water, cloth, damp cloth, white vinegar, steamer.**

**How to apply:** This is a dye stain. Mix 1 part Colour Run Remover: Coloursafe with 5 parts water. Wring out a cloth in the mixture and wipe this cloth and a damp cloth hand over hand until the stain is removed. To remove the Colour Run Remover, wipe with a cloth wrung out in white vinegar. Repeat until removed. Remove felt pads from the bedside table with a steamer and replace with new neutral-coloured felt pads.

*(TIP)* Clean the vents on your clock radio with the vacuum cleaner using the brush attachment. Dust regularly with damp pantyhose. Improve the reception by wiping the end of your aerial with a little white vinegar.

# HAMPERS/CLOTHES BASKETS

If there's space in your bedroom, keep a hamper to store dirty clothes. If clothes are really smelly, take them to the laundry right away because a nasty odour in the corner of your bedroom is not conducive to a good night's sleep. If you don't have space in your bedroom, nominate a place in the laundry for dirty clothes. Although tempting for some, never leave them in a pile on the floor.

## MIRRORS

**Q:** 'My cedar mirror frame has this white stuff on it', says Hayden. 'How do I remove it?'

> **Problem:** **White markings on timber.**
>
> **What to use:** **Damp pantyhose, fine grade sandpaper.**
>
> **How to apply:** This is a bloom caused by salt and timber oil mixing together. If the mirror frame is sealed, remove the marks by scrubbing with a pair of damp pantyhose. Reseal if needed. If it's not sealed, rub fine grade sandpaper for timber along the grain until the bloom is removed.

## JEWELLERY

Jewellery that has become dull can be brightened by adding ½ teaspoon of dishwashing liquid to a bucket of warm water. Scrub with an old toothbrush and dry each piece with a clean tea towel or cotton cloth. Don't wash items in a sink in case the plug comes loose: you don't want your precious jewellery going down the drain!

**Q:** 'I'd like some advice on a safe home-cleaning solution for my platinum, gold and diamond engagement ring', says Michelle. 'What do you suggest?'

**Problem:** **Dirty platinum, gold and diamond jewellery.**

**What to use:** **Bowl, warm water, white vinegar, sable paintbrush.**

**How to apply:** Platinum, gold and diamond jewellery is easy to clean. Fill a bowl with 1 cup of warm water and 1 teaspoon of white vinegar. Dip a sable paintbrush in the solution and gently wipe over the jewellery.

**Q:** 'My wife has a cameo brooch made of ivory', reports Roy. 'It's gone a deep yellow colour. Can it be restored to the original white?'

**Problem:** **Yellowed ivory.**

**What to use:** **Sweet almond oil, talcum powder, cotton bud, damp cotton bud.**

**How to apply:** Ivory yellows with age and you can't make it white again. Clean by mixing sweet almond oil and talcum powder to form a paste the consistency of runny cream and apply with a cotton bud. Polish off immediately with a damp cotton bud.

**Q:** 'My antique silver chain is tarnished', says Pat. 'What can I do?'

**Problem:** **Tarnished silver.**

**What to use:** **Bicarb, white vinegar, cloth.**

**How to apply:** Sprinkle a little bicarb over the tarnished area followed by a little white vinegar over the top. As it fizzes, rub with a cloth and the tarnish will come away. Buff with a cloth.

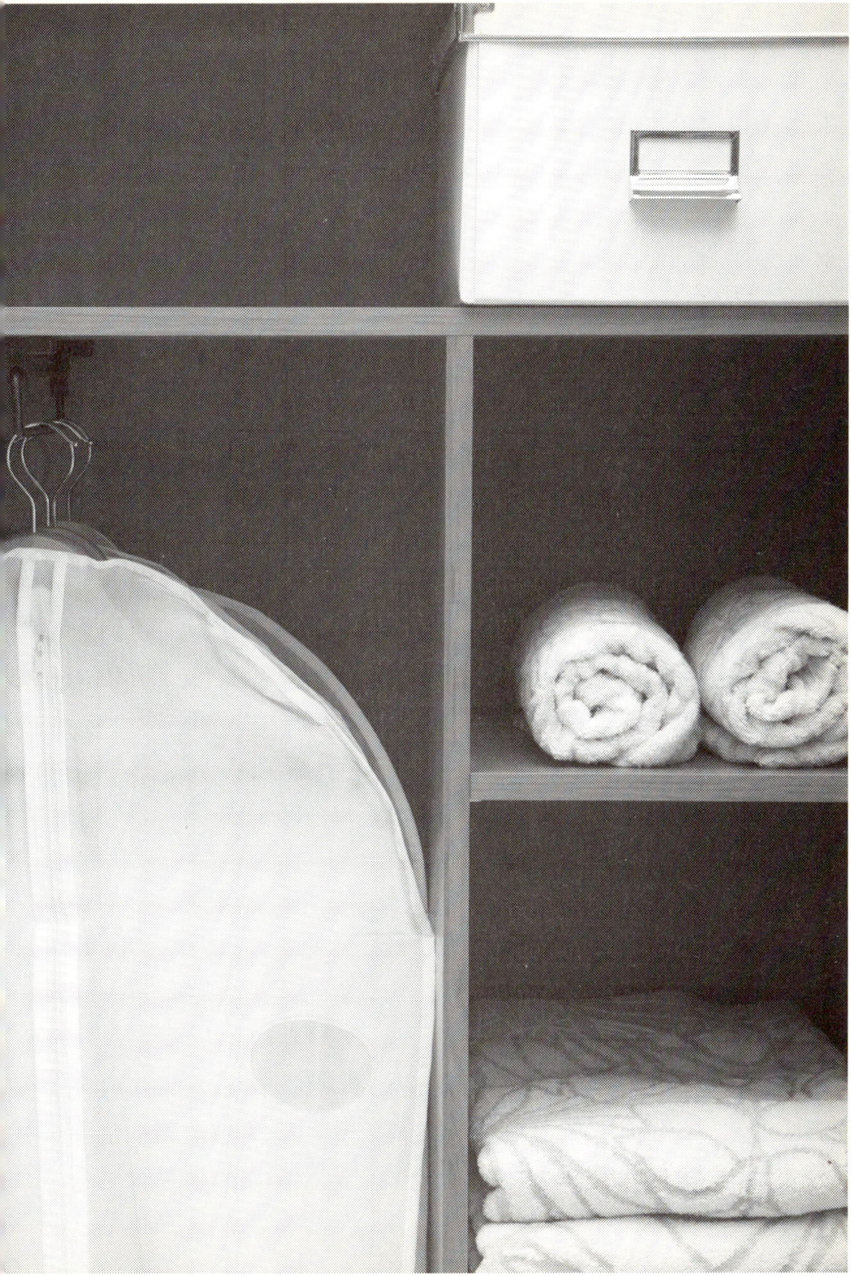

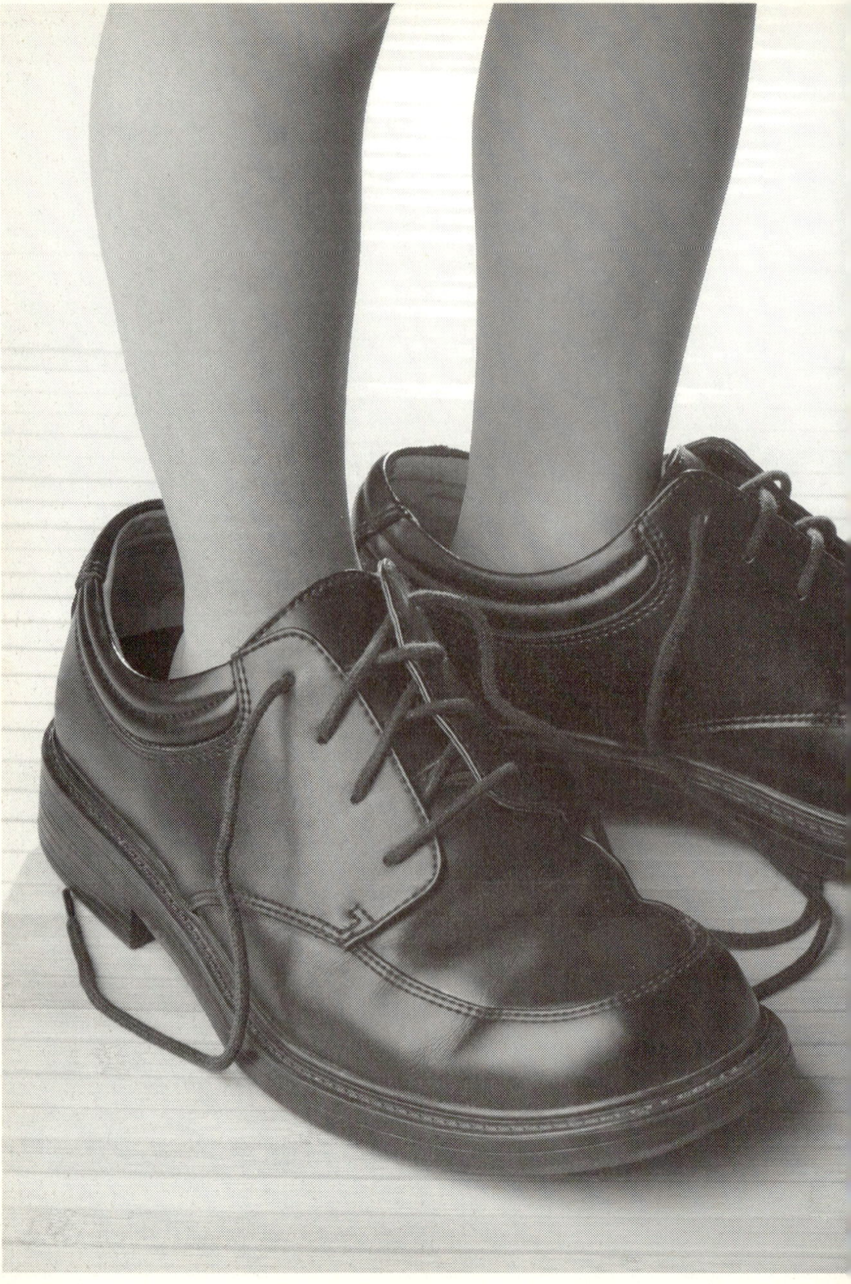

# Clothing and Shoes

If you look after your clothes and shoes, they'll last longer—a smart move if you spend a small fortune on both. Most garments have care labels with information about the type of fabric and how to best clean it, which is worth checking and following. What the labels don't include, however, is what to do when accidents happen. Whether it's finding melted choc-top on your jeans after the movies, spilling soy sauce on your jacket when eating sushi or dropping a blob of tomato sauce from your meat pie on your footy shirt, it's best to tackle stains as soon as you can. The longer you leave them, the harder they are to remove.

## DAMAGED DELICATES: Brad's story

**INCIDENT:** 'My girlfriend went away and left me to do the washing. But I didn't get to it for a few days and when I did, there were mould spots on her lightly coloured lingerie. Please help me!'

**SOLUTION:** Wipe the mouldy areas with a cloth dampened with methylated spirits. Add 1 cup of non-iodised salt to a 9 litre bucket of warm water, immerse the garments and soak overnight (salt water won't damage delicates). Gently wring but don't rinse the items, hang on the clothesline to dry and a salty crust will form. Brush the crust off with a soft brush and the mould will come away with it. Wash the lingerie in cheap shampoo and blood-heat water, rinse and dry on the clothesline.

# CLOTHING

To help you find your solution as quickly as possible, we've listed problems alphabetically. If you don't know what's caused a stain, do a stain diagnosis first (see page 362). Also, when removing stains from synthetic material, such as rayon, Lycra, nylon, elastane, spandex, etc, wipe with methylated spirits on a cloth before washing. Stains often become trapped in synthetic fibres and methylated spirits opens them up and allows them to be released.

SPOTLESS 2

**Q:** 'I spilt a jar of anchovies and olive oil on my blue denim jeans which are 98 per cent cotton and 2 per cent elastane', says Marike. 'How do I get the oily marks off?'

**Problem:** **Anchovy on denim.**

**What to use:** **Cloth, methylated spirits, cake of bathroom soap, cold water, dishwashing liquid, bicarb.**

**How to apply:** The jeans contain elastane, so wipe the stain with a little methylated spirits on a cloth first. Remove the anchovy by scribbling with a cake of bathroom soap that's been run under cold water. Then remove the oil by massaging a couple of drops of dishwashing liquid into the stain with your fingers until it feels like jelly. Rinse the jeans in cold water. Wash and dry normally.

**Q:** 'My daughter loves drinking apple juice', reports Uriah. 'And I've got several marks on my shirt. What can I do?'

**Problem:** **Apple juice on cotton.**

**What to use:** **Glycerine, cloth.**

**How to apply:** Rb the stain with a little glycerine on a cloth, leave for 20 minutes and wash and dry normally.

Clothing and Shoes

## Q: 'I've got baby oil splashes over my T-shirt', reports Sandra. 'How do you get it out?'

**Problem:** **Baby oil on cotton.**

**What to use:** **Dishwashing liquid, warm water.**

**How to apply:** Put a couple of drops of dishwashing liquid on your fingers and massage into the oil stains until it feels like jelly. Rinse under warm water then wash and dry normally.

**Problem:** **Baked beans on cotton.**

**What to use:** **Cold water, cloth, white vinegar, sunshine.**

**How to apply:** The staining is from tomato sauce, which is a vegetable dye. To remove the stain, rinse in cold water, wipe with a cloth wrung out in white vinegar and wash normally. Dry in sunshine.

**Problem:** **Banana on cotton.**

**What to use:** **Tea tree oil, cloth (peel); or glycerine, cloth (flesh).**

**How to apply:** Banana peel contains a resinous sap that is removed by wiping with a little tea tree oil on a cloth. The banana flesh causes a tannin stain and needs to be wiped with a little glycerine on a cloth before washing normally.

SPOTLESS 2

**Problem:** **Beetroot on cotton.**
**What to use:** **Cloth, white vinegar, 9 litre bucket, water.**
**How to apply:** For a small stain, wipe with a cloth wrung out in white vinegar. For a large stain, fill a bucket with cold water, add 1 cup of white vinegar and soak the garment for 20 minutes. Wash and dry normally. If you've got kids, this is a great stain removal trick to show them because they can see the beetroot colour disappearing like magic from the fabric.

## Q: 'I've got berry stains on my clothes', says June. 'How can I get them out?'

**Problem:** **Berry stains on cotton.**
**What to use:** **Cloth, white vinegar, glycerine, sunshine.**
**How to apply:** For berry stains that change colour (blueberry, blackberry), wipe with a cloth wrung out in white vinegar, then wipe with a dab of glycerine on a cloth. Wash normally and dry in sunshine. For other berries (strawberry, raspberry), wipe with a cloth wrung out in white vinegar, then wash normally and dry in the sun. Don't use soap or heat because they set berry stains.

Clothing and Shoes

**Problem:** **Bird poo on cotton.**
**What to use:** **Cold water, cake of bathroom soap (protein); or warm water, cake of bathroom soap (seed); or white vinegar, cloth, glycerine (fruit).**
**How to apply:** The treatment depends on what the bird has eaten—protein, seed or fruit. For protein (generally brown or black poo), scribble over the stain with a cake of bathroom soap that's been run under cold water. Rinse under cold water and wash and dry normally. For seed (generally white poo), scribble over the stain with a cake of bathroom soap that's been run under warm water. Rinse under warm water and wash and dry normally. For fruit (generally purple or orange poo), wipe with a cloth wrung out in white vinegar, then wipe with a little glycerine on a cloth and leave for 20 minutes. Wash and dry normally.

**Q:** 'Is there a way to get bitumen (tar) out of denim jeans?' asks Robyn. 'They have been washed in ordinary laundry powder but most of the tar didn't budge. Is it possible to salvage them?'

**Problem:** **Bitumen/tar on denim.**
**What to use:** **Disposable rubber gloves, kerosene, baby oil, dishwashing liquid, warm water.**

SPOTLESS 2

**How to apply:** Put on rubber gloves and rub equal parts kerosene and baby oil (around 1 tablespoon of each for a stain 10 cm in diameter) into the mark with your fingers. You'll see the tar beginning to spread and look worse. Add a couple of drops of dishwashing liquid and continue to massage with your fingers until it resembles jelly. Rinse in warm water. If any bitumen remains, repeat until removed. Wash and dry normally.

**Q:** 'I'm having a problem removing a stain caused by splashes of black bean sauce on a pale pink T-shirt', says Pip. 'I'd appreciate your help.'

**Problem:** Black bean sauce on cotton.
**What to use:** White vinegar.
**How to apply:** Flush the stain with white vinegar. If it proves stubborn, rub in with your fingers. Wash and dry normally.

**Q:** 'I was at the movies and got chewing gum on my trousers', says Kevin. 'How do I get it off?'

**Problem:** Chewing gum on cotton.
**What to use:** Knife/scraper, tea tree oil, tissue.
**How to apply:** Remove as much chewing gum as you can with a knife or scraper. Apply a few drops of tea tree

Clothing and Shoes

oil to a tissue and rub over the chewing gum in a circular motion. Little gum balls will form that can be plucked from the cotton. Continue until the gum is removed.

**Q:** 'I was enjoying some potato wedges dipped in chilli sauce', says Matthew. 'But, tragically, not all of the sauce made it into my mouth and went on my T-shirt instead. What can I do?'

**Problem:** **Chilli sauce on cotton.**
**What to use:** **White vinegar or lemon juice, cloth, dishwashing liquid, warm water.**
**How to apply:** Chilli sauce is high in alkaline and oil. Wipe with a cloth wrung out in white vinegar or lemon juice until most of the red colouring transfers to the cloth. To remove the oil, add a couple of drops of dishwashing liquid to your fingers and massage into the stain. Rinse in warm water.

**Problem:** **Chocolate on cotton.**
**What to use:** **Dishwashing liquid, cold water or damp cloth.**
**How to apply:** Put a couple of drops of dishwashing liquid on your fingers and massage into the stain. Rinse in cold water or with a damp cloth.

**Problem:** **Chocolate on wool.**
**What to use:** **Cheap shampoo, cold water or damp cloth.**
**How to apply:** Massage shampoo into the stain with your fingers and rinse in cold water or with a damp cloth.

**Problem:** **Coffee on cotton.**
**What to use:** **Glycerine, cotton ball.**
**How to apply:** Wipe with a dab of glycerine on a cotton ball and leave for 20 minutes before washing normally.

**Q:** 'I wore my favourite purple silk organza dress to my engagement party', reports Diana. 'But I managed to get cream from the cake in a couple of spots. Can you offer any assistance?'

**Problem:** **Cream on silk.**
**What to use:** **Dishwashing liquid, blood-heat water, white vinegar, cloth.**
**How to apply:** The staining is caused by fat in the cream. Remove by massaging the fatty spots with a little dishwashing liquid on your fingers. When it feels like jelly, rinse in blood-heat water. Silk can develop watermarks from spot removal, so dry slowly in the shade. If you do get watermarks,

Clothing and Shoes

immerse a cloth in equal parts white vinegar and water and wring out so it's just damp. Wipe over the stain, pressing heavily in the centre and easing the pressure as you move towards the outside. Dry flat in the shade.

**Q:** 'How do I remove yellow curry stains from cotton fabric?' asks Sunil.

**Problem:** **Curry stain (yellow) on cotton.**
**What to use:** **Lavender oil, cloth.**
**How to apply:** Place a couple of drops of lavender oil on a cloth and wipe over the stain until removed. Wash and dry normally.

**Q:** 'I've got custard stains on my pants', admits Ainslee. 'How can I get them off?'

**Problem:** **Custard on cotton.**
**What to use:** **NapiSan Plus, water.**
**How to apply:** Make a paste of NapiSan Plus and water and place over the stains. Leave for 20 minutes, then wash and dry normally. If the custard is flavoured, remove that stain first (consult the relevant advice elsewhere in the book eg: chocolate) and then remove the custard stain.

SPOTLESS 2

**Q:** 'How do you remove diesel from polyester and cotton clothes?' asks Jim.

    **Problem:** **Diesel on polyester and cotton.**
  **What to use:** **Disposable rubber gloves, baby oil, cloth, dishwashing liquid, warm water (cotton); or methylated spirits, cloth (polyester).**
  **How to apply:** You don't want diesel all over your hands so put on rubber gloves and wipe with a little baby oil on a cloth. Put a couple of drops of dishwashing liquid on your fingers and massage over the baby oil. When it feels like jelly, rinse in warm water. With synthetic fibres, first wipe with a dab of methylated spirits on a cloth.

**Q:** 'I practise judo three times a week', reports Tony. 'And I've got brown marks on my collar from dirt and sweat. What can I do?'

    **Problem:** **Dirt and sweat on cotton.**
  **What to use:** **NapiSan OxyAction MAX, warm to hot water.**
  **How to apply:** Mix NapiSan OxyAction MAX and warm to hot water to form a paste the consistency of peanut butter. Apply to the stain and leave for 20 minutes before washing and drying normally.

Clothing and Shoes

**Q:** 'What's the best way to get dirt stains out of a cotton sports shirt that has velvety numbers?' asks Brian. 'I don't want to damage the print by soaking it.'

**Problem:** **Dirt on cotton.**

**What to use:** **NapiSan Plus, cold water.**

**How to apply:** Mix NapiSan Plus and cold water to form a paste the consistency of peanut butter and place over the dirty marks (avoiding the velvet). Leave for 20 minutes and wash and dry normally.

**Problem:** **Egg on cotton.**

**What to use:** **Cold water, cake of bathroom soap.**

**How to apply:** Rinse in cold water and rub with a cake of bathroom soap. If needed, rub with your fingers to remove the stain. Wash and dry normally.

**Problem:** **Fish sauce on cotton.**

**What to use:** **Cake of bathroom soap, cold water, old toothbrush (protein); dishwashing liquid, cold water (oil).**

**How to apply:** Fish sauce is high in protein and oil. To remove the protein, run a cake of bathroom soap under cold water, apply to an old toothbrush and scrub over the stain. To remove the oil,

SPOTLESS 2

massage a couple of drops of dishwashing liquid into the stain using your fingers until it feels like jelly. Rinse in cold water.

## WHAT NOT TO DO...

**Q:** 'I have a white T-shirt that I think is either cotton or a poly-cotton mix. I'm not sure exactly what stains are on it (I presume they're food stains). But I applied white spirits to the stains before washing. To my horror, grey patches appeared in the places where I had dabbed the white spirits and my T-shirt smelled terrible. After this, I put the T-shirt in a bucket of water containing NapiSan OxyAction MAX and left it to soak for a week, after which I washed it again. The smell has gone but the grey stains are still there (that said, the stains have faded slightly). What can I do now?'

**A:** The reason the T-shirt turned grey is because the stain was a combination of oxide and protein. Before attempting any stain removal, do a stain diagnosis (see page 362). If in doubt, try a dab of glycerine or a dab of white vinegar on a cloth first. They're great cleaners and don't set stains. In this case, massage a little glycerine into the stains using your fingers. Leave for 20 minutes and scrub with a cake of bathroom soap that's been run under cold water. Repeat until the stains are removed.

Clothing and Shoes

**Q:** 'I've got fluorescent highlighter pen on my cotton trousers', says Mark. 'Can I get it off?'

    **Problem:** **Fluorescent highlighter pen on cotton.**

  **What to use:** **Fluorescent highlighter pen, cotton ball, white spirits; or 9 litre bucket, non-iodised salt, plastic bag, freezer.**

  **How to apply:** Fluorescent pen contains its own solvent—so, strange as it may seem, you will need to draw on the trousers again using the same pen. While the ink is wet, rub with a little white spirits on a cotton ball. Wash and dry normally. If this doesn't work, fill a bucket with water and add 1 cup of salt. Dip the stain in the salt solution, remove and place the garment in a plastic bag. Put it in the freezer and leave overnight. Remove from the plastic bag and wash and dry normally.

**Q:** 'My son purchased a leather jacket in Melbourne last week which was discounted because there's pink highlighter on both sleeves', reports Jayne. 'Can you help?'

    **Problem:** **Fluorescent pen on leather.**

  **What to use:** **White spirits, cotton bud, talcum powder, leather conditioner.**

**How to apply:** Obviously the discount was so good he didn't think about how to remove the stain. Dip a cotton bud in white spirits and rub over the pen mark, then sprinkle with talcum powder. Leave to dry and brush the talcum powder away with your hand. Repeat if necessary. If the surface of the leather becomes dry, use a good quality leather conditioner.

## Q: 'I dropped make-up on the front of my favourite white shirt', says Theresa. 'It's synthetic. What can I do?'

**Problem:** **Foundation make-up on synthetics.**
**What to use:** **Methylated spirits, dishwashing liquid; white spirits, cloth, NapiSan Plus, water.**
**How to apply:** The shirt is synthetic, so wipe with methylated spirits first. Massage a little dishwashing liquid into the stain using your fingers and rinse in just-warm water. Repeat if needed. If there's a faint shadow, wipe with a little white spirits on a cloth. Wash and dry normally. If the make-up contains colourstay, use the above technique and apply a paste of NapiSan Plus and water to the stain. Leave for 20 minutes and wash and dry normally.

Clothing and Shoes

## Q: 'How can I remove grass and other greasy stains from the knees of my trousers?' asks Phil.

**Problem:** **Grass and grease on cotton.**

**What to use:** **White spirits, cloth, dishwashing liquid.**

**How to apply:** To remove grass, wipe with a dab of white spirits on a cloth. To remove grease, put a couple of drops of dishwashing liquid on your fingers and massage into the stain until it feels like jelly. Rinse and wash and dry normally.

## Q: 'My son regularly gets mechanical grease on his woollen work jacket', reports Debbie. 'It has a cotton lining and reflector stripes on the outside over the wool. What can I do?'

**Problem:** **Grease on wool.**

**What to use:** **Dishwashing liquid, blood-heat water, cheap shampoo, blood-heat water, cheap hair conditioner, towel.**

**How to apply:** Put a couple of drops of dishwashing liquid on your fingers and massage into the stain. Rinse in blood-heat water, then wash in a little shampoo and blood-heat water. Rinse in a little hair conditioner and blood-heat water. Then rinse again in blood-heat water, gently wring out and dry flat on a towel in the shade.

SPOTLESS 2

**Q:** 'While at the hairdressers, I got hair dye on my shirt', reports Sherry. 'How do you get it out?'

> **Problem:** **Hair dye on cotton.**
>
> **What to use:** **Same hair dye, disposable rubber gloves, cheap shampoo, cold water; or hair spray.**
>
> **How to apply:** This sounds odd but it works. Hair dye contains its own solvent, so go back to the hairdresser and get the same brand and colour hair dye. Put on rubber gloves and rub a small amount of hair dye into the stain. When the stain starts to loosen, rub with a little shampoo on your fingers. Rinse in cold water and wash and dry normally. If the stain has just happened, spray with hair spray, allow to dry and brush off with the back of your hand.

**Q:** 'How do you remove hair spray from a woollen jumper?' asks Deidre.

> **Problem:** **Hair spray on wool.**
>
> **What to use:** **Cheap shampoo, blood-heat water, cheap hair conditioner, towel.**
>
> **How to apply:** Wash the garment in a little shampoo and blood-heat water. Rinse in a little hair conditioner and blood-heat water. Then rinse again in blood-heat water, gently wring out and dry flat on a towel in the shade. To minimise stress on wool fibres, always use blood-heat water.

Clothing and Shoes

**Q:** 'I got lip balm on my cotton knit dress', reports Patricia. 'How can I get it out?'

**Problem:** **Lip balm on cotton.**
**What to use:** **Dishwashing liquid, white spirits, cotton ball, blood-heat water.**
**How to apply:** Place a little dishwashing liquid on your fingers and rub into the stains. If the lip balm is coloured, wipe with a little white spirits on a cotton ball. Rinse in blood-heat water and wash and dry normally.

**Q:** 'I'm a celebrant', says Janice. 'And there's always stray lipstick at weddings. Is there something I can carry in my handbag to fix any stains before the photos?'

**Problem:** **Lipstick on cotton.**
**What to use:** **Small cloth, white spirits, pantyhose, zip-lock bag, damp cloth.**
**How to apply:** Saturate a cloth with white spirits and place in the toe of a pair of pantyhose. Cut the pantyhose, secure the cloth inside and tie off so it fits neatly into a zip-lock bag and store in your handbag ready to use. When needed, remove the cloth from the bag, wipe over the offending lipstick and then wipe with a damp cloth.

# SPOTLESS 2

**Q:** 'I know this is unusual', says Julie. 'But how do you remove lipstick from a resuscitation dummy?'

> **Problem:** **Lipstick on plastic.**
>
> **What to use:** **White spirits, cotton ball, damp cloth.**
>
> **How to apply:** While it's a good idea to learn resuscitation, consider hygiene as well. Each person should use their own mouthguard on the dummy. To remove the lipstick, wipe with a dab of white spirits on a cotton ball, then wipe with a damp cloth.

**Q:** 'How do I get Liquid Paper correction fluid out of black trousers?' asks Damien.

> **Problem:** **Liquid Paper on cotton.**
>
> **What to use:** **Liquid Paper Remover/Liquid Paper Thinner.**
>
> **How to apply:** There's a product called Liquid Paper Remover (or Liquid Paper Thinner) which is available from most shops that sell Liquid Paper. It comes with a sponge brush, which is ideal to remove the mark. Follow the manufacturer's instructions.

Clothing and Shoes

**Q:** 'I had an ink stain on my shirt that I removed with rotten milk', reports Jo. 'It's left a faint grease-like stain. What can I do?'

**Problem:** **Mark from rotten milk.**

**What to use:** **Methylated spirits, cloth.**

**How to apply:** The greasy mark indicates the garment has synthetic fibres in it and the milk has become trapped. Wipe with a little methylated spirits on a cloth and wash and dry normally.

## Mould

Sally brought her mother's silk wedding dress from the 1960s to a Stain Clinic. The dress had become part of the kids' dress-up box and the silk had mould and dirt all over it. Shannon advised her to use kitty litter to absorb the stains because the fabric was delicate and the staining extensive. Sally was stunned. The technique involves half filling a large lidded box with clean kitty litter. Cover the kitty litter with a piece of plastic wrap, punch small holes in the plastic, then place the dress on top. Put the lid on the box and leave for 3 days. The kitty litter absorbs the moisture that's causing the mould. To remove mould from silk, put coarse non-iodised salt in the toe of a pair of pantyhose and wipe over the stains. Leave to air in the sun. This technique works for any delicate or antique fabric.

# SPOTLESS 2

**Q:** 'How do I remove mould from leather jackets?' asks Barbara. 'They've been hanging in a wardrobe and there are white and mouldy looking spots on them.'

**Problem:** **Mould on leather.**

**What to use:** **Baby oil or leather conditioner, oil of cloves, microwave-safe bowl, cloth, microwave, cloth, zip-lock bag.**

**How to apply:** If the leather doesn't darken when a drop of water is placed on it, use baby oil rather than leather conditioner, it's much cheaper. Place 2 tablespoons of good quality leather conditioner or baby oil and ¼ teaspoon of oil of cloves in a microwave-safe bowl. Stir thoroughly and place a cloth on top. Place the bowl in the microwave and warm in 10-second bursts until the mixture melts into the cloth. Allow to cool, wipe the cloth over the leather and leave for 24 hours. Use another cloth to remove the mixture. Store the cleaning cloth in a zip-lock bag to use again (simply warm it again in the microwave).

Clothing and Shoes

**Q:** 'There's a big blob of mustard on my work shirt', reports Tim. 'What should I do?'

      **Problem:** **Mustard on cotton.**
**What to use:** **Dishwashing liquid, cold water, lavender oil, cloth.**
**How to apply:** Put a couple of drops of dishwashing liquid on your fingers and massage into the stain until it feels like jelly. Rinse in cold water. If any yellow mark remains, wipe with a little lavender oil on a cloth and wash and dry normally.

## Oil stains

There was confusion in *Spotless* about removing oil stains. Oils ain't oils! The higher the carbon content, the more difficult the oil stain is to remove. As a general rule, remove dark oils such as car grease with a dab of baby oil on a cloth followed by dishwashing liquid massaged in with your fingers. To remove light oils, such as olive oil, massage dishwashing liquid into the stain with your fingers. If you accidentally used baby oil on a light oil stain, fix by massaging dishwashing liquid into the stain with your fingers until it feels like jelly, then rinse in blood-heat water.

SPOTLESS 2

# Q: 'I've got old car grease stains on my overalls', says Paul. 'Can I get it out?'

**Problem:** **Old car grease/engine oil on fabric.**
**What to use:** **Baby oil, dishwashing liquid, water.**
**How to apply:** Car grease has a high carbon content, so rub the stain with a little baby oil. As soon as the stain starts to loosen and spread, massage in dishwashing liquid with your fingers. When it feels like jelly, rinse in water.

**Problem:** **Peanut butter on cotton.**
**What to use:** **Dishwashing liquid, cold water.**
**How to apply:** Remove as much peanut butter as possible. To remove the oil, put a couple of drops of dishwashing liquid on your fingers and massage into the stain until it feels like jelly. Rinse with cold water and wash and dry normally.

**Problem:** **Pear on cotton.**
**What to use:** **Glycerine, cloth.**
**How to apply:** Pear is high in tannins. Wipe with a little glycerine on a cloth and leave for 20 minutes. Wash and dry normally.

Clothing and Shoes

# Pen marks

There are different stain removal techniques for the type of pen used. We've mentioned how to remove ballpoint pen ink in *Spotless* (see page 66); here's how to remove those other pen marks.

**Permanent markers**—write over the mark using the same pen. Then wipe with white spirits on a cotton bud. Wash and dry normally.

**Artline**—wipe with methylated spirits on a cotton bud. Wash and dry normally.

**Whiteboard marker**—wipe with methylated spirits on a cotton bud. Wash and dry normally.

**Fluorescent pen**—write over the mark using the same pen, then wipe the mark with white spirits on a cotton bud. Alternatively, fill a 9 litre bucket with water and add 1 cup of non-iodised salt, dip the stain in the salt solution, gently wring and place in a plastic bag before putting in the freezer. Wash and dry normally.

**Gel pens**—soak in methylated spirits for 10 minutes and rub over the pen mark with your fingers. If the mark doesn't come out, soak again in methylated spirits for a further 10 minutes. You don't need to rub too vigorously. Repeat until removed. Wash and dry normally.

Problem: Sweat stains on poly-cotton shirt.
What to use: Methylated spirits, cloth, NapiSan Plus, water.

**How to apply:** In our climate, perspiration is a common problem and you might need to try a few different brands of deodorant before finding one that suits your body chemistry. Be aware that sweat clings more to synthetic fibres than natural ones. This shirt contains synthetic fibres, so wipe the armpits with a little methylated spirits on a cloth. Make a paste of NapiSan Plus and water, paint over the stained area and leave for 20 minutes. Wash and dry normally.

# Q: 'I spilt some pumpkin soup over my favourite shawl', says Raquel. 'What should I do?'

**Problem:** **Pumpkin on wool.**

**What to use:** **White vinegar, cold water, cloth; or lavender oil, cloth, cheap shampoo, blood-heat water.**

**How to apply:** Pumpkin is high in vegetable dye. Remove as soon as possible with equal parts white vinegar and cold water on a cloth. If the pumpkin has set, wipe with a dab of lavender oil on a cloth and leave for 20 minutes. The shawl is made of wool, so wash in shampoo and blood-heat water.

Clothing and Shoes

# Q: 'I got red wine on my linen suit', says Max. 'What can I do?'

**Problem:** **Red wine on cotton.**

**What to use:** **Cloth, white vinegar, blood-heat water.**

**How to apply:** Wipe with a cloth wrung out in white vinegar until the red colour is removed. Rinse in blood-heat water and wash and dry normally.

# Q: 'I was drying my clothes in front of the heater', reports Rebecca. 'And a cotton shirt was scorched. Can I fix it?'

**Problem:** **Scorch mark on cotton.**

**What to use:** **3 per cent hydrogen peroxide, cloth, iron.**

**How to apply:** Wring out a cloth in 3 per cent hydrogen peroxide. Place the cloth over the scorch mark and run a cool iron over the top. The burn mark will transfer to the cloth. If it doesn't, the cotton has been charred and can't be fixed. If you love the shirt, sew or appliqué a patch over the top or dye the shirt a darker colour.

**Q:** 'I've got seafood stains on my shirt', says Graham. 'What can I do?'

**Problem:** **Seafood on cotton.**

**What to use:** **Cold water, dishwashing liquid.**

**How to apply:** Seafood contains protein and oil. Rinse in cold water first. Put a couple of drops of dishwashing liquid on your fingers and massage into the stain. Rinse in cold water and wash and dry normally.

**Problem:** **Soy sauce on cotton.**

**What to use:** **White vinegar, cloth.**

**How to apply:** Wipe the stain with a cloth wrung out in white vinegar, then wash and dry normally.

**Q:** 'I was out for dinner the other night', says Lisa. 'And I managed to get squid ink over my pale blue jumper. What can I do?'

**Problem:** **Squid ink on wool.**

**What to use:** **Rotten milk, spatula, cheap shampoo, blood-heat water.**

**How to apply:** Rot some milk in the sun until it forms lumps. Place the lumps on the ink stain. When the ink has been absorbed by the milk solids, remove the solids with a spatula. Because it's made of wool, wash in a little shampoo dissolved in blood-heat water.

Clothing and Shoes

## Q: 'How can you make clothes anti-static?' asks Bill.

**Problem:** **Static in clothes.**
**What to use:** **Cheap hair conditioner, water, 1 litre spray pack.**
**How to apply:** Add 2 teaspoons of hair conditioner to the rinse cycle when washing your clothes. If you get static when wearing clothes, add ½ teaspoon of hair conditioner to a 1 litre spray pack of water and lightly mist over the clothes.

## Q: 'I have a gorgeous red pashmina', says Sally. 'But the label has fallen off, leaving a sticky residue. How can I fix this?'

**Problem:** **Sticky label on wool.**
**What to use:** **Tea tree oil, pantyhose, damp cloth, cheap shampoo, blood-heat water.**
**How to apply:** Rub the area with a little tea tree oil on a pair of pantyhose, then wipe with a damp cloth. Because it's made of wool, wash in a small amount of shampoo dissolved in blood-heat water.

## SPOTLESS 2

**Q:** 'I have a relatively new denim jacket and the fabric is quite stiff', reports Rhonda. 'Is there a way to soften it?'

**Problem:** **Stiff denim jacket.**

**What to use:** **Bicarb, laundry detergent, white vinegar, warm water.**

**How to apply:** The denim jacket is stiff because it's covered in a dressing to make it look good on the hanger in the shop. To strip away this dressing and soften the jacket, add ½ cup of bicarb to the laundry detergent, place ½ cup of white vinegar in the fabric conditioner slot and wash on a warm setting.

**Problem:** **Sunscreen on cotton.**

**What to use:** **Dishwashing liquid; or NapiSan OxyAction MAX, water.**

**How to apply:** Place a couple of drops of dishwashing liquid on your fingers and rub into the stain until it changes texture and feels like jelly. Leave for 15 minutes and wash and dry normally. Alternatively, soak in Napisan OxyAction MAX and water for 15 minutes, then wash and dry normally. The latter works better with self-tanning creams.

Clothing and Shoes

**Problem:** **Tomato sauce on cotton.**

**What to use:** **Cloth, white vinegar; or NapiSan Plus, water, sunshine.**

**How to apply:** Tomato sauce is a vegetable dye. Wipe the stain with a cloth wrung out in white vinegar. Wash normally and dry in sunshine. If the stain is stubborn, make a paste of NapiSan Plus and water and leave on the stain for 10 minutes. Wash normally and hang in sunshine.

**Q:** 'I got toothpaste on my suit', reports Hussain. 'What should I do?'

**Problem:** **Toothpaste on wool.**

**What to use:** **White vinegar, water, cloth.**

**How to apply:** Mix equal parts white vinegar and water. Wring out a cloth in the mixture and wipe over the stain. Toothpaste contains peroxide and could bleach the wool so don't leave it for long.

**Q:** 'My clothesline is under a gum tree and I have brown stains on my washing', complains Craig. 'The items are mostly made of cotton.'

**Problem:** **Tree sap (gum) on cotton.**

**What to use:** **Tea tree oil, cloth, glycerine.**

SPOTLESS 2

**How to apply:** This is both a resin and tannin stain. Wipe with a dab of tea tree oil on a cloth. Then wipe with a dab of glycerine on a cloth and leave for 5 minutes. Wash the clothes in the washing machine again.

**Prevention:** If your clothesline is under a tree and you can't move either, place an old sheet over your washing while it's drying. Ultraviolet light will still penetrate through the sheet and dry your clothes.

## Q: 'I was eating a tuna salad for lunch and dropped some tuna on my skirt', reports Deanna. 'It's left an oily mark. Can I get it off?'

**Problem:** **Tuna (in oil) on cotton.**

**What to use:** **Cold water, dishwashing liquid.**

**How to apply:** This is a protein and oil stain. To remove, rinse in cold water, then put a couple of drops of dishwashing liquid on your fingers and massage into the stain until it feels like jelly. Rinse in cold water and wash and dry normally.

Clothing and Shoes

**Q:** 'I've got Vaseline on my trousers', complains Carol. 'How do you get it out?'

**Problem:** **Vaseline on cotton.**

**What to use:** **Dishwashing liquid, warm water.**

**How to apply:** Place a couple of drops of dishwashing liquid on your fingers and massage over the spots until it feels like jelly. Rinse in warm water and wash and dry normally.

**Q:** 'I spilled hot wax on a cotton shirt', says Bill. 'The wax came off but left a white mark which I can't remove. What do you suggest?'

**Problem:** **Wax on cotton.**

**What to use:** **Paper towel, ironing board, iron, tea tree oil, cloth.**

**How to apply:** Place several sheets of paper towel on top of your ironing board and lay the wax-stained garment on top. Put several more sheets of paper towel on top of the stain and apply a warm iron. The wax will melt into the paper towel. Keep changing the paper towel until all the wax is removed. If there's a greasy mark, wipe with a little tea tree oil on a cloth before washing normally.

SPOTLESS 2

**Q:** 'I stored my clothes during winter', says Amber. 'They've now got yellow marks on them. What can I do?'

|  |  |
|---|---|
| **Problem:** | **Yellow marks on cotton.** |
| **What to use:** | **Non-iodised salt, lemon juice, sunshine; or bicarb, cold water; or CLR/Ranex, cloth, cold water, white vinegar; or methylated spirits, cold water; or glycerine, cloth.** |
| **How to apply:** | If the clothing is old or antique, the yellow will be from mineral salts used to stiffen the fabric when it was made. Place a little mountain of salt over each mark, add enough drops of lemon juice to moisten the salt and leave in the sun to dry. If the yellow marks are from milk residue (common with baby clothes), see page 286. If the yellow has been caused by contact with plastic, mix bicarb and cold water to form a paste the consistency of peanut butter, apply to the stain, allow to dry and brush off. If the fabric is sturdy, treat as though it's rust and wipe with a dab of CLR or Ranex on a cloth. Rinse with cold water as soon as the yellow mark bleeds into the rest of the fabric, then neutralise by wiping with a cloth wrung out in white vinegar. If the fabric is synthetic, wipe with a dab of methylated spirits on a cloth and rinse in cold water. If the stain is from timber shelving, wipe with a couple of drops of glycerine on a cloth, |

Clothing and Shoes

leave for 20 minutes then wash and dry normally. Don't store clothes unless they've been laundered and completely dried. Always store in acid-free paper.

**Problem:** **Yoghurt on cotton.**
**What to use:** **Cold water, cake of bathroom soap.**
**How to apply:** Rinse in cold water and rub with a cake of bathroom soap. Rinse in cold water and wash and dry normally.

**Q:** 'I've had to throw away four jumpers this year because of moth holes', complains Marian. 'And that's despite hanging mothballs around my woollens. Do you have any suggestions to stop moths in their tracks? I don't like using chemicals and would prefer natural remedies.'

**Problem:** **Moths in woollens.**
**What to use:** **Cedar chips, bay leaves, camphor flakes, whole cloves.**
**How to apply:** There are two types of jumper-chewing moths and both are repelled by a mixture of 2 large cedar chips, 2 bay leaves and 1 teaspoon of camphor flakes (store in the toe of a pair of pantyhose). The holes may also be from silverfish that are deterred with whole cloves

SPOTLESS 2

>   (add 2 whole cloves to the above mixture). To repair the hole in your jumper, see *How To Be Comfy* for instructions on how to darn or apply an appliqué.

**Prevention:** For an all-round bug deterrent, combine 2 bay leaves (moth deterrent), 5 whole cloves (kill mould spores and deter silverfish), 1 tea bag (kills dust mites), 2 heads of lavender (add fragrance and deter flying insects), 2 cedar chips (deter moths) and 1 tablespoon of bicarb (absorbs moisture and helps prevent mould) and place in a piece of muslin or the toe of a pair of pantyhose. Leave where nasties lurk.

> **TIP** If your wardrobe is prone to dampness, tie six sticks of white chalk with a ribbon and hang in your wardrobe to absorb moisture.

## Q: 'How can you stop jumpers from pilling?' asks Bill.

**Problem:** **Pilling on woollens.**

**What to use:** **Fuller's earth, 15 litre bucket, blood-heat water, soft brush; or ironing board, disposable razor.**

**How to apply:** Woollens pill if they're not washed properly or if the fibres are stressed. Stir 2 tablespoons of fuller's earth into a 15 litre bucket of blood-heat water. Immerse the garments and leave for 5–10 minutes. Rinse in blood-heat water, gently wring and dry flat in the shade. As they dry, stretch them into shape and brush away the pilling with a soft brush. If any pills remain, shave with a razor. To fix pilling in synthetic jumpers, stretch over the end of an ironing board and shave with a razor.

**TIP** To stop angora jumpers from shedding, place them in a plastic bag, remove as much air as possible and put in the freezer for 20 minutes to an hour. Remove from the freezer (brrrr!) and hang them for 10–20 minutes, to come to room temperature, before wearing.

## Caring for woollens

No one likes wearing a scratchy jumper. To restore woollens and blended woollens to their fluffy glory, wash in cheap shampoo and blood-heat water, then rinse in cheap hair conditioner and blood-heat water. Gently wring and dry flat on a towel in the shade. The reason for using cheap shampoo and hair conditioner is they have fewer oils and perfumes and are gentler on the wool fibres. It's also important to have the wash and rinse water at the same temperature to reduce stress on the wool fibres. And to prevent shrinkage or sagging, dry flat in the shade.

It's a little trickier cleaning structured woollens such as suits, coats and jackets. To clean them, fill a pillowcase with 1 kg of unprocessed wheat bran and place the garment inside. Close the

SPOTLESS 2

> top of the pillowcase and give a vigorous shake. A more passive approach involves sitting on the closed pillowcase for an hour a day over the course of a week. Just make sure you get all the bran out when you remove the garment or it might look as though you've got bad dandruff.

## WHAT NOT TO DO...

**Q:** 'I have a white wool (55 per cent wool and 45 per cent polyester) coat that I soaked in NapiSan. This turned it a shade of blotchy yellow/tan. I then soaked it in hydrogen peroxide (6 per cent and 18 per cent) and used a colour run remover but it does not seem to have helped in any way. What do I do?'

**A:** Chlorine-based bleaches burn wool, which is why the coat turned a yellowy brown colour. In this case, the fibres have been damaged. It may be beyond repair but try this solution. Mix 2 cups of 3 per cent hydrogen peroxide, 8 tablespoons of washing soda and 9 litres of blood-heat water in a bucket. Place the coat in the mixture and put a plate over the top so it stays immersed. Leave for 6 hours. Add 1 cup of white vinegar to a tub of blood-heat water and rinse the coat thoroughly. Dry flat in the shade. If the fabric is too fragile for this, dye it with a quality cold water wool dye. For an even dye, make sure the tub is large enough for the coat to move around easily.

**TIP** Use the same dye water to colour other items, such as pillowcases and sheets or tired-looking bras.

> **Caring for velvet**
>
> To clean velvet, put 1 cup of unprocessed wheat bran in a pillowcase, add the item and seal the top of the pillowcase. Sit on it for an hour a day over the course of a week. Remove and shake away the bran.

**TIP** If clothing has sequins, protect them by placing the clothes in a pair of pantyhose or a pillowcase when washing.

# SUITS

To make your suits look snappy, keep dry-cleaning to a minimum. The chemicals used in dry-cleaning weaken the fibres and shorten the life of the suit. Instead, after wearing, give a good brush before hanging on wooden hangers (wire ones don't offer enough support). And don't cram your suits into the wardrobe or they'll become wrinkled. If you're very particular, remove creases with a steamer rather than an iron because it's gentler on the fibres.

## JACKETS

**Q:** 'I've got a funky suede jacket', boasts Brad. 'But it's got general dirt markings over it. What do you suggest?

|  |  |
|---|---|
| **Problem:** | **Dirty suede.** |
| **What to use:** | **Unprocessed wheat bran, white spirits, pillowcase, cotton ball, talcum powder, brush.** |
| **How to apply:** | Mix 1 cup of unprocessed wheat bran with drops of white spirits until the mixture forms clumps that resemble brown sugar. Place the mixture in a pillowcase, add the suede jacket and then, as the Fonz used to say, sit on it! Do this for an hour a day (while watching TV or eating dinner) over the course of a week. The bran will scour the dirty marks away. Remove the jacket (somewhere outside is best) and shake until it's free of bran. If there are grubby marks on the collar, wipe with a little white spirits on a cotton ball, then sprinkle with talcum powder and when dry, wipe off with a brush. |

Clothing and Shoes

**Q:** 'I have one of those puffy jackets with a down filling which I keep in a zipped garment cover', reports Sue. 'Recently, I took it out and noticed the white jacket looks slightly yellow in certain parts. What can I do? The fabric is HyVent.'

**Problem:** **Stained HyVent fabric (waterproof).**

**What to use:** **Lemon juice, cloth, cake of bathroom soap, blood-heat water, damp cloth.**

**How to apply:** Wipe the stains with a little lemon juice on a cloth, then rub with a cake of bathroom soap that's been dipped in blood-heat water. Wipe with a damp cloth and dry in the shade.

**Q:** 'My husband's favourite leather jacket has stains on the collar from his neck', says Carol-Ann. 'Any ideas?'

**Problem:** **Sweat marks on leather.**

**What to use:** **White spirits, cloth, talcum powder, brush, saddle soap.**

**How to apply:** Wipe with a little white spirits on a cloth, sprinkle with talcum powder and brush away when dry. If the staining is extensive and has soaked into the leather, clean with saddle soap, following the manufacturer's instructions.

**Q:** 'I have a Driza-Bone coat which needs to be cleaned', reports Joanne. 'It's about 20 years old and in good condition.'

> **Problem:** **Dirty Driza-Bone.**
>
> **What to use:** **Cake of bathroom soap, cold water, pantyhose, damp cloth, white spirits, cotton ball, cloth, baby oil.**
>
> **How to apply:** Run a cake of bathroom soap under cold water and place in the toe of a pair of pantyhose. Rub over the coat then wipe with a damp cloth. For bad staining, apply a little white spirits to a cotton ball and wipe over any marks. To keep it waterproof, dab baby oil onto a cloth and wipe over the coat in even strokes.

# TIES

**Q:** 'I've spilt oily noodles on an expensive silk tie my wife bought me for Christmas', says Omar. 'Any ideas to help save the marriage would be greatly appreciated.'

> **Problem:** **Oily noodles on silk.**
>
> **What to use:** **Cheap shampoo, blood-heat water, towel, iron.**

Clothing and Shoes

**How to apply:** We may not be able to save your marriage but fixing the tie is easy. Wash in a little shampoo and blood-heat water. Rinse with blood-heat water, gently wring excess moisture and lay flat on a towel in the shade to dry. Iron on a cool setting.

# HANDBAGS

**Q:** 'I've got grease stains on a light tan leather bag', says Amy. 'The grease has left dark stains on the leather.'

**Problem:** **Grease stains on leather.**
**What to use:** **White spirits, cloth, talcum powder, brush; or leather conditioner.**
**How to apply:** What to do will depend on the type of leather. For hard-tanned leather (shiny, waxy finish), wipe with a little white spirits on a cloth. Then sprinkle with talcum powder and brush off when dry. If it's soft-tanned leather (low sheen finish/kid or kangaroo hide), oil the bag with leather conditioner and leave for 2 weeks (it takes that long to dry). The stains will lighten as the bag dries.

SPOTLESS 2

**Q:** 'I pulled out my old white Glomesh bag from the cupboard', reports Evelyn. 'And it's covered in brown stains. I have no idea what they are. Can they be removed?'

> **Problem:** **Brown marks on white Glomesh bag.**
>
> **What to use:** **CLR/Ranex, cotton bud (rust); or Colour Run Remover: Whites, cotton bud (dye); or glycerine, cloth (dirt).**
>
> **How to apply:** The brown marks could be from several sources. Do a test first to see which solvent works. For rust, use CLR or Ranex on a cotton bud. For dye, use 1 part Colour Run Remover: Whites to 5 parts water on a cotton bud. For dirt, wipe with a little glycerine on a cloth. If none of these solutions work, see a restorer.

**Q:** 'I've got mould on a suede leather handbag', says Mary. 'Any ideas?'

> **Problem:** **Mould on suede.**
>
> **What to use:** **White spirits, cotton ball, non-iodised salt, talcum powder, brush.**
>
> **How to apply:** Wipe the mouldy area with white spirits on a cotton ball. Then sprinkle on a mixture of 1 part salt to 3 parts talcum powder. Leave until completely dry and brush off.

Clothing and Shoes

# SHOES

It's annoying when you buy a new pair of shoes and they're too tight when you put them on at home. If you can't return them, try to stretch them. But we warn you—there's a lot of variation in shoes and many are delicate so we can't guarantee you won't damage them using this technique. With that disclaimer in mind, here's what you can do. If the shoes are made of hardy leather, heat the inside of the shoe with steam and rub the outside with petroleum jelly (Vaseline). Wear thick socks, put on the shoes and walk around until the shoes cool.

**Q:** 'My husband has a pair of suede boots with rubber soles', reports Elsa. 'Every time he takes a step, they squeak. Is there any way I can quieten them?'

    **Problem:** **Squeaky shoes.**

  **What to use:** **Glycerine, cotton bud; or talcum powder.**

  **How to apply:** Wipe along the seams with glycerine on a cotton bud. Alternatively, sprinkle talcum powder inside the shoes and that will gradually remove the squeak.

**Q:** 'I've got food stains on my suede shoes', says Elizabeth. 'What do you suggest?'

    **Problem:** **Food stains on suede.**

  **What to use:** **White spirits, cloth, talcum powder, brush.**

SPOTLESS 2

**How to apply:** Put a little white spirits on a cloth and wipe over in even strokes. Then sprinkle with talcum powder, leave to dry and brush off.

# Q: 'I've got chamois shoes', reports Hazel. 'And have no idea how to clean them.'

**Problem:** **Dirty chamois shoes.**
**What to use:** **Cake of bathroom soap, pantyhose, damp cloth.**
**How to apply:** Put a cake of bathroom soap into the toe of some pantyhose and rub over the shoes. Wipe with a damp cloth. Dry the shoes in the shade.

## Ugg boots/sheepskin

The best way to clean ugg boots or sheepskin shoes is in the washing machine. Put 1 teaspoon of cheap shampoo in each boot and place them into a pillowcase. Wash in cold water on the gentle cycle. When drying, stuff newspaper or old towels inside each boot and leave in the shade, so they don't go stiff.

# Q: 'I've spilt fat or oil on my new sheepskin slippers', says Morag. 'How can I clean them?'

**Problem:** **Fat/oil on sheepskin.**
**What to use:** **Cheap shampoo, damp cloth.**
**How to apply:** Massage a little shampoo into the stains with your fingers and rinse with a damp cloth. Dry the slippers in the shade or they'll go stiff.

Clothing and Shoes

If using the washing machine, wash in cold water on the gentle cycle, then dry in the shade.

# GLOVES

**Q:** 'How can I clean my red leather gloves?' asks Sammy.

**Problem:** **Dirty leather gloves.**
**What to use:** **Saddle soap.**
**How to apply:** Put the gloves on and massage your hands with saddle soap, making sure you get the saddle soap over every part of the glove. They're ready to wear. For kid gloves, use a bran ball (see page 85).

**Q:** 'I am desperate to know how to remove mould from my suede gloves', states Maxine. 'What do you suggest?'

**Problem:** **Mould on suede.**
**What to use:** **Oil of cloves, water, 1 litre spray pack, stiff brush.**
**How to apply:** Mix ¼ teaspoon of oil of cloves in a spray pack of water. Lightly mist over the gloves (don't saturate them) and leave in the shade to dry. Brush the mould off with a stiff brush. If any mould remains, repeat.

# HATS

**Q:** 'My husband owns a dark-coloured Akubra hat', reports Geraldine. 'What's the best way to clean the band on the inside of the hat?'

    **Problem:** Dirty Akubra hat.

    **What to use:** White spirits, cotton ball, talcum powder, brush; or fuller's earth, water, damp cloth.

    **How to apply:** Wipe the stains with a dab of white spirits on a cotton ball, then sprinkle with talcum powder to absorb the white spirits. Leave to dry and brush off. For light-coloured Akubras, make a paste of fuller's earth and water, leave over the dirt marks for a few minutes, then remove with a damp cloth.

**Q:** 'I've got a genuine Panama hat', reports Wally. 'But it's got sweat marks on it. What do you suggest?'

    **Problem:** Sweat marks on hat.

    **What to use:** Fuller's earth, water, damp cloth; or bran ball.

    **How to apply:** Mix fuller's earth and water to form a paste the consistency of thick cream and place on the marks. Leave for a few minutes and remove with a damp cloth. Alternatively, clean with a bran ball (see page 85).

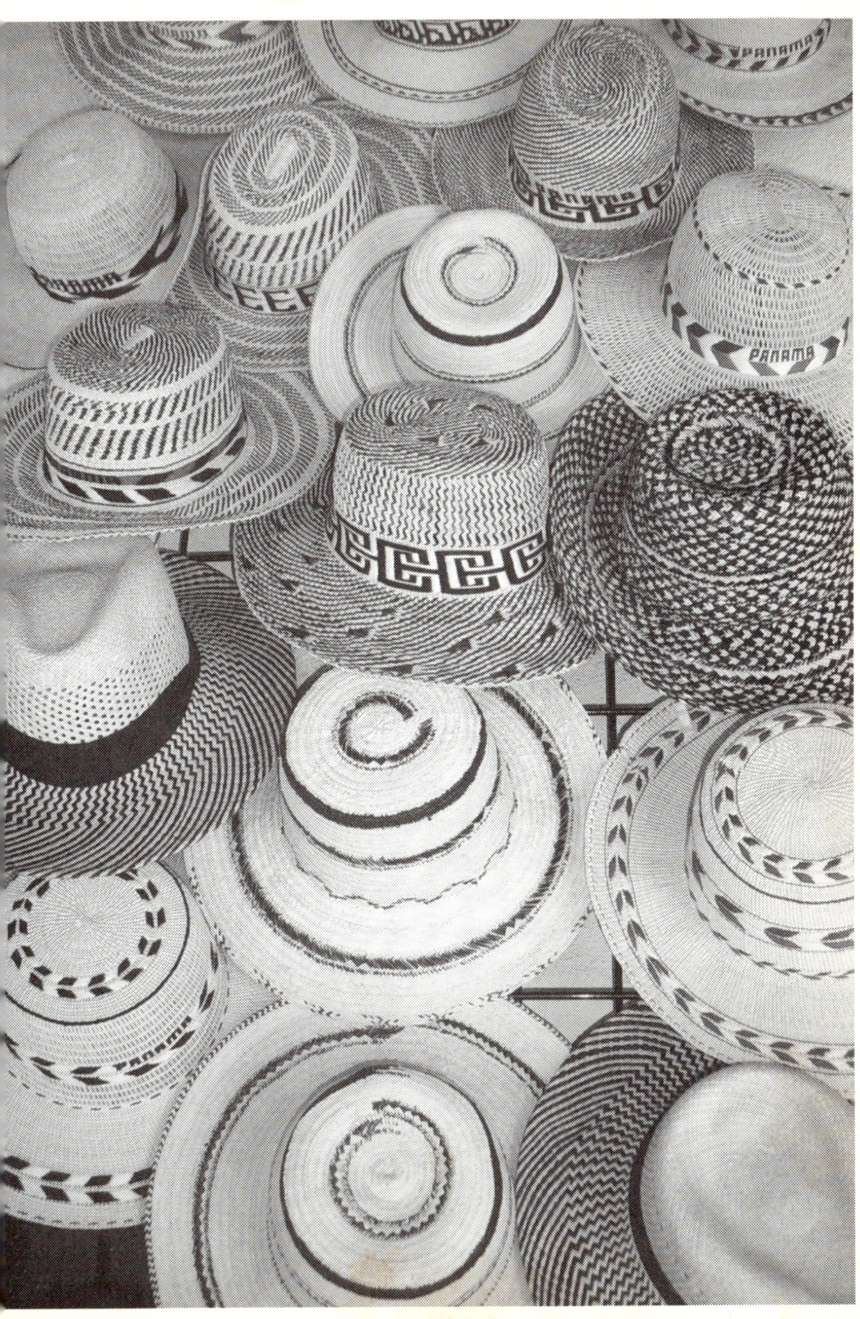
PANAMA
PANAMA
PANAMA

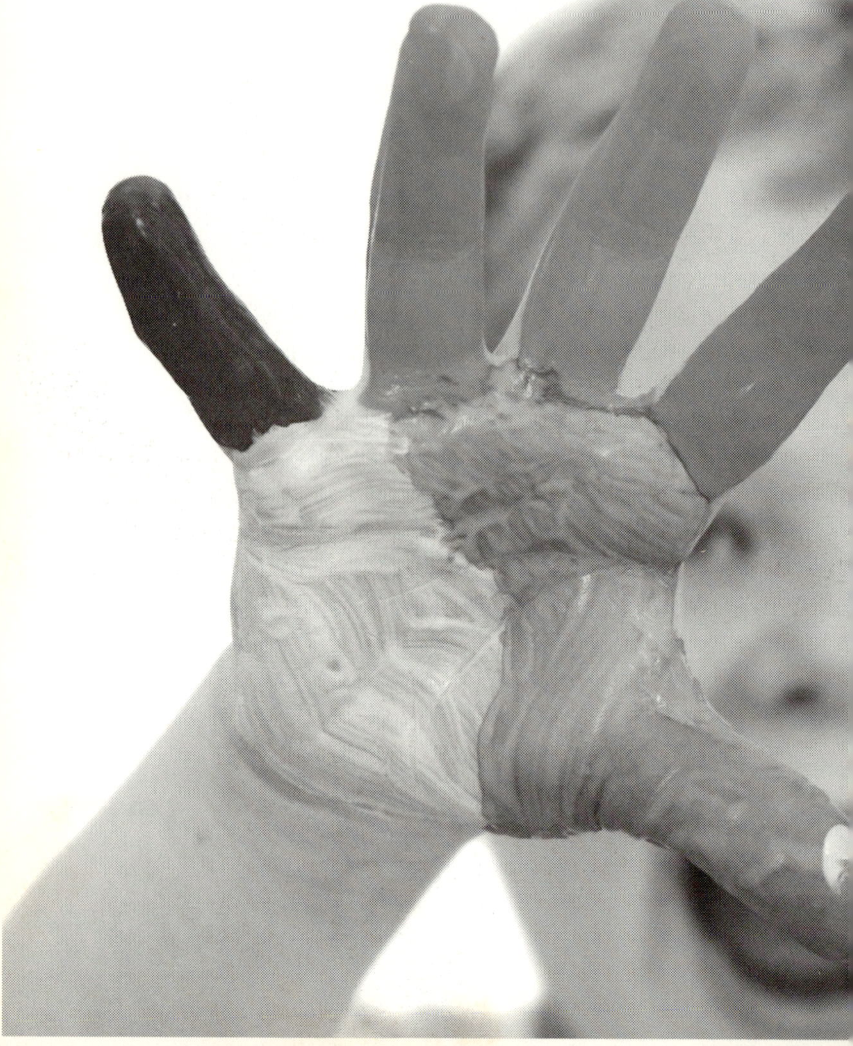

Kids' Stuff

Children are messy! Even the most vigilant parents can find themselves removing Vegemite smears from the couch or crayon marks from a wall. And let's not forget projectile vomit or muddy footprints tracked through the house on a rainy day; it's all part of the rich tapestry of family life. It doesn't matter if the stains are accidental or from a rush of creativity from your child, you can find the solutions here!

## SMELLY TEDDY: Jane's story

**INCIDENT:** 'We have a much-loved old teddy bear which is starting to smell. Is there a way to make him less stinky?'

**SOLUTION:** Mix 1 cup of unprocessed wheat bran with drops of white vinegar until the mixture forms clumps that resemble brown sugar. If the teddy smells mouldy, add 2 drops of oil of cloves. Put the mixture into a pillowcase and place the smelly teddy inside. Secure the top of the pillowcase and shake well. Remove the ted (preferably outside or over a bin) and shake away the bran. If the teddy bear is still smelly, find a dry cleaner that works with conservation pieces.

# ROUTINE CLEAN

Babies and young children are extremely vulnerable to bacteria so a clean home is very important. Use tea tree oil—a non-toxic antibacterial and antiseptic—instead of harsh chemical cleaners. Dilute 1 teaspoon of tea tree oil in 1 litre of water and store in a spray pack. Lightly spray over hard surfaces and wipe with a clean cloth. Regular vacuuming is important as children are susceptible to dust and dust mites. Wipe over suckable surfaces each day because bacteria breed in saliva. Used nappies should be removed and dealt with as soon as possible.

**TIP** You may not know that the most common cause of oral thrush in babies (white cloudy marks on gums and cheek linings) is from people sticking their fingers in the baby's mouth. Don't allow it!

Clean toddlers' rooms twice a week. Vacuum and spray with the tea tree oil and water solution and wipe with a cloth. Don't use bleaches or other heavy chemical cleaners which can be harsh on little lungs. Help toddlers learn where clothes and toys go by placing labels on drawers with the name and picture of what's in each drawer. They could even draw the pictures themselves.

From when your children reach the age of four, keep this word in mind: 'washable'. If you're searching for inspiration, look around your local kindergarten, where floors, walls and toys are washable. From this age, encourage your children to put their own toys and clothes away. Show them how to sweep the floor in their room and make a game of removing marks on walls. To get them excited about cleaning, mix bicarb and white vinegar together, they'll love to watch the fizzing.

**TIP** Before removing a Band-Aid, wipe across the outside with tea tree oil and leave for 5 minutes. The Band-Aid will come off easily with no tears.

Kids' Stuff

# COTS

Use a mattress protector because it's easier to wash than the mattress; having said that, you still need to air the mattress each day. Wash sheets and bedding in washing detergent for sensitive skin and dry in the sun rather than in the dryer because UV light kills bacteria. If you can't dry things in the sun and have to use the dryer, iron items afterwards so that the steam heat can help kill any remaining bacteria. If there's a problem with dust mites, put 2 tea bags in a 1 litre spray pack of water, allow to steep for 5 minutes, remove the tea bags and lightly mist over mattresses and pillows.

Make sure the cot is sturdy and safe. Stiff hinges can lead to accidents, so keep them well oiled with baby oil by adding a drop and allowing it to work through the hinges and slides.

## *SPOTLESS CLASSIC*
### Baby vomit on sheets

What to do will depend on the type of vomit. If the vomit is just milk, a normal wash on a cold cycle should do the job. For bad staining, rub with a cake of bathroom soap, add some cold water and scrub. Wipe with white vinegar on a cloth. If there's other food in the vomit, do a stain diagnosis (see page 362).

## BED-WETTING

If your child wets the bed, protect the mattress with a breathable waterproof mattress cover. To remove urine, wipe both sides of the mattress with white vinegar on a cloth and sprinkle with talcum powder. Leave in the sunshine until dry then vacuum. To clean a mattress made of tea tree bark, sprinkle with bicarb, leave in the sunshine and then vacuum.

## HIGHCHAIRS

Highchairs tend to be sealed in material that can be cleaned easily. Clean up food spills as soon as possible because they are more difficult to remove when the food sets and hardens. See *Spotless* for tips on what to do if you don't get to the food in time. If your child makes a huge mess when eating, place a flattened garbage bag underneath the highchair to catch the rejected food.

## PLAYPENS/SECURITY GATES

Most playpens and security gates are made with powder-coated aluminium and are easy to clean with a damp cloth.

## PRAMS/STROLLERS

Prams, strollers and baby packs have removable parts that can be washed and kept clean. If there's mould on a pram, wipe with a strong salt solution (1 kg of non-iodised salt per 9 litres of water) with a couple of drops of oil of cloves added to prevent mould.

Allow to dry. Brush the salt crust off with a stiff brush and the mould will come away with it.

**Q:** 'We use a sheepskin in our daughter's pram', says Tessa. 'Is there a way to wash it so it doesn't go hard?'

| | |
|---|---|
| **Problem:** | **Washing sheepskin.** |
| **What to use:** | **Blood-heat water, cheap shampoo, soft hairbrush.** |
| **How to apply:** | Hand wash in blood-heat water with 1 teaspoon of cheap shampoo added, then rinse in blood-heat water and gently wring. The rinse water temperature must be the same as the wash water. To dry, lie it flat in the shade and brush regularly with a hairbrush. If the sheepskin dries too quickly, it will go stiff. |

# BABY BOTTLES

After using a sterilising kit, rinse the bottles with boiled water or the contents will taste like a swimming pool and might be spat back at you. Preserve rubber nipples by wiping with non-iodised salt before rinsing in boiled water.

# NAPPIES

Most Australian babies wear disposable nappies. If your baby wears cloth nappies, shake the solids into the toilet, rinse, then place the soiled nappy in a nappy bucket with a lid that seals, to await washing. Don't leave the nappies sitting in the bucket for more than a day because urine can weaken the fabric. Nappies are unlikely to have greasy stains on them so use less nappy soaker and opt for an enzyme-free detergent to avoid residue build-up and nappy rash. If you like to wash with bicarb, white vinegar or essential oils but have a new-style nappy, check that these won't affect its elasticity. Don't be seduced by antibacterial products: they aren't necessary when cleaning nappies. It's best to dry nappies on the clothesline where the sun sterilises and removes stains. It's also gentler on the nappy fibres, so they'll last longer.

> **TIP** To disguise the smell of a nappy bucket, mix 2 tablespoons of bicarb, ½ teaspoon of dried sage, ½ teaspoon of dried thyme and 2 drops of lavender oil on a saucer and place near the bucket.

# TOYS

You can clean chewable toys by wiping them with pantyhose dipped in 1 teaspoon of tea tree oil per litre of water. Many new toys contain oils and plastics that stain. One of Jennifer's friends was horrified when her daughter brought playdough home from a birthday party filled with a green liquid. The liquid found its sticky way under the bed, went hard and stuck to the carpet. How could she remove it? If you don't know what a stain is made of, feel it with your fingers. If it feels oily, massage dishwashing liquid into the stain with your fingers until it feels like jelly, then wipe with

Kids' Stuff

a damp cloth. If it still sticks, wipe with white spirits on a cloth. If there's fluorescent colouring, place ice-cubes in a zip-lock bag and leave over the area until the ice almost melts. Remove the zip-lock bag and wipe with a strong salt solution (1 cup of non-iodised salt in 1 litre of water) on a cloth. Dry with paper towel.

Shannon stores children's toys in clear plastic stackable boxes with lids to keep dust at bay. Because the container is clear, your kids can see what's inside. These boxes can even be stored under the bed.

**TIP** When visiting a doctor's surgery, take your own toys to reduce the risk of contact with germs from other children.

## Q: 'How do you prevent sling shot rubbers from drying out?' asks Rob.

**Problem: Preserving rubber.**
**What to use: Salt, talcum powder.**
**How to apply:** Wipe the rubber with equal parts salt and talcum powder. Store in the shade.

## Q: 'My children's favourite plastic bath toys have mould on the inside', says Maria. 'What can I do?'

**Problem: Mouldy bath toys.**
**What to use: Oil of cloves, 9 litre bucket, warm water.**

**How to apply:** Add 2¼ teaspoons of oil of cloves to a bucket of warm water. Place the toys inside, squeeze so water gets inside and leave for 2 hours. Remove, squeeze out the water and set aside to dry.

*TIP* If electronic games get wet, unscrew the back cover and leave on a tray in the sun. Turn the parts regularly so they don't corrode and wipe across the electric board with a dry paintbrush. When you put it back together, it should work again. You may need to replace the batteries. Clean the outside of electronic games with a drop of glycerine on paper towel.

## FLOORS

**Q:** 'How do I remove playdough from a beautiful silk and wool woven rug?' asks Sarah. 'It's been there for a few months.'

**Problem:** **Playdough on rug.**
**What to use:** **Vacuum cleaner, non-iodised salt, pantyhose.**
**How to apply:** When playdough dries out, it becomes powdery and easy to vacuum. If necessary you can scrub it with a little salt on pantyhose and vacuum thoroughly. Repeat until the play dough is removed.

# CLOTHES

Use pure soap flakes or laundry detergent for sensitive skin (to make your own, see page 359) when washing babies' clothes. You can remove excess washing powder by adding ½ cup of white vinegar to the rinse cycle. Another issue with baby clothes is scratchy seams. Run the back of your hand along the inside of clothing to feel for any scratchy bits. If there's any irritation, use iron-on cotton binding to cover the seams.

**Q:** 'I had some woollen baby clothes in storage', reports Rebecca. 'And they've got rusty marks on them. What can I do?'

**Problem:** **Rust on wool.**

**What to use:** **Blood-heat water, cheap shampoo, towel; or non-iodised salt, lemon juice, sunshine.**

**How to apply:** Place the garments in blood-heat water and massage 1 teaspoon of shampoo over the stain. Rinse in blood-heat water, gently wring out and dry flat on a towel in the shade. For stubborn stains, cover with a little mountain of salt and add drops of lemon juice until the salt is moistened. Dry in the sun. Hand wash in shampoo and blood-heat water, rinse well, wring out and dry flat in the shade.

SPOTLESS 2

**Q:** 'Disaster!' exclaims Judy. 'My son has orange Texta on a 100 per cent cotton light grey track suit. What can I do?'

> **Problem:** **Texta on cotton.**
>
> **What to use:** **Methylated spirits, cotton ball.**
>
> **How to apply:** Wipe the marks with methylated spirits on a cotton ball. Wash normally.

**Q:** 'My son's baby shawl has been packed away for 30 years', reports Sue. 'I recently unwrapped it to find a dark yellow stain on it. What can I do?'

> **Problem:** **Yellow stain on wool.**
>
> **What to use:** **Cheap shampoo, blood-heat water, towel.**
>
> **How to apply:** The stain is likely to be old milk. To remove, wash with 1 teaspoon of shampoo in 9 litres of blood-heat water. Rinse in blood-heat water, gently wring out and dry on a flat towel in the shade.
>
> **Prevention:** To avoid yellowing marks, store clothes in acid-free paper which is available at newsagents.

**Q:** 'My son had a cold', reports Lisa. 'And I rubbed Vicks VapoRub onto his chest. But it also got onto his T-shirt. How can I get it out?'

> **Problem:** **Vicks VapoRub on cotton.**

**What to use:** **Dishwashing liquid.**

**How to apply:** Put a couple of drops of dishwashing liquid on your fingers and massage into the stain until it feels like jelly. Wash and dry normally.

**Q:** 'My 6 year old dripped vivid blue icy pole down the front of his T-shirt', reports Anne. 'How can I get it out?'

**Problem:** **Blue icy pole on cotton.**

**What to use:** **Sunshine, white vinegar, cloth.**

**How to apply:** These stains are usually removed by the washing machine as long as they're dried in sunshine which fades the stain. If the stain remains, wipe with white vinegar on a cloth, wash normally and hang it on the clothesline in the sun to dry.

**Q:** 'My daughter got chocolate ice-cream on her favourite cotton T-shirt', says Alice. 'She is heartbroken. Is there a way to get the stain out?'

**Problem:** **Chocolate ice-cream on cotton.**

**What to use:** **Cake of bathroom soap, cold water.**

**How to apply:** Dip a cake of bathroom soap in cold water and scribble on the stain as though you're using a big crayon. Wash and dry normally.

SPOTLESS 2

**Q:** 'When I washed my daughter's school windcheater, the burgundy dye ran into the white collar and it's now pink.' says Christine. 'Can I fix it?'

| | |
|---|---|
| **Problem:** | **Dye run in cotton.** |
| **What to use:** | **9 litre bucket, water, Colour Run Remover: Coloursafe.** |
| **How to apply:** | Soak overnight in a bucket of water and Colour Run Remover. Use twice as much Colour Run Remover as suggested by the manufacturer. Wash and dry normally. |
| **Prevention:** | To make clothes colourfast, mix 4 cups of non-iodised salt in a 9 litre bucket of water, place clothes in the bucket and leave for 5 minutes. Wash normally. Salt removes excess surface dye and acts as a setting agent. |

**Q:** 'My son plays cricket', reports Tania. 'And I'm finding it difficult to remove the red markings from the cricket ball. Do you have a suggestion?'

| | |
|---|---|
| **Problem:** | **Cricket ball marks on cotton.** |
| **What to use:** | **White spirits, cotton ball.** |
| **How to apply:** | Cricket balls are made of dyed red leather and the ball is often polished with the bowler's sweat or saliva. Rub the marks with a little white spirits on a cotton ball then wash and dry normally. White spirits also removes grass stains. |

Kids' Stuff

**TIP**  To stop white Lycra becoming see-through when you get sweaty, spray it with a light mist of hair spray. Allow to dry before wearing.

# Q: 'My daughter's white socks are really dirty', says Anne. 'Is there a way to get the whiteness back?'

| | |
|---|---|
| **Problem:** | **Dirty white socks.** |
| **What to use:** | **Cake of bathroom soap, water.** |
| **How to apply:** | Put a cake of bathroom soap in the toe of one sock and run under water. Put your hand in the other sock and rub the two together for about 15 seconds. Remove the cake of soap then wash and dry normally. |
| **Prevention:** | Socks often become dirty around the toes because dye from school shoes leaches into the socks when little toes get sweaty. To prevent this, lightly spray inside each shoe with hair spray and allow to dry before wearing. |

**Q:** 'I have a white tulle dress (to be used as a flower girl's dress) that had several artificial flowers attached to it with what appears to be a heat glue gun', says Margaret. 'I've managed to remove the flowers using hot water but cannot remove the glue. Do you have any suggestions?'

| | |
|---:|:---|
| **Problem:** | **Glue on tulle.** |
| **What to use:** | **Heatproof jug, boiling water, pantyhose.** |
| **How to apply:** | Fill a heatproof jug with boiling water and stretch the gluey tulle over the mouth of the jug. Allow the steam to loosen the glue then remove the tulle and rub the glue with a pair of pantyhose. The glue will roll off the pantyhose. |

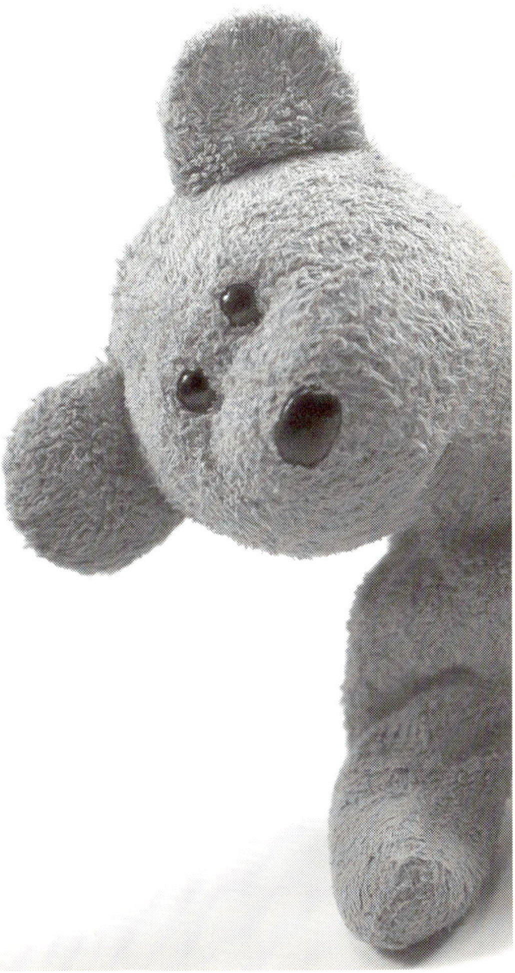

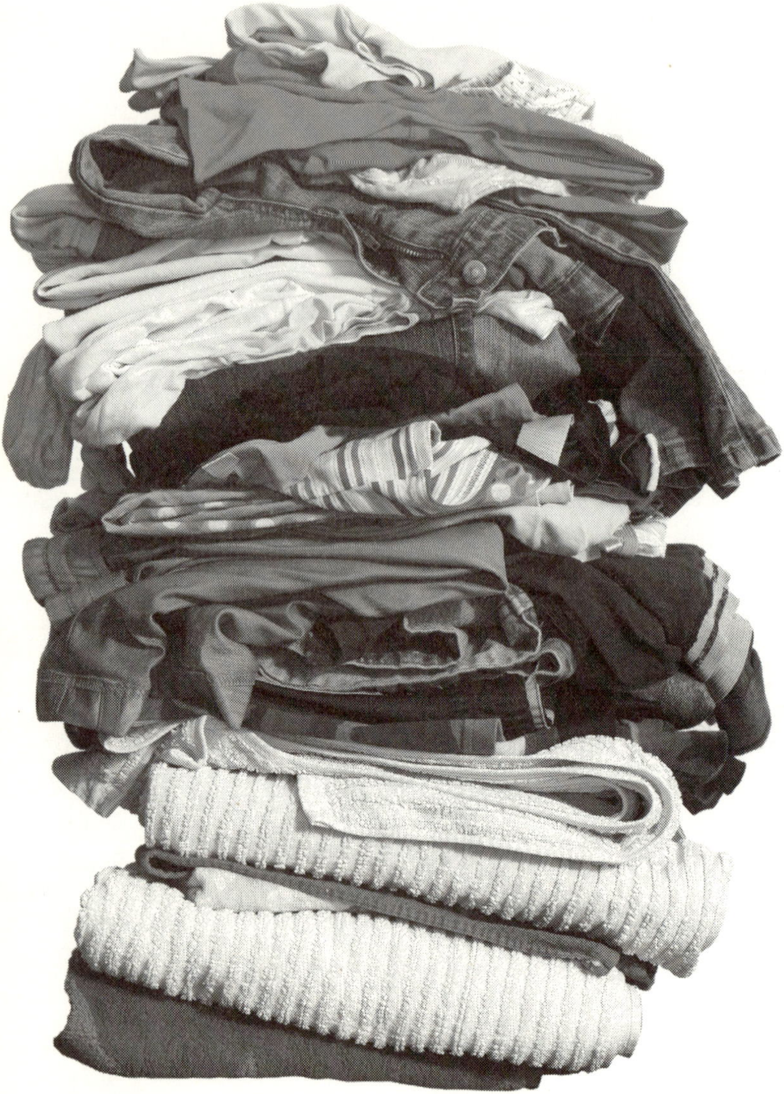

# The Laundry

Shannon still remembers the first time she saw her grandmother remove an ink stain using rotten milk solids. She thought it looked like magic as the black ink was drawn into the white milk. And today, all those years later, rotten milk is still an effective way to remove ballpoint pen ink (other inks have different solvents) from fabric. Jennifer's friend got dye from a new suede handbag over her expensive cream skirt and her dry-cleaner said it couldn't be cleaned without damaging the fabric. She used the rotten milk technique and it worked a treat. With other stains, don't rush in and make a bigger mess. Instead, work out what the stain is made of and then apply the correct solution.

## TISSUE ISSUE: Jake's story

**INCIDENT:** 'I know it's stupid. But I didn't bother to check the pockets before putting some clothes in the washing machine. Of course, there was a random tissue that has spread everywhere. How do I remove all that fluff from the wash?'

**SOLUTION:** There are two things to clean here: the interior of the washing machine and the contents of the wash. To remove the fluff from the washing machine, put your hand inside the toe of a pair of pantyhose and wipe over the drum. To remove the fluff from your clothes, put on a pair of disposable rubber gloves, wash your gloved hands with a cake of bathroom soap and water and shake dry. Stroke over the linty fabric and the lint will attach to the rubber gloves.

# WASHING

We've already outlined basic washing techniques in *Spotless* but here's a summary of the essentials:

- Cooler temperatures are gentler on fabrics. To work out the appropriate temperature, consult the garment labels on the items you are washing. Only cotton and linen can handle very hot temperatures;
- Remove stains before washing clothes. If very dirty, soak before washing but only soak wool and silk for 20 minutes. If the item contains synthetic fibres, wipe with a dab of methylated spirits, then treat the stain before washing;
- Less dirt will be removed from clothes if the washing machine is overloaded;

SPOTLESS 2

- Sort clothes into different fabric types, then separate whites from colours. After sorting, check pockets (you don't want a stray tissue in the wash), close zippers and do up buttons.

*TIP* Have a separate basket for stained items that need to be spot-cleaned before washing.

## Soaking

You may think the longer you soak your clothes, the more dirt is removed but this is not the case. The more delicate the fabric, the less time it should sit soaking (the exception is in salt water). Twenty minutes is generally enough time for an item to soak. Never soak woollens for more than 20 minutes because the fibres will shrink, even in cool water. And be aware that proprietary products such as NapiSan contain chlorine and can leave yellow marks on wool and silk. It's better to clean them with cheap shampoo in blood-heat water. To remove the yellow marks, see Clothing and Shoes, page 262.

## Colourfast

If you have new clothes and you're not sure if they're colourfast, try this test. Wring out a white cloth in white vinegar and place the cloth over an inconspicuous part of the garment and iron. Colour will transfer to the cloth if it's not colourfast. Alternatively, wring out a white cloth in white vinegar and pinch it over an inconspicuous part of the garment. The colour will transfer to the cloth if it's not colourfast. To make an item colourfast, place in a 9 litre bucket of water with 2 cups of non-iodised salt. Soak for 1 hour and wash normally.

# Colour Run

Jennifer was really annoyed when her shirt became pink after a rogue red item found its way into the washing machine. If you have a similar disaster, use the proprietary product, Colour Run Remover (which used to be called Runaway). There are two varieties: Colour Run Remover: Whites and Colour Run Remover: Coloursafe. Rather than add Colour Run Remover to the washing machine as suggested by the manufacturer, soak items in a tub or bucket with twice the amount of product recommended. If the item is made of wool or silk, soak for 20 minutes in blood-heat water. For other fabrics, soak overnight.

At our Stain Clinics many people complain about the 'lamington look' of lint on their clothes. To prevent this, clean the lint filter on your washing machine before each wash and remove lint from the drum by wiping with damp pantyhose. Use one-third less washing powder than is recommended by the manufacturer and dissolve the powder particles in water before adding to the wash. Another tip is to use a gentle wash cycle. If clothes are washed too vigorously with too much washing detergent, they become statically charged and collect lint. To remove the static charge in clothes, place 1 teaspoon of cheap hair conditioner in a 1 litre spray pack of water and lightly mist over the clothes as they dry. To remove really tough lint, put on disposable rubber gloves, wash your gloved hands with a cake of bathroom soap and water, shake dry and wipe your hands across the fabric. The lint will stick to the rubber gloves.

# Quick stain removal guide for fabrics

This is only a brief guide to stain removal. For more detailed instructions, consult the relevant advice in the book.

### Banana
Wipe with a little glycerine and leave for 15 minutes, then wash normally.

### Barbecue sauce
Wipe with a little white vinegar, wash normally and hang in sunshine to dry.

### Beer (including dark beer)
Paint a paste of NapiSan OxyAction MAX and water on the stain and leave for 15 minutes, then wash normally.

### Beetroot
Soak in white vinegar until the stain is removed, then wash normally.

### Bird droppings
It depends on what the bird has eaten—either protein, seed or fruit. With protein (generally black or brown poo), scribble over the stain with a cake of bathroom soap and cold water. With seed (generally white poo), scribble over the stain with a cake of bathroom soap and warm water. With fruit (generally purple or orange poo), wipe with a cloth dampened with white vinegar, then wipe with a dab of glycerine on a cloth and leave for 20 minutes before washing normally.

### Blood
Rub the stain out with cold water and a cake of bathroom soap then wash normally on the cold setting. If you can't put it through

the wash, use a thin paste of cornflour and cold water to draw out the stain. Allow to dry and brush away. For old blood stains, use cold water and a cake of bathroom soap and vigorously rub the stain against itself.

### Carrot
Wipe with a little white vinegar and hang in the sun. Carrot stains respond to UV rays.

### Chewing gum
Harden the gum with an ice-cube and cut as much off as possible with scissors or a blade. Then apply a little tea tree oil with a rolled up pair of pantyhose and work the remaining gum out by rubbing it in circles. White spirits also works.

### Chilli sauce
Wipe with white vinegar or lemon juice until most of the red colouring transfers to the cloth. To remove the oil, add a couple of drops of dishwashing liquid to your fingers and massage into the stain until it feels like jelly before washing normally.

### Chocolate
Scrub with a cake of bathroom soap and cold water, then scrub with a cake of bathroom soap and hot water before washing normally.

### Chocolate ice-cream
Scrub with a cake of bathroom soap and cold water before washing normally.

### Collar grime
Mix NapiSan OxyAction MAX and water to form a paste the consistency of peanut butter. Apply to the stain and leave for 20 minutes. Wash and dry normally.

### Cooking oil
Soak up as much oil as possible with paper towel. Apply a little dishwashing liquid and massage into the stain with your fingers until it feels like jelly. Rinse with a little warm water. Wash normally.

### Coffee/tea
For fresh stains, use a little glycerine applied with a cotton ball, then wash normally. For old stains, use a little glycerine, followed by a little white spirits and a little dishwashing liquid, then wash normally.

### Crayon
Mix 2 drops of tea tree oil with 1 teaspoon of dishwashing liquid and massage over the crayon marks with your fingers, then rinse with water and wash normally.

### Deodorant
Apply a little white spirits with a cotton ball before washing. For stiffened armpits, apply a paste of NapiSan Plus and water, leave for 15 minutes before washing normally.

### Dog poo
Dip a cake of bathroom soap in cold water and scribble over the stain as though using a crayon, then rub before washing normally.

### Egg yolk
Use a cake of bathroom soap and cold water first, then a couple of drops of dishwashing liquid and warm water.

### Fruit juice
Wash in white vinegar and hang in the sunshine to dry. UV light breaks down fruit colouring. For stone fruits and fruits with high tannin levels, treat the stain with a little glycerine first.

### Grass
Sponge with a little white spirits before washing normally.

### Gravy
Dip a cake of bathroom soap in cold water and scribble over the stain. Put a couple of drops of dishwashing liquid on your fingers and massage into the stain until it feels like jelly. Then wash normally.

### Grease
Apply dishwashing liquid to the stain and rub with your fingers to emulsify. Rinse under cold water.

### Hair dye
Use the same brand and colour hair dye (hair dye contains its own solvent). When the stain starts to loosen, rub with a little anti-dandruff shampoo on your fingers. If the stain has just happened, spray with hair spray before washing normally.

### Ink/ballpoint pen
Apply rotten milk solids or a little white spirits to the stain. Use a little glycerine first on red ink.

### Lipstick/make-up
Apply a little white spirits with a cotton ball.

### Mascara
Sponge the stain with methylated spirits, then blot with paper towel.

### Mayonnaise
Massage a little dishwashing liquid into the stain with your fingers and wash in cold water. The massaging makes the mayonnaise water-soluble.

### Milk
Wash normally on the cold cycle.

### Mud
For red clay mud, apply a dab of white spirits then wash. For black mud, wash in the washing machine.

### Nail polish
Use pure acetone on a cotton bud or ball, not nail polish remover.

### Paint
For water-based paint, use a dab of methylated spirits. For oil-based paints, use a dab of turpentine.

### Pen marks
Solutions vary according to the type of pen. **Permanent markers**—write over the mark using the same pen. Then wipe with white spirits on a cotton bud. Wash and dry normally. **Artline**—wipe with methylated spirits on a cotton bud. Wash and dry normally. **Whiteboard marker**—wipe with methylated spirits on a cotton bud. Wash and dry normally. **Fluorescent pen**—write over the mark using the same pen, then wipe the mark with white spirits on a cotton bud. Alternatively, fill a 9 litre bucket with water and add 1 cup of non-iodised salt, dip the stain in the salt solution, gently wring and place in a plastic bag before freezing in the freezer. Wash and dry normally. **Gel pens**—soak in methylated spirits for 10 minutes and rub with a cotton bud dipped in methylated spirits. Repeat until removed. Wash and dry normally.

### Rubber
Dampen and rub with coarse non-iodised salt.

### Rust
Use CLR or Ranex or lemon juice and non-iodised salt.

### Sap
Sponge with a little tea tree oil.

### Shoe polish
Use a little methylated spirits applied with a cotton ball.
Alternatively, use a little tea tree oil applied with a cotton ball.

### Soft drink
Treat as though it's a fruit stain because soft drinks are coloured with vegetable dyes.

### Soy sauce
Wipe with white vinegar before washing normally.

### Sunscreen
Massage a little dishwashing liquid into the stain with your fingers, then wash with warm water.

### Sweat
Make a paste of NapiSan Plus and water, leave on the stain for 15 minutes, then wash in the washing machine. To prevent sweat marks, experiment until you find a deodorant that works for you. Everyone's body chemistry is different which means some people will need a deodorant and others will need an antiperspirant. Make sure your deodorant has dried before putting on your clothes.

### Tar
Massage in a little baby oil followed by a little kerosene on a cloth.

### Tomato sauce
Wipe with white vinegar and wash normally. Dry in sunshine.

### Tumeric
Wipe with a little lavender oil before washing normally.

### Urine
Wash normally and dry in sunshine.

### Vegemite
Will generally come out in the wash. If stubborn, put a couple of drops of dishwashing liquid on your fingers and massage into the stain. Then wash normally.

### Vomit
Wash normally and dry in sunshine or use NapiSan Plus if the stains are stubborn.

### Watermelon
Quickly deteriorates and ferments causing a smell. Sponge with white vinegar and sprinkle with bicarb to remove the stain and the smell.

### Wax
Place ice-cubes on the wax until the ice starts to melt. Scrape away as much wax as possible with a blunt knife, then lay sheets of paper towel over your ironing board. Place the stained material over the ironing board and cover with more paper towel before ironing with a cool iron. If a greasy mark remains rub it with a little tea tree oil.

### Wine
For new red wine spills, absorb moisture with paper towel, then wipe with a little white vinegar on a cloth. For old red wine spills, wipe with a dab of glycerine on a cloth and sprinkle with bicarb. It will turn grey. Allow to dry, wipe with a little white vinegar and vacuum. For white wine stains, both old and new, sponge with white vinegar on a cloth.

## Cleaning the washing machine

If you think about all the dirt and grime that passes through your washing machine, it's no surprise it needs to be cleaned. Each month, add ½ cup of bicarb to the wash slot and ½ cup white vinegar to the rinse slot and wash on a quick cycle. If you get a random tissue or disposable nappy washed through the machine, allow the drum to fill with water, add 2 tablespoons of cheap hair conditioner, 2 tablespoons of bicarb and leave filled for 1 hour before rinsing and wiping with pantyhose. Don't forget to clean the exterior, seals and hinges of the machine. To clean the seals, wrap an old tea towel around a plastic knife, dip in white vinegar and work under and around the seals. Wipe hinges with 2 drops of machine oil and clear away any fluff and dirt. If you keep your washing machine clean, you won't need to call the repairer as often.

**Q:** 'I've got mould in the rubber seal of my front loading washing machine', says Sue. 'What should I do?'

| | |
|---|---|
| **Problem:** | **Mould on rubber seal of washing machine.** |
| **What to use:** | **Oil of cloves, water, 1 litre spray pack, pantyhose, damp salt.** |
| **How to apply:** | Mix ¼ teaspoon of oil of cloves with water in a spray pack and lightly spray over the area. Leave for 24 hours. Rub with a pair of pantyhose dipped in damp salt. Respray with oil of cloves solution and leave to dry. |

SPOTLESS 2

**Q:** 'We have a rather old washing machine and one of the last loads stained all our clothes', says Meg. 'We believe it's from a build-up of all the fabric softeners which have collected grease and dirt during various washes. What can we do to remove these stains?'

**Problem:** **Washing machine staining clothes.**

**What to use:** **Damp pantyhose, bicarb, white vinegar.**

**How to apply:** To remove the current grime, wipe the inside of the drum with damp pantyhose. Make sure you get behind the seals. Run an empty load with ½ cup of bicarb in the washing slot and ½ cup of white vinegar in the fabric conditioner slot using a quick cycle. Instead of using fabric softener, try this washing formula. Use one-third the quantity of your regular detergent and for a large top loader, add ½ cup of bicarb and ½ cup of white vinegar; for a large front loader, add 2 tablespoons of bicarb and 2 tablespoons of white vinegar.

*TIP*

New flannelette sheets can leave a load of fluff in your washing machine. To avoid this, wash them on a heavy duty cycle with ½ cup of bicarb added to the laundry detergent and ½ cup of white vinegar in the fabric softener slot. Dry on the clothesline, not in the dryer. Many flannelette sheets contain polyester and if placed in the dryer they wear more quickly and pill.

**Q:** 'We live in the mining town of Newman', says Penny. 'And our washing machine is caked in red dirt from iron ore. Is there anything we can flush through the machine to remove the dirt?'

>**Problem:** **Red dirt in washing machine.**
>
>**What to use:** **Bicarb, white vinegar, bucket, water.**
>
>**How to apply:** Place 1 cup of bicarb in the washing water and 1 cup of white vinegar in the fabric conditioner slot of the machine. Remove heavy dirt by soaking the clothes in a bucket of water saved from the bath or shower before placing them in the washing machine. It means your machine won't have to work as hard. Reuse the bucket water over your garden.

## Fabric care symbols

Be aware that these vary from country to country.

## Washing

- 95°C cotton wash—maximum and most effective temperature
- 60°C
- 40°C
- 40°C with bar—synthetics wash
- 40°C with broken bar—wool wash

- hand wash only symbol
- chlorine may be used
- do not use chlorine

## Ironing
- hot iron
- warm iron
- cool iron

## Dry cleaning
- must be professionally cleaned
- do not dry-clean

## Dryer
- may be tumble dried
- dry on high heat setting
- dry on low heat setting
- do not tumble dry

**Q:** 'I washed a spandex/viscose top in warm water', says Rhonda. 'But I accidentally used the fast spin on the washing machine. It's now stretched about two sizes bigger. Can I possibly shrink it back to the right size?'

## The Laundry

**Problem:** **Stretched synthetic fabric.**
**What to use:** **Methylated spirits.**
**How to apply:** Soak the garment in methylated spirits for 20 minutes, remove and squeeze but don't wring out. Dry flat in the shade. Most synthetic fibres have a memory and return to their original shape. When dry, wash normally using a gentle spin.

**TIP** When trying to get a whiter than white look, many people reach for bleach. But most bleaches and mould-removal products simply whiten the mould rather than kill the spores that allow mould to grow. A better option is to use oil of cloves, which kills mould spores.

## Q: 'I get a sudsy residue on dark clothes when washed in my washing machine', reports Annabelle. 'What's wrong?'

**Problem:** **Soap residue on clothes.**
**What to use:** **Less washing detergent; or repairer.**
**How to apply:** A sudsy residue on clothes could mean you're using too much washing detergent, the lint filter hasn't been cleared or something is wrong with your washing machine. Try using one-third less washing detergent and clean the lint filter. If the problem persists, water may not be entering the

washing machine at the right rate and you'll need to consult a repairer.

**Q:** 'I've got black tar in my washing machine', complains Jenny. 'It came from my son's work clothes. What can I do?'

|  |  |
|---|---|
| **Problem:** | **Tar in washing machine.** |
| **What to use:** | **Baby oil, pantyhose, talcum powder.** |
| **How to apply:** | Wipe the tar with a dab of baby oil on pantyhose. When it softens, puff some talcum powder over the top. Rub with clean pantyhose and the tar will come away in little balls. |

**Q:** 'I didn't hang my washing out right away', reports Mandy. 'Apart from being a bit smelly, my daughter's cream-coloured shirt has mouldy spots on it. Can it be fixed?'

|  |  |
|---|---|
| **Problem:** | **Mouldy spots on cotton.** |
| **What to use:** | **Warm water, NapiSan Plus; or non-iodised salt, water, 9 litre bucket, brush.** |
| **How to apply:** | Soak in warm water and NapiSan Plus for 20 minutes. If any mould remains, combine 1 kg of non-iodised salt with a bucket of water and soak the shirt in the solution overnight. Remove, gently wring (but don't rinse) and hang in the sun to dry. A salt crust will form as |

it dries. Brush the salt off and the mould will come with it. Wash and dry normally.

# TOWELS

We're constantly asked at Stain Clinics how to make towels less scratchy. One of the main reasons they become scratchy is washing detergent residue. To fix, add ½ cup of bicarb to the washing detergent and ½ cup of white vinegar to the fabric conditioner slot. If towels have become yellow with age, add ¼ cup of lemon juice to your normal wash and hang in the sun to dry.

**Q:** 'I perform massages and use white towels', says Ngaire. 'What's the best way to remove massage oils from them?'

    **Problem:** **Massage oil on towels.**
**What to use:** **Dishwashing liquid; or bucket, warm water, dishwashing liquid, tea tree oil.**
**How to apply:** Place a couple of drops of dishwashing liquid on the oil stain and rub with your fingers until it feels like jelly. Wash normally. If the stain is substantial, get a large bucket (big enough for you to get your feet in) and fill with warm water and 2 teaspoons of dishwashing liquid. If the oils are dense, add 1 teaspoon of tea tree oil to the mixture. Place the towels in the bucket, put your feet inside and stomp up and down. Tip the entire contents of the bucket into the

washing machine and wash normally. The stains will be removed and your feet will be nice and clean as well!

**(TIP)** It's best not to use orange oil to remove oil stains because over time, the orange oil can leave a residue and stain if not completely rinsed out. Instead, place a couple of drops of dishwashing liquid on your fingers and massage into the oil. Wash and dry normally.

# SINK

**Q:** 'I have a plastic laundry tub', says Bob. 'And it's got a blue-green stain on it. Can it be removed?'

**Problem:** **Stained plastic.**
**What to use:** **Glycerine, talcum powder, pantyhose, damp cloth.**
**How to apply:** Mix glycerine and talcum powder to form a paste the consistency of runny cream. Polish the stain with a pair of pantyhose and repeat until removed. Wipe with a damp cloth.

# HAND WASHING

It doesn't take much more effort to hand wash your more delicate clothes and they'll thank you for it. First, spot clean any stains. Then fill a laundry tub or bucket with blood-heat water and add a small quantity of cheap shampoo. Gently wash the garment by hand and leave for around 10–20 minutes to soak; any longer and the fibres will reabsorb the dirt and the cold water will strain delicate fibres. Then rinse in clean blood-heat water. The temperature of the rinse water must be the same as the temperature of the wash water. Remove the rinse water by placing the garments in the washing machine and using the spin cycle. Either hang the garments on the clothesline or lay them flat on a towel in the shade to dry. Avoid using the dryer if you can. If it's raining, use a clothes drying rack or hang the items from a coat-hanger in the bathroom.

**TIP** If you hand wash after gardening, you'll clean your hands and clear your pores as well.

# DRY-CLEANING

It's common for clothing manufacturers to include a 'dry-clean only' label so they're not liable for any damage but some of the garments sent to the dry-cleaner can be hand washed. The exception is structured or tailored clothing which should go to a dry-cleaner because of the shape of the garment. With fabrics such as rayon, silk or viscose, test first by rubbing a wet cotton bud into a seam and leaving it to dry. If the fabric crinkles, it can't be hand washed because the fabric will shrink. Be careful with darker coloured rayon, silk and viscose garments which may lose colour if hand washed. You can hand wash wool, linen, cashmere and cotton.

## HANGING OUT THE WASHING

Keep this in mind when hanging out the washing: if you hang your clothes as flat as possible, you'll have less ironing to do because there'll be fewer creases. Keep the clothes basket at waist height and store pegs beside the basket. Don't leave pegs on the clothesline because UV light and rain cause them to deteriorate. Hang each item by the strongest section of the garment: trousers and skirts should be hung from the waistband; shirts should be hung from the tails and pegged on the side seams or hung on a coat-hanger. Woollens are best dried flat on a white towel.

## TUMBLE DRYING

Apartment living means many people don't have a clothesline and use a clothes dryer instead but it's better for clothes to be dried naturally. Drying racks are cheap to buy and easy to put up and down. If you do use the dryer, make sure you remove any lint and don't allow clothes to become bone dry or they'll be stiff.

If you get a dry powdery build-up in the lint catcher or around the seals on the dryer or across dried clothes, this is excess soap, which indicates that the rinse cycle on the washing machine isn't working properly. Reduce the amount of washing detergent you use by one-third and add ½ cup of white vinegar in the fabric conditioner slot.

The Laundry

# IRONING

It's hard to imagine a time when irons had to be heated on the stove before being used; now, they're Teflon coated and super steaming with multiple functions. Some are even smart enough to turn themselves off if you forget. We can't wait for the day when they can do the ironing by themselves.

Before you begin ironing, consult the care label on the garment and set the iron to the correct temperature. Begin ironing clothes that require the least amount of heat and work your way up—that way you avoid scorching your clothes.

As a general rule, iron the least important part of the garment first because you're more likely to crease that part as you move the garment around. Iron the most important part last—the part that people see the most. If you're in a hurry, fill a spray pack with 1 litre of water and 1 teaspoon of lavender oil and mist over your clothes before you put them on. Shannon loves using this technique: it removes creases—and it keeps mozzies and flies away.

If there are white flecks coming out of your iron, that's aluminium oxide. To fix, pour a weak tea solution—1 tea bag in 1 cup of warm water left to steep for 30 seconds—or equal parts white vinegar and water into the iron. Turn the iron on and press the steam button until the liquid has worked through the iron. Add clean water and continue to press the steam function until the iron sprays clean water. To prevent this problem, remove water from your iron after using it. If the holes are blocked, add 2 drops of CLR or Ranex to the water, turn the iron on, hold it horizontally and push the steam button down. Rinse with clean water.

SPOTLESS 2

If clothes become shiny from ironing, immerse a clean white cloth in white vinegar, wring out well and place over the shiny area. Run a cool iron over the top. This also gives clothes a quick spruce up if they've been in the cupboard for too long.

If you scorch clothes while ironing, immerse a clean cloth in 3 per cent hydrogen peroxide, wring out tightly, place over the mark and iron on a cool setting.

**Q:** 'I've got an iron mark that's stiff and shiny on my polyamide/elastane trousers', says Leonie. 'What can I do?'

| | |
|---|---|
| **Problem:** | **Iron melt.** |
| **What to use:** | **Cotton cloth, white vinegar, iron.** |
| **How to apply:** | Hopefully the fibres are melted rather than burnt. Immerse a cloth in white vinegar, wring out and place over the area. Use a cool iron over the top. If the mark won't come out, it's permanently damaged. To save the garment, soak a piece of cotton corduroy in white vinegar, place over the garment, cord side down, and apply a hot iron. This creates a ridging pattern over the fabric which covers the scorch mark. |

**Q:** 'I've got a burn stain on my iron', says Josie. 'It looks like black muck. How can I get it off?'

| | |
|---|---|
| **Problem:** | **Burn on iron.** |
| **What to use:** | **Old towel, pantyhose, bicarb, white vinegar.** |

**How to apply:** Turn the iron off and allow to cool. Put an old towel over your ironing board and pull a pair of pantyhose over the end of the ironing board until taut. Sprinkle bicarb on the pantyhose and spray the surface of the iron with white vinegar. Wipe the cold iron over the pantyhose. Repeat if necessary.

## LINEN PRESS

**Q:** 'I have a collection of my mother's 70-year-old hand-embroidered linen doilies and tea towels', says Lynda. 'Some have dark rust-coloured spots on them. Can they be removed?'

**Problem: Rust-coloured stains on old linen.**

**What to use: Non-iodised salt, lemon juice, sunshine.**

**How to apply:** Place a little mountain of salt over each spot and squeeze drops of lemon juice on top until the salt is just moistened. Leave in the sunshine to dry. Repeat if necessary. This can take up to 2 days but is a gentle solution that won't damage the fabric.

**Prevention:** Store items in acid-free paper or wrapped in an old cotton sheet. Add a couple of white chalk sticks to absorb moisture.

SPOTLESS 2

**Q:** 'I must have put a damp towel in the linen cupboard', says Gail. 'I think the mould spores must still be on the shelf. How do I fix it?'

**Problem:** Mould on towels in linen press.

**What to use:** **Non-iodised salt, water, 9 litre bucket, stiff brush (towels); oil of cloves, water (shelves), 1 litre spray pack.**

**How to apply:** Mix 1 kg of salt with a bucket of water, add the towels and leave overnight to soak. Remove, gently wring (but don't rinse) and hang the towels on the clothesline. When dry, they'll be covered in a salt crust. Brush away the crust with a stiff brush. Wash the towels normally. To remove the mould spores from the shelves, put ¼ teaspoon of oil of cloves into a spray pack of water and lightly spray the shelves. Leave for 24 hours before wiping and re-stacking.

**TIP** If there's rising damp in the rear wall of the linen press or the linen is sweating from lack of ventilation, place a tub of silicone crystals or a bouquet of white chalk sticks on the shelves.

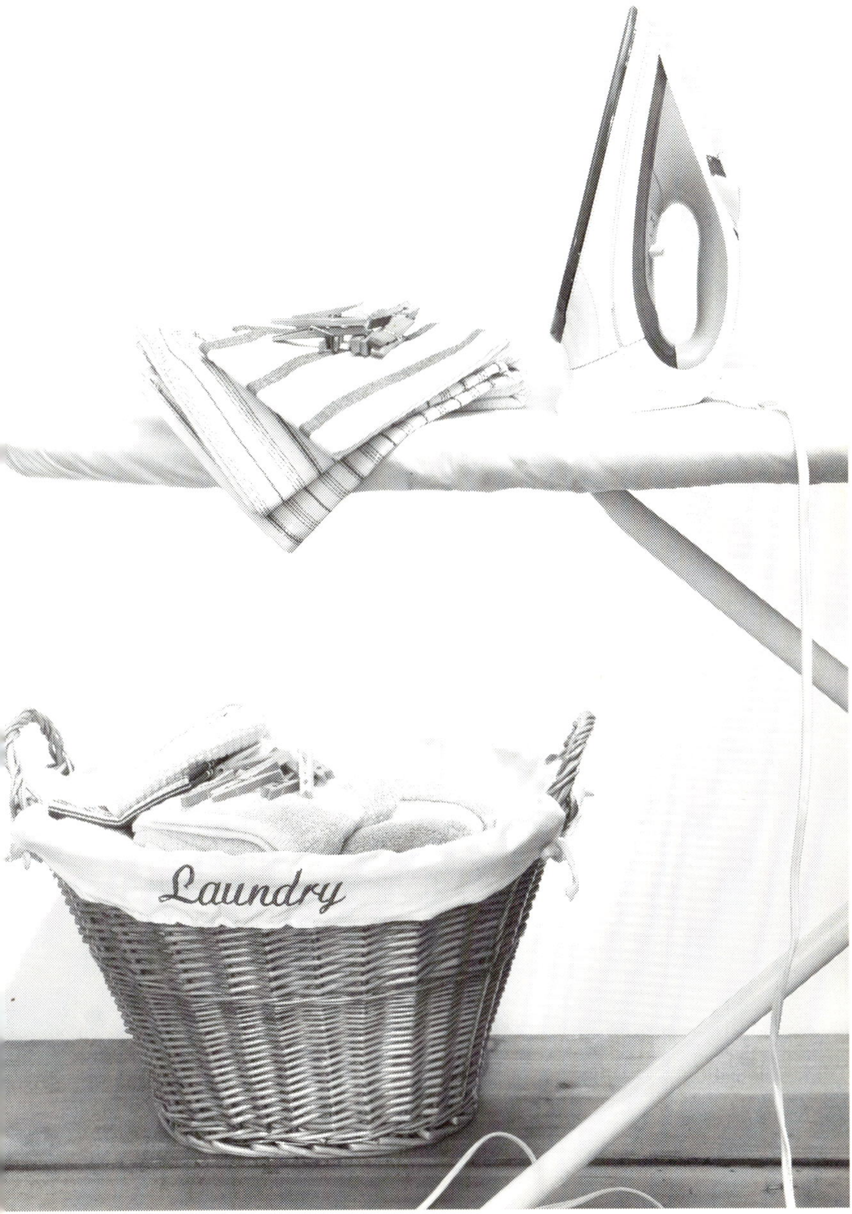
Laundry

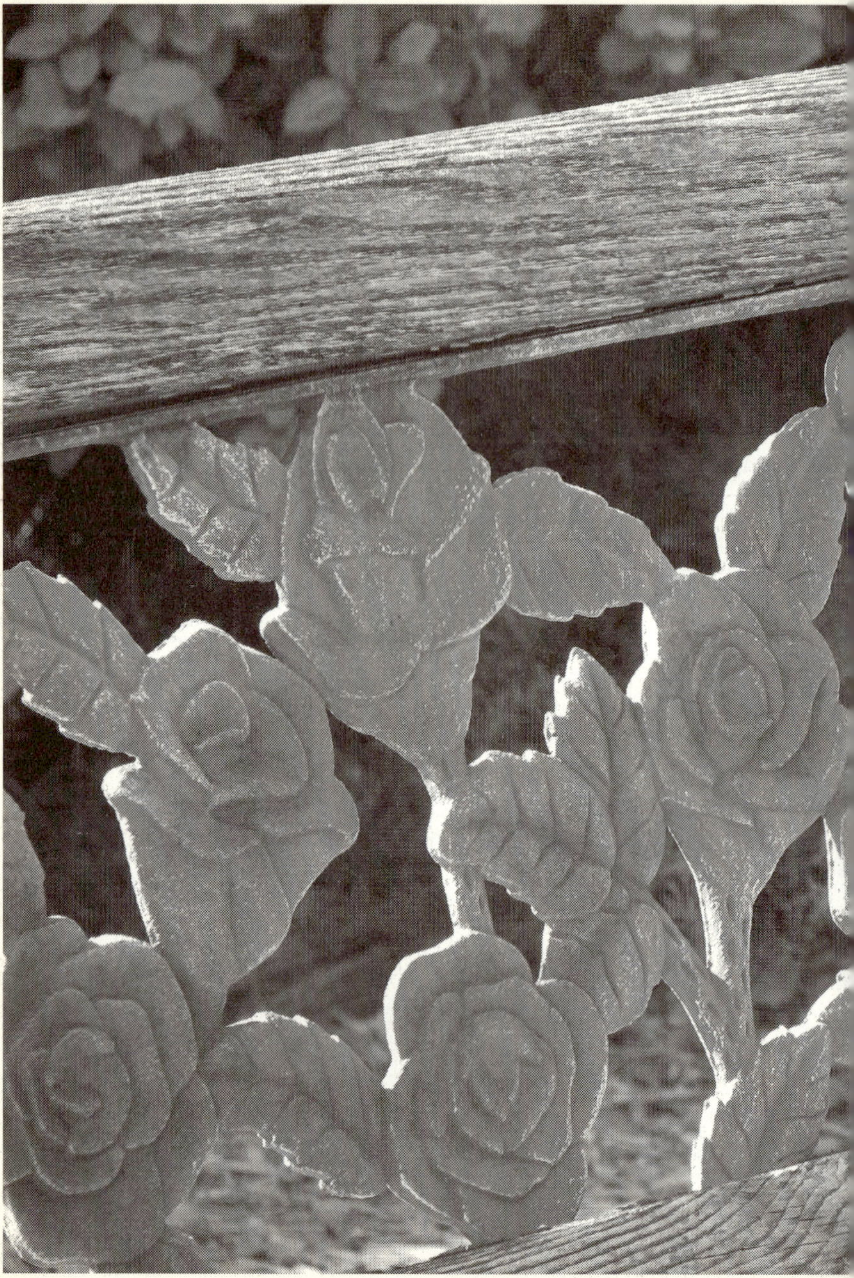

# Outside

The backyard is generally a place for fun, be it hosting a barbie, digging about in the garden, jumping on the trampoline or kicking around a soccer ball. But there's also work to do including hanging out the washing, cleaning up after the barbie, mowing the lawn, sweeping the paths, looking after the compost and maintaining the pool. You might have to remove accidental spills from the car, caravan or boat as well. After dealing with spills and stains, you'll be able to enjoy many a relaxing hour in your patch of paradise.

## RASCALLY RABBITS: Kylie's story

**INCIDENT:** 'We live on the edge of bushland and love the tranquillity. But our deck has become a bit of a haven for rabbits. The particular problem is rabbit urine staining the timber. How can we get it out?'

**SOLUTION:** Remove by scrubbing with white vinegar on a stiff brush. If the urine has penetrated into the timber, mix plaster of Paris and water to form a paste the consistency of peanut butter. For each cup of mixture, add 2 teaspoons of white vinegar. Place a 1 cm thick layer over the stain. Leave to completely dry and brush away with a broom.

# TIMBER DECKING

Hold on to your old tea bags. Black tea is great to clean unsealed timber because the tannins in tea react with the tannins in timber and restore colour. Place 2 cups of black tea in a 9 litre bucket of warm water and sweep over the surface with a stiff broom. You can also clean unsealed timber with 1 cup of white vinegar and ½ teaspoon of eucalyptus oil in a 9 litre bucket of water. If the timber is sealed, put 1 teaspoon of dishwashing liquid into a 9 litre bucket of warm water, sweep the surface with a stiff broom, then rinse with water. Don't use dishwashing liquid on unsealed timber because it will dry it out.

SPOTLESS 2

**Q:** 'The oil surface on my 3-year-old pine timber decking has gone black and grimy', admits Bob. 'How can I clean it?'

    **Problem:** **Dirty timber.**

**What to use:** **Dishwashing liquid, black tea, warm water, 9 litre bucket, stiff broom.**

**How to apply:** Mix 1 teaspoon of dishwashing liquid and 1 cup of black tea in a bucket of warm water. Sweep the mixture over the timber with a broom. Rinse with water, then re-oil the timber.

**Q:** 'We love spending time on the outside deck', reports Paul. 'But so do some kookaburras. What's the best way to deal with kookaburra poo?'

    **Problem:** **Kookaburra poo on timber.**

**What to use:** **Stiff scrubbing brush, cake of bathroom soap, cold water, deck scrubber.**

**How to apply:** Kookaburras eat a lot of protein. Remove as much poo as possible with a brush. Rub a cake of bathroom soap and cold water over the bristles of a deck scrubber or brush and scrub over the stain. If the area is exposed to sunlight, shade it with an umbrella while you're cleaning because heat sets kookaburra poo. If the poo has penetrated the surface, you'll have to scrub for longer.

Outside

# CEMENT AND BRICK PAVERS

To clean pavers, sprinkle with a little bicarb followed by a little white vinegar. As the mixture fizzes, sweep with a stiff broom. If there's any mould, mix ¼ teaspoon of oil of cloves in a 1 litre spray pack of water and spray over the area. Respray after 24 hours.

Clean pathways with 2 cups of water and 1 tablespoon of dishwashing liquid in a bucket of sand. Mix thoroughly, spread over the path and sweep with a stiff broom. Collect the sand and reuse it.

**Q:** 'When it rained, our new spotted gum decking oozed brown stains on the sandstone coloured concrete composite pavers', reports Jamie. 'What can I do to fix this?'

|   |   |
|---|---|
| **Problem:** | **Brown stains on pavers.** |
| **What to use:** | **Glycerine, deck scrubber or stiff scrubbing brush, eucalyptus oil, old toothbrush, dishwashing liquid, 9 litre bucket, water.** |
| **How to apply:** | The brown stains are tannin marks and can be difficult to remove. Scrub with glycerine on a deck scrubber or brush, leave to soak for 20 minutes and scrub again. If there's gum sap (it looks shiny and resinous), remove with eucalyptus oil on a toothbrush. Add 1 teaspoon of dishwashing liquid to a bucket of water and |

SPOTLESS 2

scrub with a deck scrubber or stiff brush. Repeat if the stain remains. There is a proprietary product that removes stains from pavers which is available from hardware stores. Wear protective clothing when using it. Tannin stains become harder to remove with time so tackle them as soon as possible.

**TIP** If there are gum leaf stains, use eucalyptus oil on an old toothbrush to remove them.

**Q:** 'I've got oil and petrol from a lawnmower that's leaked onto pavers and stained them', reports Sam. 'How do I remove them?'

**Problem:** **Oil and petrol on pavers.**
**What to use:** **Plaster of Paris, water, dishwashing liquid, broom.**
**How to apply:** Mix plaster of Paris and water to form a paste the consistency of peanut butter. For every cup of mixture add 1 teaspoon of dishwashing liquid and stir. Spread a 1 cm thick layer over the stains and leave to dry. Sweep away with a broom; the oil and petrol will be absorbed into the mixture.

Outside

**Q:** 'I've got cooking oil on my brick pavers', reports Keith. 'How can I get it out?'

    **Problem:** **Cooking oil on pavers.**
  **What to use:** **Plaster of Paris, water, dishwashing liquid, broom.**
  **How to apply:** Mix plaster of Paris and water to form a paste the consistency of peanut butter. For every cup of mixture, add 1 teaspoon of dishwashing liquid. Place a 1 cm thick layer over the stain and leave to dry. Sweep away with a broom.

**Q:** 'Our umbrella stand has left rust marks on our pavers', reports Rachel. 'How can I get it out?'

    **Problem:** **Rust on pavers.**
  **What to use:** **Talcum powder, disposable rubber gloves, CLR/Ranex, water.**
  **How to apply:** Cover the rust with a sprinkle of talcum powder and, wearing rubber gloves, moisten the powder with CLR or Ranex. Leave for 2 hours and rinse with water. You may need to repeat.

    **Problem:** **Bore water stain on brick.**
  **What to use:** **White vinegar, water, bucket, stiff broom.**

SPOTLESS 2

**How to apply:** Because bore water is high in mineral salts, it causes white marks on bricks. To remove, mix equal parts white vinegar and water in a bucket. Sweep over the bore water stain with a broom.

# Q: 'Help!' exclaims Michael. 'Eggs were thrown on the front brick wall of our home. How do we remove them?'

**Problem:** **Egg on brick.**
**What to use:** **Cake of bathroom soap, stiff brush, cold water, glycerine.**
**How to apply:** If you get to it before the egg fries, rub a cake of bathroom soap and cold water over a stiff brush and scrub over the egg until it's removed. Don't use dishwashing liquid or spray products. If the egg has set, wipe with glycerine on a stiff brush. Leave for 20 minutes. Then use a cake of bathroom soap, cold water and a stiff brush as described above.

**TIP** Don't use hydrochloric acid as a cleaner. It strips the top surface and leaves orangey marks. If you have used it, neutralise with equal parts bicarb and water.

Outside

# GLAZED TILES

To clean tiles, lightly sprinkle with bicarb, spray with white vinegar and, while fizzing, scrub with a broom. Don't overuse the bicarb and vinegar or you'll get residue. If you do, wipe with a clean damp cloth.

**Q:** 'What's the best way to remove bark and eucalyptus leaf stains from ceramic patio tiles?' asks Jim.

| | |
|---|---|
| **Problem:** | **Bark and leaf stains on tiles.** |
| **What to use:** | **Glycerine, broom, dishwashing liquid, 9 litre bucket, water; eucalyptus oil.** |
| **How to apply:** | This is a tannin stain. Apply a little glycerine directly to the stain and scrub with a broom. Add 1 teaspoon of dishwashing liquid to a bucket of water and sweep backwards and forwards over the stain with a broom. If the leaves are eucalyptus, add 1 tablespoon of eucalyptus oil to the solution. |

# UNSEALED TILES

**Q:** 'Our outside balcony has unsealed matt black ceramic tiles', says Neil. 'But some of the tiles are turning white-ish. The house is near the coast so there's salt in the air. Any suggestions?'

SPOTLESS 2

**Problem:** White marks on tiles.
**What to use:** White vinegar, stiff broom; or sweet almond oil, stiff broom, cloth; tile sealer.
**How to apply:** The white markings could be from salt, lime scale build-up or glass cancer. If it's from salt or lime scale, wash with white vinegar on a broom. If this doesn't work, it's glass cancer, which means the surface has been damaged. To deal with this, wipe with sweet almond oil on a stiff broom and polish with a cloth. Seal with a good quality tile sealer.

# CONCRETE

**Q:** 'How can I remove battery rust stain from my concrete driveway?' asks Rob.

**Problem:** Rust on concrete.
**What to use:** White vinegar, deck scrubber or stiff broom, disposable rubber gloves, CLR/Ranex, water.
**How to apply:** To remove battery acid (which is actually an alkaline), scrub with white vinegar on a deck scrubber or broom. Put on rubber gloves and sweep with CLR or Ranex on a broom and rinse with water.

Outside

**Problem:** **Fluorescent float paint on concrete.**
**What to use:** **Non-iodised salt, water, cloth, ice-cubes, zip-lock bag, cake of bathroom soap, broom.**
**How to apply:** Mix 1 cup of salt with 1 cup of water and apply with a cloth. Place ice-cubes in a zip-lock bag and put on top of the stain and leave until the ice melts. Remove and rub a cake of bathroom soap over the bristles of a broom, add water and scrub over the stain. Repeat until removed.

# SLATE

**Q:** 'I've got slate tiles', says Harry. 'What's the best way to clean them?'

**Problem:** **Dirty slate.**
**What to use:** **Bicarb, white vinegar, broom, water, non-iodised salt, marble wax.**
**How to apply:** Sprinkle on bicarb, followed by white vinegar and scrub with a broom, then rinse thoroughly with water. If mouldy, add 1 cup of salt to the rinse water. Seal with marble wax.

# STONE

**Q:** 'It looks as though wax has been splashed over my mother's headstone', reports Valda. 'It's gone into the granite and left a grease mark on the stone about the size of a hand. Can you help?'

**Problem:** **Wax on granite.**

**What to use:** **Tea tree oil, pantyhose, Brasso, cloth.**

**How to apply:** Scrub the wax stains with tea tree oil on a pair of pantyhose. You may need to repeat if the wax returns to the surface. If there are watermarks, rub with a little Brasso on a cloth. It will look worse before it looks better.

**Q:** 'How do you remove graffiti on white marble?' asks Stephen.

**Problem:** **Graffiti on marble.**

**What to use:** **White spirits, pantyhose; or plaster of Paris, methylated spirits; or rotten milk, damp cloth.**

**How to apply:** If the graffiti was applied with Texta, oil-based paint or spray paint, use white spirits polished on and off with a pair of pantyhose. If the graffiti is from water-based paint, mix plaster of Paris and water to the consistency of peanut butter. For every cup of mixture, add 1 teaspoon of methylated spirits. Paint a 1 cm thick layer over the stain and allow to dry then brush away. If the graffiti is ink-based, place rotten milk solids over the stain. The ink will be absorbed into the solids. Remove and wipe clean with a damp cloth.

# METAL

**Q:** 'My powder-coated railings have become white and dullish', reports Alan. 'What can I do?'

**Problem:** **Dull powder-coated rails.**
**What to use:** **White vinegar, water, 2 x 1 litre spray packs, cloth, sunblock lotion, warm water.**
**How to apply:** The dullness is from sun damage. Mix equal parts white vinegar and water in a spray pack, spray over the stain and wipe with a cloth. Add 1 tablespoon of sunblock to a spray pack of warm water and lightly mist over the rail. The sunblock lotion protects the railing from further sun damage.

**Problem:** **Bird droppings on wrought iron.**
**What to use:** **Glycerine, white vinegar, cold water, bucket, deck scrubber or stiff scrubbing brush, cake of bathroom soap.**

SPOTLESS 2

**How to apply:** Mix 1 teaspoon of glycerine, 1 teaspoon of white vinegar and 1 cup of cold water in a bucket. Scrub the mixture over the stains with a deck scrubber or brush and allow to dry. Rub a cake of bathroom soap over a deck scrubber or brush, dampen with cold water and scrub over the stain. Bird droppings are high in protein so use only cold water.

# OUTDOOR FURNITURE

Most outdoor furniture is built to withstand the elements but, as with skin, it starts to look a bit shabby if damaged by the sun. When not in use, store underneath an umbrella or veranda. See page 213 of *Spotless* for instructions on how to clean different finishes.

**Q:** 'There's some salad dressing on our oil-finished table', says Sandra. 'And I'm finding it difficult to remove. What can I do?'

**Problem:** **Salad dressing on oil-finished timber.**
**What to use:** **Plaster of Paris, water, dishwashing liquid, broom, cold black tea, cloth.**
**How to apply:** Mix plaster of Paris and water to form a paste the consistency of peanut butter. For each cup of paste add 1 teaspoon of dishwashing liquid. Cover the stain with a 1 cm thick layer of paste, allow to dry and brush off with a broom. Before

re-oiling, wipe the timber with cold black tea on a cloth and allow to dry.

## Q: 'Over time, the white vinyl cushions on our outdoor setting have turned a red-brown colour', says Lisa. 'Is there anything you would recommend to clean them?'

**Problem:** **Stained white vinyl.**

**What to use:** **CLR/Ranex, water, cloth, disposable rubber gloves; or glycerine, talcum powder, cloth.**

**How to apply:** The stain could be from mineral discolouration or sun damage. If it's been caused by mineral discolouration, wearing disposable rubber gloves, mix 1 part CLR or Ranex to 5 parts water, place on a cloth and wipe over the stains. If it's been caused by sun damage, it's difficult to repair. Reduce the staining by polishing with a paste of equal parts glycerine and talcum powder applied with a cloth. Rub off with a cloth.

**Prevention:** Keep outdoor cushions under cover when not using them.

## Q: 'We were entertaining outside', says Sally. 'And managed to get both red wine and citronella candle wax on a cotton tablecloth. What can be done?'

| | |
|---|---|
| **Problem:** | **Red wine and wax on cotton.** |
| **What to use:** | **White vinegar, cloth, glycerine (red wine); freezer/ice-cubes, zip-lock bag, plastic knife, paper towel, iron, tea tree oil (wax).** |
| **How to apply:** | Remove the wine stain first by wiping with a cloth wrung out in white vinegar. If the stain is stubborn, add 2 drops of glycerine directly to the stain, leave for 20 minutes, then wipe with white vinegar on a cloth. To remove the wax, place the tablecloth in the freezer. If it won't fit in the freezer, put ice-cubes in a zip-lock bag and place over the wax. When the wax is cold, remove as much as possible with a plastic knife. Put several layers of paper towel on either side of the stain and run a hot iron over the top. Repeat until all the wax is absorbed into the paper towel. If a greasy mark remains, wipe on tea tree oil with your fingers, then wash normally. |

# UMBRELLAS, AWNINGS AND SHADE CLOTH

The main issue with umbrellas, awnings and shade cloth is mould. To remove it, see *Spotless*, pages 214–15.

# BARBECUES

We know it's the last thing you want to do, but it's important to clean your barbecue after each use—a grotty barbecue doesn't produce tasty food. Before firing it up, sprinkle sand over pavers around the barbecue to absorb any oil splatter. If you do get oil splatter, see page 327. Also see pages 215–16 in *Spotless* for instructions on how to clean your barbie.

**TIP** Spread barbecue ash around plants such as azaleas, camellias or citrus. They love it.

# FLYSCREENS

Flyscreens keep bugs out of your home but they can be dirt traps too, so clean removable ones on both sides with a vacuum cleaner using the brush attachment and wipe with lemon oil to keep spiders at bay.

To clean fixed screens, close the window or door, dampen the screen with water and sweep with a soft broom. With soft flyscreens, use a Slurpex instead of a broom.

To fix a ripped flyscreen, see page 250 in *How To Be Comfy*.

# UNDER AND AROUND THE HOUSE

**Q:** 'I live in an old house', says Renee. 'When we have lots of rain, the house smells like wet carpet and is musty. How can I prevent the musty smell?'

SPOTLESS 2

> **Problem:** **Musty smell in house.**
> **What to use:** **Bicarb, lavender oil, oil of cloves, water, 1 litre spray pack, long-nozzled spray pack.**
> **How to apply:** The smell is from mould spores in the soil under the house. If you have carpet, sprinkle with bicarb before vacuuming. Add 1 teaspoon of lavender oil and ¼ teaspoon of oil of cloves to a spray pack of water and lightly mist over the carpet. Leave for 10 minutes and vacuum. If you can, pull up the carpet and replace it with floorboards. To get under the house, use a long-nozzled spray pack and add ¼ teaspoon of oil of cloves per litre of water. Spray through the vents at the side of the house to reach the soil underneath.

# Q: 'We get our water directly from the river', reports Stuart. 'At the moment, the water has blue-green algae in it which has stained our vinyl-clad house. The cladding is a cream vinyl with a woodwork groove mark in the texture.'

> **Problem:** **Blue-green algae on vinyl cladding.**
> **What to use:** **Bicarb, water, cloth, methylated spirits, glycerine, white vinegar, water, 1 litre spray pack; 3 per cent hydrogen peroxide, pantyhose, broom.**

Outside

**How to apply:** Mix equal parts bicarb and water and wipe with a cloth. Combine 1 cup of methylated spirits, 1 teaspoon of glycerine, 1 cup of white vinegar and 2 cups of water in a spray pack. Spray the mixture over the bicarb and, while fizzing, wipe with a cloth. If there's grey staining, add 1 teaspoon of 3 per cent hydrogen peroxide to the spray pack. For a large area, put pantyhose over the head of a broom and scrub the area after it's been sprayed with the mixture.

*(TIP)* When cleaning hard-to-reach light bulbs, place a paper cup over the end of a broom handle and secure with masking tape. Place paper towel inside the cup and wipe over light bulbs.

# SPORT AND CAMPING

Many people have exercise bikes and treadmills at home and you can get your heart-rate up just cleaning them. Wipe regularly with a damp cloth, clean plastic surfaces with a little glycerine on a cloth and wipe rubber in a salt solution (1 cup of salt per 9 litre bucket of water) on a cloth.

**Q:** 'How do I remove mould on leather boxing gloves?' asks Alicia.

**Problem: Mould on leather.**
**What to use: Oil of cloves, baby oil, cloth.**

**How to apply:** Mix ¼ teaspoon of oil of cloves and 1 tablespoon of baby oil, dab a little on a cloth and rub over the gloves. Save the mixture for next time.

## Q: 'My white soccer boots are now covered in black stud marks', say Frank. 'Can I get the marks off?'

**Problem:** **Black marks on leather.**

**What to use:** **Glycerine, pantyhose, damp pantyhose.**

**How to apply:** Wipe a dab of glycerine over the marks with rolled up pantyhose. Remove with clean damp pantyhose.

## Q: 'Our tennis court has synthetic grass', reports Anne. 'And there are big patches of mould in all the corners. What do you suggest?'

**Problem:** **Mould on synthetic grass.**

**What to use:** **Swimming pool chlorine tablet, 9 litre bucket, warm water, stiff broom.**

**How to apply:** Wear protective clothing and be careful not to splash the mixture on your clothes. Add ¼ tablet of swimming pool chlorine to a bucket of warm water and allow to dissolve completely. Rub the mouldy area with a broom and leave for 15 minutes. Rinse with water. Don't use oil of cloves on synthetic grass because it can break it down.

Outside

**Q:** 'Flying fox poo landed on my new canvas tent', says Nathan. 'What should I do?'

**Problem:** **Flying fox poo on canvas.**
**What to use:** **Cake of bathroom soap, cold water, stiff scrubbing brush; non-iodised salt, 9 litre bucket, water, cloth.**
**How to apply:** Flying fox poo is high in tannins and protein. Remove by dipping a cake of bathroom soap in cold water, rub over the bristles of stiff brush and scrub. When the stain is removed, make the canvas waterproof by mixing 1 cup of salt in a bucket of water. Wipe the salt solution over the canvas with a cloth.

**Q:** 'On a recent camping holiday, I got diesel on my swag', says Ron. 'What do you suggest?'

**Problem:** **Diesel on swag.**
**What to use:** **Methylated spirits, cloth, bath, blood-heat water, dishwashing liquid, salt, sunshine.**
**How to apply:** Wipe the stain with methylated spirits on a cloth. Fill a bath with blood-heat water and 2 teaspoons of dishwashing liquid. Place the swag in the bath and walk up and down on it. Add 1 cup of salt to the water. Rinse in blood-heat water and dry in sunshine. Turn regularly to prevent clumping in the swag padding.

SPOTLESS 2

# WATER FEATURES

**Q:** 'I have a glazed fountain', says David. 'And there's water staining on it. What should I do?'

> **Problem:** **Water stain on glazed fountain.**
> **What to use:** **Bicarb, white vinegar, nylon brush.**
> **How to apply:** Remove water from the fountain, sprinkle with equal parts bicarb then white vinegar and, while fizzing, scrub with a nylon brush. Refill fountain with water.

**Q:** 'My water feature has a brown stain on it', reports Kelvin. 'How can I get it off?'

> **Problem:** **Brown stain on water feature.**
> **What to use:** **Glycerine, eucalyptus oil, old toothbrush.**
> **How to apply:** It's likely to be a tannin stain from gum leaves. Remove water from the water feature. Mix 1 teaspoon of glycerine with ½ teaspoon of eucalyptus oil and scrub the marks with a toothbrush until removed.

**Q:** 'We've got a fibreglass baptismal font at our church', reports Ken. 'How can I clean the rust water marks from it?'

> **Problem:** **Rust on fibreglass.**

Outside

**What to use:** **Bicarb, white vinegar, old toothbrush; or glycerine, Gumption, old toothbrush.**

**How to apply:** Sprinkle with a little bicarb followed by a little white vinegar (equal parts) and, while fizzing, rub with a toothbrush. If the stain is really stubborn, mix equal parts glycerine with Gumption and scrub with a toothbrush.

## Q: 'How do I remove algae from a birdbath?' asks Val.

**Problem:** **Algae in birdbath.**

**What to use:** **Pantyhose, non-iodised salt.**

**How to apply:** Remove water from the birdbath, then wipe over the algae with a rolled up pair of pantyhose. To prevent the problem, add a pinch of salt to each litre of clean water. The birds won't be deterred by the tiny amount of salt.

# SWIMMING POOL AND SPA

## Q: 'We've got a fibreglass-lined pool', reports Tony. 'And there are rust marks. What can we do?'

**Problem:** **Rust marks on fibreglass.**

**What to use:** **Biro eraser, disposable rubber gloves, CLR/Ranex, cloth.**

SPOTLESS 2

**How to apply:** Rub the rust with a biro eraser. If this doesn't work, you'll need to empty the pool and, wearing rubber gloves, apply CLR or Ranex to the rust with a cloth.

*(TIP)* If there's sunblock clogging the spa filter, backflush with white vinegar.

# PETS

We know it's obvious, but make sure pet bedding is kept clean. Food bowls are easier to clean if you wipe them with a little cheap cooking oil on a cloth. Regularly change kitty litter and wipe the tray with bicarb before replacing kitty litter.

**Q:** 'What's the best way to clean and deodorise a dog kennel?' asks Marina.

**Problem:** **Smelly dog kennel.**
**What to use:** **Oil of cloves, dried mint, hot water, 1 litre spray pack, pantyhose.**
**How to apply:** Mix ¼ teaspoon of oil of cloves, 2 tablespoons of dried mint and 1 litre of hot water. Allow to cool. Add to a spray pack and spray every surface. Wipe with pantyhose. The oil of cloves kills mould spores and the mint kills fleas. Do this once a month.

# PESTS

It's a bit harder to keep pests at bay in the outdoors. Here are some natural solutions to deter common barbecue stoppers.

### Mosquitoes

Lavender oil is a great mozzie deterrent. Add a few drops to a cloth and wipe around the chairs and table. Alternatively, place 1 teaspoon of lavender oil in a 1 litre spray pack of water and lightly mist around the area. You can also rub lavender oil directly over your wrists. Plant lavender, basil, pennyroyal, *Pelargonium citrosum* (citronella plant) and tansy around entertainment areas.

### Spiders

Spiders hate lemon oil. Add a couple of drops of lemon oil or rub the outside of a lemon over the head of a broom and sweep over areas where spiders lurk. Don't forget bins, shed shelves and tools. Repeat every 3 months. To access spiders under the house, mix ¼ teaspoon of lemon oil in a 1 litre spray pack of water and squirt through vents and access areas.

### Flies

To kill flies, put white or black pepper (not red or green) onto a piece of paper painted with sugar and water. The sugar attracts the flies and the pepper kills them. Pepper contains piperine which is a toxin to flies.

### Ants

Mix equal parts powdered borax and icing sugar for sweet ants or equal parts powdered borax and grated parmesan cheese for savoury ants. Or find the nest and pour boiling water down it.

**Warning:** Borax is toxic and should not be placed where children or pets could eat it.

### Snails/slugs

Wipe petroleum jelly (Vaseline) around areas where snails and slugs wander—they won't cross it. Renew every couple of months. Protect plants by crushing a clove of garlic in a 1 litre spray pack of water. Allow to steep for 2 hours, strain and spray over plants. To make a trap for snails, cut an orange in half, remove the flesh and half-fill the two orange skins with beer. The snails will be attracted by the beer, climb in and won't be able to get out.

### Fruit flies

Use a glass jar with a plastic or metal lid. Punch holes at 2 mm intervals on the lid and half fill the jar with 1 tablespoon of Vegemite and ½ cup of white vinegar. Tie string around the lip of the jar and hang from a tree or branch. Fruit flies are attracted to the yeast and acetic acid mix, fly into the jar through the holes and become trapped.

# SHED

When working in the shed, sweep up timber shavings and sawdust or you could be in for a nasty tumble. Remove glue and rust from tools and lightly wipe with machine oil. To remove sap and dirt from secateurs' blades, rub with lemon juice and an old cork coated in coarse non-iodised salt.

Outside

**TIP** Don't stand on electrical leads. Not only could you get a nasty shock, it damages the leads. Wear goggles, masks and gloves, when required.

# CARS

Cars are vulnerable to spills and stains especially if you allow food and drink in them. If you have to suddenly apply the brakes and that café latte goes all over the seat and floor, the milk will really begin to stink, so fix the spill as soon as you can.

**Q:** 'I managed to spill a cup of coffee in the car the other morning', says Bev. 'There's a nasty sour smell now.'

**Problem:** **Coffee spill in car.**

**What to use:** **Cake of bathroom soap, cold water, damp cloth, glycerine, cloth, talcum powder, vacuum cleaner.**

**How to apply:** Rub the stain with a cake of bathroom soap dipped in cold water, then wipe with a damp cloth. Rub with a dab of glycerine on a cloth and sprinkle with talcum powder. Allow to dry, then vacuum. The soap will remove the milk, the glycerine will remove the coffee and the talcum powder will absorb the glycerine.

SPOTLESS 2

**Q:** 'I need to change the electronic toll tag on my car window', says Arthur. 'And I can't remove the plastic base. What do you suggest?'

> **Problem:** Glue/plastic base on windscreen.
>
> **What to use:** Tea tree oil, thin screwdriver (or similar), heat gun.
>
> **How to apply:** Work tea tree oil into the glue at the back of the plastic base and leave for 24 hours. Carefully work a screwdriver behind the base and lever it away from the glass. If it doesn't come away, aim a heat gun over the plastic. Only use the heat gun in short bursts or you could crack your windscreen.

**Q:** 'Our newly acquired second-hand car has a very, very strong perfumed smell', reports Meredith. 'It's giving me migraines. What can I do?'

> **Problem:** Perfumed smell in car.
>
> **What to use:** Black tea, cold water, lavender oil, 1 litre spray pack, cloth, bicarb, vacuum cleaner, damp tea bag.
>
> **How to apply:** Mix 1 cup of cold black tea, 2 cups of cold water and ¼ teaspoon of lavender oil in a spray pack. Spray onto a cloth and wipe over hard surfaces. Lightly mist over the upholstery, dust with bicarb and leave for 20 minutes. Then vacuum

Outside

thoroughly. If the perfume has been absorbed into the air-conditioning and venting system, hang a damp tea bag near the air intake. Deodorisers are often placed under seats (or hung from the rear-vision mirror), so check there and remove them.

**Q:** 'What's the best way to remove the smell of cigarettes from a car?' asks David.

| | |
|---|---|
| **Problem:** | **Cigarette smell in car.** |
| **What to use:** | **Bicarb, vacuum cleaner, disposable rubber gloves, cigarette ash (yes, that's right), white vinegar, cloth, damp cloth.** |
| **How to apply:** | Sprinkle bicarb over the upholstery, leave for 20 minutes, then vacuum. Put on rubber gloves and mix equal parts cigarette ash and white vinegar. Wipe the mixture over hard surfaces with a cloth and wipe clean with a damp cloth. You'll also need to remove smoke from the air-conditioning and venting system. To clean the filtration mat, wash with equal parts cigarette ash and white vinegar, leave for 5 minutes and rinse thoroughly with water. Allow to dry before replacing. If you can't remove it, see a specialist for a replacement pad. |

SPOTLESS 2

**Q:** 'How can I clean sweaty stains from the fabric of my car seats?' asks Jo.

> **Problem:** **Sweat stains on car seats.**
> **What to use:** **Bran ball, vacuum cleaner.**
> **How to apply:** Make a bran ball (see page 85), rub back and forth across the seats to remove the stains, then vacuum.

**Q:** 'There's butter on the back seat of my car', says Debbie. 'How can I get it out?'

> **Problem:** **Butter in car.**
> **What to use:** **Dishwashing liquid, old toothbrush, damp cloth, paper towel.**
> **How to apply:** Put a couple of drops of dishwashing liquid on your fingers and massage into the stain until it feels like jelly. If the stain is stubborn, scrub with a toothbrush, wipe with a damp cloth and dry with paper towel.

**Q:** 'How do I fluff up woollen sheepskin car seat covers?' asks Jo.

> **Problem:** **Cleaning sheepskin car seat covers.**
> **What to use:** **Unprocessed wheat bran, pillowcase, stiff hairbrush; or cheap shampoo, tub, blood-heat water, stiff hairbrush; or bran ball.**

**How to apply:** Place 1 kg of unprocessed wheat bran in a pillowcase and add the sheepskin covers. Secure the top and give a really good shake. Remove the sheepskin covers from the pillowcase and shake out the bran. Brush covers with a hairbrush. If they won't fit in a pillowcase, wash in 1 teaspoon of shampoo in a tub of blood-heat water. Rinse in blood-heat water and dry in the shade. As they dry, brush with a hairbrush. If the car seat covers can't be removed, rub with a bran ball (see page 85).

**Q:** 'I'm a truck driver with a BigFoot ute', says Joe. 'What's the best way to clean alloy wheels?'

**Problem: Dirty alloy wheels.**

**What to use: Pantyhose, cold black tea.**

**How to apply:** Dip a pair of pantyhose in cold black tea and polish over the alloy.

*TIP* To make your windscreen wipers last longer, mix 1 cup of salt in a 9 litre bucket of hot water and immerse the wipers for 5 minutes. Allow to dry and wipe with a dab of glycerine on a cloth.

SPOTLESS 2

**Q:** 'How can I remove pizza smells from the car after collecting takeaway?' asks Brad.

  **Problem:**  **Pizza smell in car.**
 **What to use:**  **Bicarb, vacuum cleaner.**
 **How to apply:**  The smell is from an oily residue in the steam which is absorbed by the upholstery. To remove, sprinkle bicarb over the upholstery, leave for 20 minutes and vacuum. To avoid the problem, put the piping hot pizza box in a paper bag so the steam can't escape.

**Q:** 'How can I remove chocolate milk stains from my car seat?' asks Susie.

  **Problem:**  **Chocolate milk in car.**
 **What to use:**  **Cake of bathroom soap, cold water, old toothbrush, paper towel.**
 **How to apply:**  Dip a cake of bathroom soap in cold water and scribble over the stain as though using a crayon. Scrub with a toothbrush and dry with paper towel. Chocolate milk contains protein so use only cold water.

**Q:** 'A mouse died in the ventilation system of our car', reports Trudy. 'We removed the mouse but can't get rid of the terrible smell. Help!'

| | |
|---|---|
| **Problem:** | **Dead mouse smell in car.** |
| **What to use:** | **2 small containers or trays, bicarb, tea bag, lavender oil.** |
| **How to apply:** | This is a tough one! Keep the windows open (when you can). Fill 2 containers or trays with bicarb and place under the front seats of the car. Dampen a tea bag with lavender oil and hang in front of the air-conditioning intake vents. Replace each day until the smell goes. |

**Q:** 'There's flying fox poo on my garage roller door', reports Charlie. 'How can I get it off?'

| | |
|---|---|
| **Problem:** | **Flying fox poo on powder-coated steel.** |
| **What to use:** | **Dishwashing liquid, warm water, pantyhose, glycerine, cloth.** |
| **How to apply:** | Apply a couple of drops of dishwashing liquid and a little warm water to the stain with a pair of pantyhose. Follow by wiping with a dab of glycerine on a cloth. |

# CARAVANS AND BOATS

**Q:** 'How do I remove mould spots on orange synthetic life jackets?' asks Brad.

**Problem:** **Mouldy synthetic life jackets.**

**What to use:** **Non-iodised salt, 9 litre bucket, water, stiff brush.**

**How to apply:** Mix 1 kg of salt in a bucket of water, add jackets and soak for 20 minutes. Remove and give a good scrub with a brush. Leave to dry without rinsing the salt off. When dry, brush the salt crust away and the mould will come with it.

**Q:** 'I've got seagull droppings all over my canvas boat cover', complains Jeff. 'What can I do?'

**Problem:** **Seagull poo on canvas.**

**What to use:** **Cake of bathroom soap, cold water, stiff brush.**

**How to apply:** Dip a cake of bathroom soap in cold water and scribble over the stain as though using a crayon. Scrub with a brush and rinse in cold water.

Outside

**Q:** 'I've got black sediment coming out of the water tank in my campervan', says Karen. 'What can I do?'

> **Problem:** **Black sediment in water tank.**
>
> **What to use:** **Salt, 9 litre bucket, water, glycerine.**
>
> **How to apply:** Add ½ cup salt to a bucket of water and flush through the water tank. Combine ½ teaspoon of glycerine and a bucket of water, pour into the tank and leave for 12 hours. Empty and rinse with clean water.

**Q:** 'We recently purchased a second-hand caravan', reports Merv. 'The spare wheel was left on the vinyl floor for a long time and has left a mark. Can you help?'

> **Problem:** **Tyre mark on vinyl.**
>
> **What to use:** **Non-iodised salt, talcum powder, glycerine, old toothbrush, damp cloth.**
>
> **How to apply:** The colour from the tyre has leached into the vinyl floor. Mix 2 tablespoons of salt, 2 tablespoons of talcum powder and 1 tablespoon of glycerine and scrub into the stain with a toothbrush. Leave for 20 minutes, then remove with a damp cloth. Repeat if necessary.

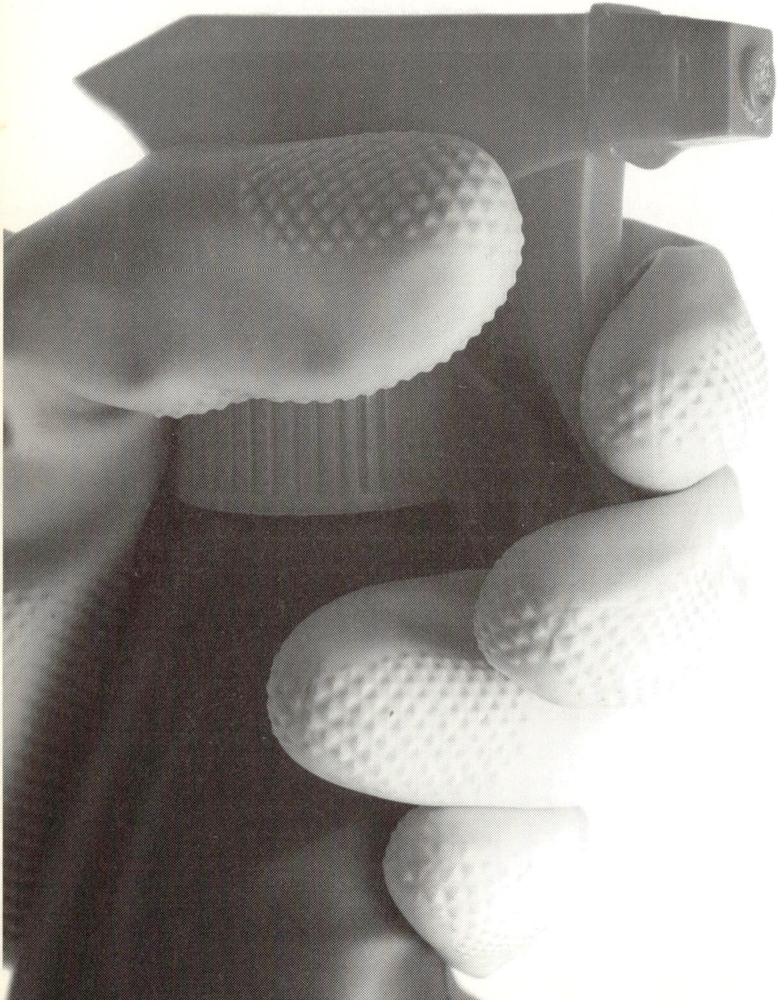

# Formulas

This is a summary of the many cleaning formulas used throughout the book. We do advise, however, that you consult the detailed guidelines for dealing with your stain. Don't rush in and create another stain by using the wrong solution!

## BLEACH
Mix 8 tablespoons of washing soda (sodium carbonate) and 2 cups of 3 per cent hydrogen peroxide.

## BRAN BALL
Put 1 cup of unprocessed wheat bran in a bowl and add white vinegar, 1 drop at a time, until the mixture resembles brown sugar—it should be clumping but not wet. Place the mixture into the toe of a pair of pantyhose and tie tightly. Rub the pantyhose across a surface like an eraser. This mixture can be reused again and again. Add drops of white vinegar to re-moisten.

## CAR WASH SOLUTION
Mix 3 cups of strong black tea, 1 teaspoon of tea tree oil, 1 teaspoon of dishwashing liquid in a 9 litre bucket of warm water.

## CARPET CLEANER
Carpet steam-cleaning machines can be hired at supermarkets. They come with a bottle of chemicals but use only half the amount the manufacturer suggests and top up with 2 teaspoons of eucalyptus oil, 2 tablespoons of white vinegar, 2 tablespoons of bicarb and 2 tablespoons of methylated spirits. If you have mystery stains on your carpet, add 2 teaspoons of glycerine. This solution is also a great multi-purpose spot cleaner so leave it in a 1 litre spray bottle and use as required.

## GLYCERINE SOLUTION (TO REMOVE TANNIN STAINS)
Mix 2 tablespoons of glycerine to 2 cups of water in a 1 litre spray pack and lightly mist over areas. Leave for 20 minutes.

## HARD SURFACE CLEANER
Do not use on marble.
Combine 1 teaspoon of lavender oil, 1 cup of white vinegar and 1 litre of water in a spray pack, lightly mist over hard surfaces and wipe with a clean cloth.

## LAUNDRY DETERGENT FOR DELICATES AND SOFT WOOLLENS
Mix ½ cup of pure soap flakes, ¼ cup of cheap shampoo, 2 teaspoons of bicarb and 2 teaspoons of white vinegar in a clean relabelled detergent bottle. Add 2 litres of water, shake and it's ready to use. Add fragrance, such as 2 teaspoons of lavender oil, but be careful adding eucalyptus oil because it strips colour and oils from fabric. Adding ½ teaspoon of tea tree oil is a good disinfectant and antiviral. For a regular size lightly soiled load, use 1 tablespoon of detergent for a top loader and ½ tablespoon for a front loader.

## LAUNDRY DETERGENT FOR SENSITIVE SKIN
Combine 1 tablespoon of pure soap flakes, juice of 1 lemon and 2 tablespoons of bicarb in a large jar. Add 2 cups of warm water, mix well and label the jar. For a regular size lightly soiled load, use 1 tablespoon of detergent for a top loader and ½ tablespoon for a front loader.

## MOULD REMOVER FOR FABRICS
Add 1 kg of non-iodised salt to a 9 litre bucket of water. Add item, soak, remove from salt solution but don't rinse or wring the

item. Hang in sunshine until dry and scrub off the salt crust—the mould will come away with it.

## MOULD REMOVER FOR HARD SURFACES

Mix ¼ teaspoon of oil of cloves in a 1 litre spray pack of water. Spray and leave for 24 hours before respraying. Wipe with a clean cloth.

## RICE STARCH

Cook white rice in plenty of boiling water, drain and reserve the water. Add 1 cup of the reserved rice water to 2 cups of water and stir. To starch items, add ½ cup of rice starch to the rinse cycle of your washing machine.

## ROTTEN MILK SOLIDS

Place an opened carton of milk in the sun and leave until it forms solids. The time it takes to rot will vary—up to a few days. Place the solids over biro ink stains and the ink will be absorbed into the solids. Wash normally. Warning: the rotten milk does smell and you might have to block your nose when using it. But once it's washed out, the smell disappears!

## SEALANT DIAGNOSIS

Surfaces can be sealed with varnish, polyurethane, shellac or wax. To work out which sealant has been used, take a pin or needle, hold in a pair of pliers and heat on the stove. Touch the pin or needle to an inconspicuous part of the item and work out what smell it creates. If it smells like burnt plastic, it's coated in polyurethane. If it smells like an electrical fire, it's an oil-based varnish. If it smells like burnt hair, it's shellac. If it smells like a snuffed candle, it's wax. To repair polyurethane, apply a little Brasso with a lint-free cloth and rub swiftly over the mark in the direction of the grain. It will look worse before it looks better. Brasso partially melts polyurethane and allows it to refill the tiny air holes that create white water marks. Shellac, varnish and wax can be repaired using beeswax. Warm beeswax in a bowl in the microwave until it just softens and apply with the skin side of a piece of lemon peel. Rub in the direction of the grain using speed, not pressure.

## SHAMPOO FOR BLONDES
Add 4 teaspoons of crushed maiden hair fern leaves to 3 cups of boiling water. Allow to steep for 5 minutes, then strain. Combine 1 tablespoon of this mixture with 1 tablespoon of brown sugar and use to wash your hair.

## SHAMPOO FOR BRUNETTES
Place 4 teaspoons of chopped rosemary leaves in 3 cups of boiling water. Allow to steep for 5 minutes, then strain. Add 1 tablespoon of the rosemary mixture to 1 tablespoon of brown sugar and use to wash your hair.

## SHOE FROU
Mix 2 tablespoons of bicarb (absorbs odours and moisture), 2 tablespoons of talcum powder (absorbs moisture and keeps a silky feel), 1 drop of tea tree oil (kills tinea), 1 drop of oil of cloves (kills mould spores) and 1 drop of lavender oil (adds fragrance and deters insects). Place the mixture in the centre of a small piece of muslin or cotton voile and tie with string or ribbon to enclose. Pat in smelly shoes.

## SILK AND WOOL (BURNT/YELLOWED)
Chlorine-based bleaches burn silk and wool and turn them a yellowy brown. To repair burns, soak items in a 9 litre bucket of

warm water with 2 cups of 3 per cent hydrogen peroxide and 8 tablespoons of washing soda. Immerse the items and cover with a plate to keep them in the solution. Leave for around 6 hours. Add 1 cup of white vinegar to a tub of warm water and rinse thoroughly. Hang in the sunshine to dry. If the fabric is too damaged, another option is to dye items with a quality silk dye in the colour of your choice.

## SPIDER DETERRENT

Wipe 2 drops of lemon oil or the skin of a lemon over a broom head and sweep over areas where spiders lurk. Alternatively, mix ½ teaspoon of lemon oil with water in a 1 litre spray pack and mist over areas where spiders lurk. Lemon oil doesn't kill spiders, it just deters them.

## STAIN DIAGNOSIS

Before tackling a stain, take some time to work out its components. Use your nose, fingers and eyes. The colour, pattern, smell and texture will help you identify the stain. And remember: there could be several parts to a stain that will need to be removed in a particular order. That order starts with proteins and finishes with resins. The order is important because what you use affects the chemical signature of the stain. If you've applied the wrong solvent, you must remove it before using the correct solvent. Here are the five main types of stain:

**Proteins**—these have a dark ring around the edge and include blood, semen, seeds, nuts, meat, cheese, milk, dairy and fish. To remove the stain, apply cold water and a cake of bathroom soap. Whatever you do, don't use warm or hot water or you'll set the stain.

**Carbohydrates**—these stains are darker in the centre, lighter around the edge and feel stiff. They include sugar, fruit juices, cakes, biscuits, lollies, soft drinks, alcohol, honey and many plants. They also include starches, such as potato, rice, corn, ground corn, wheat-based products (pasta and couscous), floury grain foods and wallpaper paste. To remove sugar stains, use warm water and a cake of bathroom soap. To remove starchy stains, use cold water and soap. If in doubt, use cold water first.

**Fats and oils**—these stains spread evenly across a surface, feel greasy between your fingers and, when you wash the stained garment, they continue to spread—that's why a greasy chip mark on your T-shirt gets bigger every time you wash it. Stains include cooking oils (lighter in colour) and mechanical oils (darker in colour and more viscous). To remove lighter oils, rub dishwashing liquid into the stain with your fingers until it feels like jelly. For darker or thicker oils, use mineral oil (baby oil) to dilute the stain before emulsifying with dishwashing liquid.

**Pigments**—these stains include ink, paint, dye, rust and oxide and each requires a different solution. For ink stains, place rotten milk solids over the stain and the ink will be absorbed into the solids. Alternatively, rub with white spirits on a cotton bud. Permanent pen markers contain their own solvent, so write over the mark and while it's wet, wipe with white spirits on a cotton bud. For water-based paint, use methylated spirits on a cotton bud or cotton ball. For oil-based paint, use white spirits or mineral turpentine on a cotton bud or cotton ball. To remove rust, use CLR or Ranex. If a stain is vegetable based, wipe with white vinegar on a cloth. For an oxide stain, wipe with glycerine on a cloth and remove any remaining colour by exposing the stain to ultraviolet light. Protect the area around the ultraviolet light with cardboard.

**Resins**—these stains include sap, chewing gum, wax and glue and feel sticky to touch. For plant-based resins, such as tree sap, use a dab of glycerine or dab of tea tree oil. The solvent for shellac is methylated spirits. Glues used in children's crafts are made of carbohydrates, so use warm water and a cake of bathroom soap and scribble over the stain. To remove silicone, cut it using a utility knife.

## TIMBER FLOOR WASH

Mix 2 cups of strong black tea, ½ cup of white vinegar with warm water in a 9 litre bucket.

## TOWEL SOFTENER

For a large top loader, add ½ cup of bicarb to the wash slot and ½ cup of white vinegar to the conditioner slot of the washing machine. For a small top loader, add 2 tablespoons of bicarb and 2 tablespoons of white vinegar. For a large front loader, add 2 tablespoons of bicarb and 2 tablespoons of white vinegar. For a small front loader, add 1 tablespoon each of bicarb and white vinegar.

## WARDROBE SACHET

Mix 2 bay leaves (deter moths), 5 whole cloves (kill mould spores and deter silverfish), 1 tea bag (kills dust mites), 1–2 heads of lavender (adds fragrance and deters flying insects), 2 cedar chips (deter moths), 1 tablespoon of bicarb (absorbs moisture and helps prevent mould) in a bowl. Place the mixture in the centre of a small piece of muslin or cotton voile and tie up with string or ribbon.

## WINDOW CLEANER

1 cup of methylated spirits or 1 cup of white vinegar in a 1 litre spray pack of water.

## WOOLLENS (HOW TO UNSHRINK)

Add 2 tablespoons (dark colours) or 4 tablespoons (light colours) of fuller's earth to 15 litres of blood-heat water. Immerse the garment for 15 minutes, remove, rinse in blood-heat water and gently wring out. Lay the garment on a towel flat in the shade to dry. As it dries, stretch back into shape.

# Uses for Essential Oils

| Fragrance | Properties | Where to use | How to use |
| --- | --- | --- | --- |
| Lavender Oil | Relieves headache, helps relaxation and smells clean. It's a great insecticide for mozzies and flies | Bedroom, living area, bathroom, cupboards, on your skin | 1 teaspoon of lavender oil per 1 litre spray pack of water |
| Rose Oil | Creates a cosy romantic feel | Bedroom, living area, on your skin | 1 teaspoon of rose oil per 1 litre spray pack of water |
| Cinnamon, vanilla and herbals | Encourage appetite | Kitchen, dining room | Use in sachets or simply wipe directly onto surfaces |

| Fragrance | Properties | Where to use | How to use |
|---|---|---|---|
| Oil of cloves | Anti-bacterial, anti-mould. Has a festive scent | Anywhere you find mould | ¼ teaspoon of oil of cloves per 1 litre spray pack of water. Lightly mist over mould and leave to dry. Mould spores will die and drop off in a couple of days |
| Cedar or pine chips | Clean scents that prevent insects | Particularly good for moths in cupboards and wardrobes. Great for sick rooms as they make breathing easier | Place in sachets or saucers |
| Bay leaves | Kill pantry moths | Pantries, kitchen cupboards and wardrobes | Place a dry leaf on each shelf |
| Tea tree oil | Clean fresh smell and is a great disinfectant, antibacterial and antifungal | Just about anywhere | 1 teaspoon of tea tree oil per 1 litre spray pack of water |

## Formulas

| Fragrance | Properties | Where to use | How to use |
|---|---|---|---|
| Fruit oils | Warm welcoming fragrance, although apart from lemon they do encourage insects | Kitchen, dining room | 1 teaspoon of fruit oil per 1 litre spray pack of water. Lightly mist as an air freshener |
| Lily, freesia, lily of the valley and the other strong floral oils | Good at temporarily masking very nasty odours and are wonderful on clothes | Anywhere there is a nasty pong or wardrobes and drawers to scent your clothes | ¼ teaspoon of floral oil per 1 litre spray pack of water. Lightly mist as an air freshener |
| Bicarb | Absorbs gaseous smells | Anywhere there is a nasty pong | Place 2 tablespoons on a saucer near the offending odour |

# Index

acetone 6
Akubra hat 272
alloy wheels 351
almond oil, sweet 19, 194, 198
aluminium, corroded 34–5
angora 261
antibacterial cleaners 24
ants 61, 345–6
apple juice 228
Artline 249

babies *see* children
baby bottles 281
baby oil 6, 229
bags *see* handbags
baked beans 229
ballpoint pen *see also* pen marks
  quick stain removal guide 301
bamboo flooring 132
bamboo furniture 101
banana 229, 298
Band-Aid removal 278
barbecue grill, cleaning 35
barbecue sauce 138, 298
barbecues 337
basin, yellow marks on 79
bathroom 64
  bath 68–70
  drains 81
  hand basin and vanity 78–9
  mirror 77
  shower 70–5
  spa bath 70
  stained tiles 133
  stained timber 65
  taps 75
  tiles 75–7
  toilet 65–7
  towels 80
  walls 80
bay leaves 6, 365
bedroom
  bed 207
  bedhead scratches 208–9
  bedside table spills 219
  blankets and throws 216–17
  carpet, in 124
  chests of drawers 218–19
  clean 206, 207
  clothes baskets 219–20
  doonas and bedcovers 212
  mattress airing and cleaning 207, 209
  mattress protector 207
  mirrors 220
  pillows 215–16

rust stain on valance 208
sheepskin underlay 217
sheets 210–11
silk doona cover 213–14
wardrobes 218–19
beer 298
beeswax 6
beetroot 138, 230, 298
benchtop ovens 35
benchtops 40
  CaesarStone 44
  granite 47–8
  laminate/formica 41–4
  marble 44–6
  Quantum quartz 44
  Silestone 44
  stainless steel 48
berry stains 230
Bessemer plates 55
Betadine 139
bicarbonate of soda 6, 367
billiards 111
bird poo
  canvas, on 354
  cotton, on 231
  quick stain removal guide 298
  timber, on 324
  wrought iron, on 333–4
biro *see also* pen marks
  blinds, on 198–9
  leather, on 97–8
bitumen 231–2
black bean sauce 232
blankets and throws 216–17
bleach 7, 358, 140
blenders 34–5
blinds
  cleaning 198–202
  food stains 199–200
  mildew on 201
  roman blinds 202
blood
  carpet stain 141
  quick stain removal guide 298–9
  timber chopping board 50
  timber floor 126
blue-green algae 338–9
boats
  mouldy synthetic life jackets 354
  seagull poo on canvas 354
body oil 93
books/bookshelves 121
borax 7
bore water stain 70, 327–8

bran balls 85–7, 187, 188, 199, 358
Brasso 7
bronze firescreens 105
broom 7, 125–6
brushes
  hairbrush 13
  stiff 18
  toothbrush 20
buckets 7
bug deterrent 260
burn marks
  laminate, on 42–3
  white sink 50
burnt pans 31–2
burnt smell 36
burnt/stained glass 107
butter
  carpet stain 141–2, 173–4
  cars, in 350

CaesarStone benchtop 44
calcium deposits 9, 34
camphor 8
camphorated oil 217
camping
  diesel on swag 341
  flying fox poo 341
cane flooring 132
cane furniture 101
canvas 341, 354
car wash solution 358
caravans
  black sediment in water tank 355
  tyre mark on vinyl 355
carnauba wax 8, 134
carpet
  cleaner 358
  cleaning 134–5, 166–7, 176, 358
  DIY steam cleaning 135–6
  professional steam cleaning 136–7
  steam cleaner 8
  vacuum cleaner 20, 134, 136, 161
carpet beetles 166
carpet stains 134–7, 166–7
  barbecue sauce 138
  beetroot 138
  Betadine 139
  black tea 166
  bleach 140
  blood 141
  butter/margarine 141–2
  chocolate 142
  coffee 142–3

# Index

cordial 143
cough medicine 143–4
crayon 144
curry 145
dog poo 145–6
dye 146–7
egg 147
Fanta 148
felt pad stain on 219
fluorescent pen 148
food colouring 181
fruit 149
glue 150
glycerine 149–50, 166–7
graphite powder 150–1
grass 151–2
gravy 152
grease 152–3
hair gel 153–4
hair serum 154
ice cream 155
ink 155–6
insects 156–7
jam 157
jelly beans 157–8
lubricant (personal) 158
mayonnaise 159
milk 160–1
mould 159–60
mud 161
nappy rash cream 161–2
orange juice 162–3
pot plant mark 162–3
red wine stain 164
rubber 164–5
rust 165
scuff marks 168
shoe polish 168
silicone 167
soot 168
sorbolene cream 169
soup 169–70
sugar 168
suntan lotion 170–1
timber stain 171
tomato sauce 172
toner ink 172
tree sap 173
urine 173
vegemite 173–4
vomit 174
water 174–5, 179
zinc cream 175
carrot 299
cars
 alloy wheels, cleaning 351
 butter in 350
 chocolate milk stains 352
 cigarette smells 349

coffee spill in 347
dead mouse smell 352–3
glue/plastic base on windscreen 348
perfumed smell in 348–9
pizza smell 352
sweaty stains on seats 350
windscreen wipers 351
woollen sheepskin care seat covers 350–1
cast-iron pots 32
cat deterrent 217
cat hair on blankets 216–17
cat urine 130–1
cedar chips 8, 366
ceiling 202–3
cement and brick pavers 325–8
Cera Wax 8
ceramic bath 70
chalk sticks 9
chamois 270
cheese, melted 92
chewing gum 232–3, 299
children
 baby bottles 281
 bed wetting 280
 clothing 285–90
 cots 279
 floors 284
 highchairs 280
 nappies 281–2
 playpens/security gates 280
 prams/strollers 280–1
 routine cleaning 277–8
 toys 282–4
chilli sauce 233, 299
chocolate
 carpet stain 142
 cotton, on 233
 ice-cream on cotton 287
 milk on car seat 352
 quick stain removal guide 299
 wool, on 234
chopping boards 50
cigarette
 ash 9
 burn on timber 127
 smell 100–1, 349
cinnamon oil 52, 365
citronella candle wax 335–6
cleaning formulas 358–65
clothes baskets 219–20
clothing
 angora 261
 apple juice, on 228
 baby, washing 285
 baby oil splashes 229

baked beans 229
banana 229
beetroot 230
berry stains 230
bird poo 231
black bean sauce 232
car grease 248
care labels 227
chewing gum 232–3
children 285–90
chilli sauce 233
chocolate 233–4
coffee 234
collar grime 299
cream 234–5
curry 235
custard 235
denim 228, 231, 254
diesel 236
dirt 236–7
dry-cleaning 313
egg 237
fish sauce 237–8
fluorescent highlighter pen 239–40
gloves 271
grass and grease 241
hair dye 242
hair spray 242
hand washing 312–13
handbags 267–8
hats 272
jackets 264–6
leather 239–40, 246
lint 297
lip balm 243
lipstick 243–4
Liquid Paper 244
make-up 240
moths in woollens 259–60
mould 227, 245–6
mustard 247
oil stains 247
peanut butter 248
pear 249
pen marks 249
pilling on woollens 260–1
poly-cotton 249–50
polyester 236
pumpkin soup 250
quick stain removal guide 298–304
red wine 251
rotten milk mark 245
scorch mark 251
seafood 252
sequins, on 263
shoes *see* shoes
silk 234–5

369

SPOTLESS 2

soap residue on 309–10
soy sauce 252
stain diagnosis 227, 238
static 253
sticky label 253
suits 263
sunscreen 254
sweat 236, 249–50
synthetic material 240, 308–9
ties 266–7
tomato sauce 255
toothpaste 255
tree sap 255–6
tumble drying 314
tuna (in oil) 256
Vaseline 257
velvet 263
wax 257
what not to do 238
yellow marks 258–9
cloves 10
 oil of 16, 366
CLR 9, 165, 208
cockroaches 33, 199
coffee machines 33, 34
coffee stains
 car, in 347
 carpet, on 142–3
 cotton, on 234
 laminate, on 41
 quick stain removal guide 300
coffee tables 102–3
Coke 66
collar grime 299
Colour Run Remover 10, 297
colour runs 297
computers 119–20
concrete
 battery rust stain 330
 cleaning and polishing 134
 fluorescent paint 331
 rubber marks under carpet 165
cooking oil
 brick pavers, on 327
 quick stain removal guide 300
cooktop
 ceramic/induction, cleaning 28
 electric, cleaning 29
 electric, rings on 29
 gas, cleaning 29–30
copper, blackened 105
cordial 88, 143
cork floors 125–6, 176
cornflour 10
cosmetics *see* make-up

cots 279
cotton ball 10
cotton buds 11
cotton/linen upholstery 88–91
couches
 bran ball, use of 85–6
 cotton/linen upholstery 88–91
 cushions 86–7
 jacquard 94
 leather 95–100
 stains, generally 85–6
 sweat/body oil 93
 tapestry 95
 throws 101
 vinyl 90–1
 watermarks on microsuede 85
 wool 95
cough medicine 143–4
crayon marks
 carpet stain 144
 cotton, on 89
 microsuede, on 93
 quick stain removal guide 300
cream 234–5
cricket ball marks 288
crockery
 Bessemer plates, stained 55
 cleaning 53
 crystal bowls sticking together 54
 tannin stains on bone china 54
crystal 54
cupboards (kitchen)
 cinnamon oil on vinyl wrap 51–2
 cleaning 51
 dead mouse smell 53
 warping and discolouration 26, 52
 yellowed melamine 52
curry stains 145, 235
curtains 199–202
 cleaning 199–202
 cockroach poo 201
 dry-cleaning smell 202
 rubber-lined 201
 shower 74
 silk 200
 tip to prevent bushfire smoke damage 202
 velvet 199
cushion covers 86–7
custard 235
cutlery 59

damask 116–17
Damp Rid 182
decanters 111–12
deck scrubber 11
decking 323–4
denim
 anchovy on 228
 bitumen on 231–2
 stiffness 254
 tar on 231–2
denture tablets 11
deodorant stains 300
desks 120–1
diamond jewellery 221
diesel 236, 341
dining tables
 bleach marks from moisture 114
 green dye on timber 116
 heat/water marks 112–14
 marble 114s–15
 peas on timber 115
dishwasher 36–7
dishwashing liquid 11, 47–8
dog kennel 344
dog poo
 carpet, on 145–6
 quick stain removal guide 300
 tiles, on 133
dog saliva 198
dog urine 133
doonas and bedcovers 212, 213–14
doorknobs 187
doors 187
 easy soundproofing 187–8
 garage 353
 rattling 188
 rust on hinges 187
 strip seal 187
drains 81
Driza-Bone 266
dry-cleaning 313
drying clothes 314
dye
 carpet, on 146–7
 cotton, run in 288
 green, on timber 116
 hair *see* hair dye
 leather, on 98
 linen, on 86–7
 running, prevention 98
 using 263

ear drop stains 91
egg
 brick, on 328
 carpet, on 147

370

# Index

cotton, on 237
quick stain removal guide 300
electrical leads 347
electricity 188
electronic games 284
electronic toll tags 348
engine oil
  carpet stain 153
  timber 128-9
entertainment systems 108-9
  stereos 108-9
  TVs 108
eraser (pencil and biro) 11
espresso/coffee machines
  calcium scale 34
  cleaning 33
essential oils, uses for 365-7
eucalyptus oil 12

fabrics
  care symbols 307-8
  mould remover 359-60
  stain removal guide 298-304
Fanta 148
fax machines 120
fibreglass 69, 343-4
fire screens, bronze 105
fireplaces 104, 105
fish sauce 237-8
flies 345, 346
floors
  bamboo, cane and palm, 132, 176
  carpet see carpet; carpet stains
  cleaning guide 176-8
  coir 183
  concrete 134
  cork 125-6, 176
  linoleum, vinyl and self-levelling plastics 124, 183-8
  marble/limestone 134, 178
  rammed earth 134
  rugs and mats 179-83
  tiles 124, 132-3, 177
  timber see timber floors
  types 124, 132-3
floral oils 367
fluff 295, 306
fluorescent pen see also pen marks
  carpet stain 148
fly specks 202-3
flying fox poo 341, 353
flyscreens 337
formica see laminate/formica benchtops
formulas 358-65

french polish
  cleaning 113-14
  heat/water marks 112-13
fruit juice 228, 300
fruit oils 367
fuller's earth 12, 365
furniture
  couches/chairs 85-101
  metal-framed 102
  oriental 104
  outdoor 334-6
  timber 103-4

garage door 353
garbage disposal unit 51
garden shed 346-7
garlic smell 57
gel pens 249, 302 see also pen marks
germs 24, 283
glass
  burnt/stained 107
  chandelier 189
  lamp bases 188
  melted polyester 106-7
  splashback 30
  windows see windows
glass ware 60
Glomesh 268
gloves 271
glue
  stain on carpet 150
  tulle, on 290
  walls, on 189-90
glycerine 12
  cleaning formula 359
  stain on carpet 149-50, 166-7
gold jewellery 221
graffiti 332-3
granite benchtops 47-8
granite mantlepieces 106
graphite powder 150-1
grass 151-2, 241, 301
gravy 152, 301
grease
  carpet stains 153, 158-9
  cotton, on 241
  dark or light coloured 152-3
  engine oil on timber 128-9
  leather, on 267
  linen, on 86-7
  lubricant (personal) 158
  old car grease 248
  quick stain removal guide 301
  wool, on 241
grill, cleaning 28
grout 49, 76-7
grout rake 12

guitars 110
gum leaf stains 326, 329
Gumption 12

hair conditioner (cheap) 13
hair dryer 13, 208
hair dye
  cotton, on 242
  laminate, on 43-4
  quick stain removal guide 301
  timber floor, on 127-8
hair gel 153-4
hair serum 154
hair spray 186, 242
hairbrush 13
hand washing 312-13
handbags
  Glomesh 268
  grease stains 267
  mould on suede 268
hats 272
heat/water marks 112-13, 126-7
heaters 106
  burnt/stained glass 107
  heater oil on towels 107-8
  melted polyester 106-7
herbal oils 365
highchairs 280
highlighter pen see also pen marks
  fluorescent, on cotton 239
  leather, on 239-40
hydrochloric acid 328
hydrogen peroxide (3%) 13
  cigarette burn 127
HyVent fabric 265

ice cream
  carpet stain 155
  chocolate 299
  cotton, on 287
ice cubes
  cleaning melted plastic 25
  wax stain on hardwood floor, 131-2
icy pole, blue 287
ingredients, useful 6-21
ink see also pen marks
  carpet stain 155-6, 172
  lino, on 185
  quick stain removal guide 301
  toner 172
insects see also pests
  carpet beetles 166
  carpet stain 156-7
  cockroaches 33, 199

371

SPOTLESS 2

deterrent 260
flies 345, 346, 346
moths in woollens 259–60
iron 13
  burn on 316–17
  mark on velvet curtains 199
  melt 316
  white flecks coming from 315
ironing 315–16
ivory, yellowed 221

jacquard 94
jam 157
jars 57
jelly beans 157–8
jewellery 220–2
  dirty platinum, gold and diamond 221
  tarnished silver 222
  yellowed ivory 221
juicer 39–40

kerosene 13
kettle/electric jug 32–3
kitchen 24
  appliances 32–40
  benchtops 40–9
  chopping boards 50
  cooktop *see* cooktop
  crockery 53–5
  cupboards 26, 51–3
  cutlery 59–60
  garbage disposal unit 51
  glass ware 60
  grill 28
  jars 57
  knives 60
  lunch bags 58–9
  melted plastic 25
  oven, cleaning 25–6
  pantry 60–1
  plastic containers 57
  pots and pans 30–2
  rangehood and extractor fan 30
  sink 50–1
  smoky smell 27–8
  splashback 30
  teapot 55–6
  tiles and grout 49
  yellowing oven door 26
kitty litter 13
knives 60

laminate/formica benchtops
  burn marks 42–3
  cleaning 41
  coffee 41
  coloured plastic 42

hair dye 43–4
  mould 43
  superglue 41–2
lamps and light shades 188–9
laundry *see also* washing
  drying clothes 314
  hand washing 312–13
  hanging out washing 314
  ironing *see* ironing
  quick stain removal guide 298–304
  sink 312
  tumble drying 314
  washing machine *see* washing machine
laundry detergent 13
  delicates and soft woollens 359
  sensitive skin, for 359
lavender oil 14, 365
leadlight cement on glass 194–5
leather
  biro mark 97–8
  black marks on 340
  bleached 96
  conditioner 14
  couch 95–100
  dye on 98
  gloves 271
  grease stains 267
  highlighter pen 239–40
  ink stain 120–1
  mould 246, 339–40
  nail polish 97
  paint 99
  plaster powder 99–100
  rockwool material 99–100
  scratches 95
  sweat marks 265
lemon juice 14
lemon oil 14
  spider deterrent 191
light bulbs 339
light switches 192
lime scale 9, 32–3
limestone floor 134, 178
linen
  grease and dye on 86
  red wine on clothing 251
  rust-coloured stains 317
  upholstery, red wine on 88–9
linen press 317–18
  rising damp 318
linoleum
  choice as flooring 124
  cleaning 178, 183–8, 186
  crepe paper stain 184
  general cleaning guide 178

hair spray removal 186
ink printing stain 185
rust stain 185
scuff marks 184–5
sticky, 186
stiletto heel marks 183–4
lint 297
lip balm 243
lipstick 243, 244, 301
lubricant (personal) 158
lunch bags 58–9
Lycra 289

macramé wall hanging 192
macrosuede 91–4
make-up
  quick stain removal guide 301
  synthetic clothing, on 240
  towels, on 80
mantlepieces 106
marble
  chips in 46
  dull, in shower 72
  graffiti, on 332–3
  mantlepieces 106
  marking on 114–15
  stain prevention 46
  watermarks on 78
marble benchtops
  chips in 46
  protection 44–5
  rust on 46
  stain prevention 46
  tea stains 45–6
marble floor 134, 178
marble floor wax 14, 134
margarine 141–2
mascara 215–16, 301
massage oil 311–12
mattress 207, 209, 210
mattress protector 207, 279
mayonnaise 159, 301
metal-framed furniture 102
metal lice comb 14, 153
metal railings 333
methylated spirits 15
mice 53, 352–3
microsuede 85, 91–2, 93–4
microwave 36
mildew 116–17
milk
  carpet stain 160–1
  quick stain removal guide 302
  rotten 17, 185, 245, 294, 360
  skim 104
mineral oil *see* baby oil
mirror

372

# Index

cedar frame 220
  silicone on 77
mixers/blenders 35–6
mosquitoes 345
moths 259–60
mould
  bathroom walls 80
  carpet stain 159–60
  ceilings 203
  clothes, on 227, 245
  cotton, on 310–11
  curtains 199
  laminate, on 43
  leather, on 246, 339–40
  mattress, in 210
  mildew on blinds 201
  oil of cloves 309
  plastic bath toys 283–4
  remover for fabrics 359–60
  remover for hard surfaces 360
  showers 70–1, 73
  silicone 70–1, 73
  suede 268, 271
  synthetic grass, on 340
  synthetic life jackets 354
  tablecloth 116–17
  towels on 318
  wallpaper 191
mud 161, 302
musical instruments 110
mustard 247

nail polish
  leather, on 97
  microsuede, on 93–4
  quick stain removal guide 302
  timber floor, on 130
naphthalene 217
NapiSan OxyAction MAX 15
NapiSan Plus 15
nappies 281–2
nappy rash cream 161–2
noise reduction 187–8
non-iodised salt 15, 182, 199, 208
nubuck 91–2, 93
nylon brush 15

odours *see* smells
oil stains
  cinnamon oil 51–2
  cooking fat/oil on timber 129
  essential, uses for 365–7
  floral 367
  grease *see* grease
  massage 311–12
  orange oil, using 312

pavers, on 326–7
  quick stain removal guide 300
  rules for treatment 247
  sheepskin slippers 270
  silk, on 266–7
orange juice 162–3
orange oil 312
oriental furniture 104
ornaments 103
oven 25–6, 27

paint
  fluorescent, on concrete 331
  leather, on 99
  quick stain removal guide 302
paint fumes 193
palm flooring 132
Panama hat 272
pantry 60–1
pantyhose/stockings 16
paper, musty 121
paper towel 16
pavers
  bore water stain 327–8
  brown stains on 325–6
  cement and brick 325–8
  cleaning 325
  cooking oil on brick 327
  egg on brick 328
  gum leaf stains 326
  oil and petrol on 326
  rust marks 327–8
peanut butter 125, 248
pear 248
pen marks
  biro 97–8, 198–9
  clothing 249
  couches, on 87, 91–2, 97
  fluorescent pen 249, 302
  highlighter 239–40
  ink 155–6, 172, 185
  quick stain removal guide 302
  Texta pen 91–2, 286
pencils, coloured 89–90
pennyroyal, oil of 16, 61
permanent markers 249, 302
pests 345–6
petroleum jelly 16, 187
pets 344
photocopiers 120
pianos 110
pilling on woollens 260–1
pillow protectors 215
pillowcase 16
pillows 215–16
pine chips 366

pizza smell 352
plaster of Paris 17, 126
plastic
  bath toys 283–4
  coloured, on laminate 42
  containers 57–8
  lipstick, on 244
  melted 25
  ring on hotplate 25
  stained 312
  white marks on 38
plastic bag 17
plastic wrap 17
platinum jewellery 221
playdough on rug 284
playpens 280
polished concrete 134
poly-cotton 249–50
polyester 236
polyurethene coated timber
  cigarette burn 127
  cleaning of 125–30
  hair dye stain, 127–8
  nail polish on 130
  pot plant mark 162–3
pots and pans 30–2
prams 280–1
printers 120
pumpkin soup 250

Quantum Quartz benchtop 44
quilt cover 209

rammed earth floors 134
Ranex 17, 165, 208
rangehood and extractor fan 30
red wine
  carpet stain 164
  cotton, on 335–6
  decanter, in 111–12
  linen clothing 251
  linen upholstery, on 88–9
  quick stain removal guide 304
refrigerator 37, 38
respirator mask and straps 214–15
rice starch 360
rings on electric cooktop 29
rose oil, use for 365
rotten milk technique 17, 185, 245, 294, 360
rubber gloves, disposable 11
rubber marks
  carpet stain 164–5
  quick stain removal guide 302
  timber, on 109

373

rubber, preserving 283
rugs and mats
  cleaning 176, 179-83
  coir 183
  flokati rug 179-80
  sisal 181-2
  Turkish rug 180
Runaway *see* Colour Run Remover
rust
  carpet stain 165
  cast-iron pots 32
  CLR and 9, 165, 208
  concrete, on 330
  door hinges 187
  fabric, on 208
  fibreglass, on 343-4
  lino, on 185
  metal 189
  pavers, on 327
  quick stain removal guide 303
  screws, on 187
  shower tiles 71
  stainless steel benchtop 48
  unsealed marble 46
  wool, on 285

saddle soap 17
saline solution 17
salt 17, 186, 210
  non-iodised 15, 182, 199, 208
sandstone, brick 106
sandwich makers 33
scanners 120
scorch mark 251
Scotchgard 136
scraper 18
scuff marks
  carpet, on 168
  lino, on 184-5
seafood 252
seagull poo 354
sealant diagnosis 360-1
security gates 280
septic tank 66-7
sequins 263
shampoo
  blondes, for 361
  brunettes, for 361
  cheap 18, 180, 199
  hair dye stain, 127-8
shed 346-7
sheepskin
  car seat covers 350-1
  pram, in 281
  slippers 270
  underlay 217
  washing 281

sheets 210
  baby vomit, on 279
  bore water stains 111-12
  doonas and bedcovers 212
  flannelette 306
  liquid foundation stains 213
  ointment stains 212
  stain diagnosis 314
  tea stains 111
  yellowed 111
shoe frou 361
shoe polish
  carpet stain 168
  liquid, stain on enamel bath 69
  quick stain removal guide 303
shoes
  chamois 270
  deodorisers 361
  food stains on suede 269-70
  sheepskin boots 270-1
  squeaky 269
  stretching 269
  ugg boots 270
shower
  cleaning tip 73
  curtains 74
  dull marble in 72
  head, green-coloured marks 74-5
  mould 70-1
  rubber suction mat marks 72
  rust marks on shower tiles 71
  screens 73
shower screens 73
Silestone benchtop, streaky 44
silicone 18
  carpet stain 167
  joins, cleaning 51
  mirror, on 77
  showers, in 70-1, 73
  tiles, on 76
silk
  burnt/yellowed 361-2
  cream on 234-5
  doona cover 213-14
  mould 245
  oil on 266-7
silver
  cleaning 118
  restoring 118
  tarnished jewellery 222
  teapot, cleaning 56
sink (kitchen)
  silicone joins 51
  tobacco burns 50
sisal 181
  cleaning 176, 181-2

graphite powder on 150-1
slate tiles 331
Slurpex 18
smells
  benchtop ovens 35
  cat urine on timber floor 130-1
  cigarettes 100-1, 349
  coffee 347
  dead mouse 53, 352-3
  dishwashers 36-7
  dry-cleaning smell in curtains 202
  garlic 57
  microwave 36
  musty paper 121
  musty smell in house 337-8
  nappy bucket 282
  paint fumes 193
  perfume, strong 348-9
  pizza 352
  refrigerator 38
  salmon juice on cloth 58
  smoky smell 27-8
  urine 65-6
  water soaked carpet 179
smoke damage 202
smoke stains 202-3
smoky smell 27-8
snails/slugs 346
socks 289
soft drink 303
soot 168
sorbolene cream 169
soup 169-70
soy sauce 252, 303
spa bath 70
spider deterrent 191, 345 362
splashback 30
sport
  leather boxing gloves 339-40
  soccer boots 340
  synthetic grass 340
spot-cleaning, clothes 296
squeaky shoes 269
squid ink 252
Stain Clinics 2
stain diagnosis 2, 279, 362-4
  clothing 227, 238
  importance of 238
stain removal techniques 3, 298-304
stainless steel
  benchtop 48
  scratches on cutlery 59-60
  splashback 30
stains
  carbohydrates 363
  fats and oils 363

# Index

pigments 363–4
proteins 362
resins 364
static 253
stereos 108–9
sticky labels
 appliances, on 37
 wool, on 253
sticky tape residue 109
sticky Tupperware 58
sticky vinyl floor 186
stiletto heel marks 183–4
stockings see pantyhose/ stockings
stone splashback 30
strollers 280–1
suede
 food stains 269–70
 gloves 271
 handbag 268
 jacket 264
sugar 168
sugar soap 19, 194
suits 263
sunscreen 254, 303
suntan lotion 170–1
superglue 41–2
supersuede 91–4
swag, diesel on 341
sweat
 cotton, on 236
 hat, on 272
 leather, on 265
 nubuck, on 93
 poly-cotton, on 249–50
 quick stain removal guide 303
 stains in cars 350
sweet almond oil 19, 194, 198
swimming pool/spa 343–4
synthetic fabric 227
 make-up, on 240
 stretched 308–9
synthetic grass 340

tablecloths 117–18, 335–6
tables
 coffee 102–3
 dining 112–16
 outdoor 334–5
talcum powder 19, 25, 26
tannin levels in flooring 126
tapestry 95
taps, bathroom 75–6
tar 231–2, 303
tarnished silver 222
tea bag 19
tea stains
 cotton, on 90

quick stain removal guide 300
 sealed marble benchtop 45–6
 sheets 111
 teapot 55
tea tree oil 19, 366
teapot 55, 56
teddy bear, smelly 277
televisions 108
Texta pen see also pen marks
 cotton, on 286
 nubuck, on 91–2
throws 101
ties 266–7
Tiger Balm in hair 79
tiles
 bark and eucalyptus stains 329
 bathroom 75–6, 124
 cleaning 132–3, 177
 dog urine/poo 133
 general cleaning guide for 176–8
 glazed 329
 grease on 49
 grout, cleaning 49
 metal marks, 133
 rust marks 71
 slate 331
 splashback 30
 unglazed, 132, 177
 unsealed 329–30
 white marks on 329–30
timber
 bleach mark 114
 blood on 50, 126
 dent in 126
 engine oil 128–9
 floors see timber floors
 furniture 102–3
 grease 128–9, 152
 green dye, on 116
 green stains on 115
 hair dye stain, 127–8
 heat/water marks 112–13
 lacquered 104
 mantlepieces 106
 moisture 114
 nail polish on 130
 rabbit urine stains 323
 rubber marks on 109
 salad dressing, on 334–5
 scratches 208–9
 stain in carpet from 171
 toothpaste and soap stains 65
 wax on 110, 131–2
 white cloudy mark 103
 white markings on cedar 220

timber decking 323
 kookaburra poo 324
 oil surface 324
timber floors
 blood/meat stain, 126
 cat urine 130–1
 cigarette burn 127
 cleaning of 125–6, 176
 cooking fat/oil 129
 polyurethane coated see polyurethene coated timber
 wash for 364
 wax on 126, 131–2
 waxed 126
tissues 19
toddlers see children
toilet
 cleaning 65–6
 septic tank 66–7
 urine stains 65–6
 water stain on back of 67
tomato sauce
 carpet, on 172
 cotton, on 255
 quick stain removal guide 303
tomato stains 58
toothbrush 20
toothpaste stains 65, 255
towels
 heater oil 107–8
 liquid foundation make-up on 80
 massage oil on 311–12
 mould 318
 softener 364
 stiff and scratchy 311
toys
 cleaning 282–3
 electronic games 284
 plastic bath, mould on 283–4
 rubber, preserving 283
tree sap
 carpet, on 173
 cotton, on 255–6
 quick stain removal guide 303
tumble drying 314
tumeric 304
tuna oil 256
Tupperware, sticky 58
turpentine 20

ugg boots 270
ultraviolet light 20
 rust on fabric 208
 urine 130–1, 179
 wax stain on hardwood floor, 131–2

375

# SPOTLESS 2

umbrellas, awnings and shade cloth 336
unprocessed wheat bran 20
upholstery *see* fabrics; furniture
urine
  bed wetting 280
  carpet, on 173, 181
  cat urine 130–1, 181
  dog urine on tiles 133
  quick stain removal guide 304
  smell 65, 130–1
  stains 65, 132–3
  timber, on 323

vacuum cleaner 20
  carpet cleaning 134, 136
  routine cleaning 277
vanilla oil, use for 365
vanity (bathroom), watermarks on 78
varnished floors 125, 130, 131–2
Vaseline *see also* petroleum jelly
  cotton, on 257
vegemite
  carpet, on 173–4
  quick stain removal guide 304
velvet, caring for 263
Vicks VapoRub
  cat deterrent 217
  cotton, on 286–7
  stain on coir rug 183
vinyl
  buckled 117–18
  cigarette smoke smell 100–1
  stained 335
  tyre mark on 355
vinyl cladding 338–9
vinyl flooring 124
  choice as flooring 124
  cleaning 178, 183–8, 186
  crepe paper stain 184
  general cleaning guide 178
  hair spray removal 186
  ink printing stain 185
  rust stain 185
  scuff marks 184–5
  sticky, 186
  stiletto heel marks 183–4
vomit
  baby milk on jacquard 94

carpet, on 174
quick stain removal guide 304
sheets, on 279
wallpaper 189, 190, 191
walls
  cleaning 189–93
  glue on 189–90
  light switches 192
  mark from fly spray unit 190
  rust stains 193
  spider deterrent 191
wardrobe 218–19
  moisture prevention 260
  sachet 364
washing
  colour runs 297
  colourfast check 296
  fabric care symbols 207–8
  hand washing 312–13
  hanging out 314
  soaking 296
  soapy residue on clothes 309–10
  spot-cleaning 296
  techniques 295–6
  tissue in 295
  tumble drying 314
washing machine
  cleaning 305
  mould on rubber seal 305
  red dirt in 307
  removing fluff from 295
  staining clothes from build-up 306
  stretched synthetic fabric 308–9
  tar in 310
washing soda 20
water
  carpet, on 174–5, 179
  marks on microsuede 85
  marks on sealed marble 78
  marks on timber 102, 128
  yellow watermarks on basin 79
water bottle, leaking 209
water features
  algae in birdbath 343
  brown stain on 342–3
  water stain on glazed fountain 342
water filter 25, 39
water hyacinth furniture 101
watermelon 304

wax
  carnauba 8, 134
  cotton, on 257, 335–6
  granite, on 332
  quick stain removal guide 304
  timber, on 110, 131–2
waxed floorboards
  cleaning 125–6
  stain removal 127–30, 131–2
wheat bran, unprocessed 20
white spirits 21, 151–2
white vinegar 21
whiteboard marker 249, 302
  *see also* pen marks
whiting 21
wicker furniture 101
windows 193–202
  blinds 198–9, 201
  cleaner 365
  cleaning 193–9
  corrosion on aluminium 195
  curtains 199–202
  dog saliva mark 198
  gloss paint on aluminium 197
  leadlight cement on glass 194–5
  masking tape removal 197
  old tint film 196
  scratches 196
  sugar soap removal from glass 194
wine *see also* red wine
  quick stain removal guide 304
wool
  burnt/yellowed 361–2
  caring for woollens 261–2
  pilling 261
  unshrinking 365
  what not to do 262
wrought iron 333–4

yellow curry stains 235
yellow marks
  cotton, on 258–9
  wool, on 286
yellowing oven door 26
yellowing towels 311
yoghurt 259

zinc cream 175
zip-lock bag 21